Making Government Work

Making Government Work

Lessons from America's Governors and Mayors

Edited by
PAUL J. ANDRISANI, SIMON HAKIM,
and EVA LEEDS

ROWMAN & LITTLEFIELD PUBLISHERS, INC.
Lanham • Boulder • New York • Oxford

ROWMAN & LITTLEFIELD PUBLISHERS, INC.

Published in the United States of America
by Rowman & Littlefield Publishers, Inc.
4720 Boston Way, Lanham, Maryland 20706
http://www.rowmanlittlefield.com

12 Hid's Copse Road
Cumnor Hill, Oxford OX2 9JJ, England

Copyright © 2000 by Rowman & Littlefield Publishers, Inc.

British Library Cataloguing in Publication Information Available

Library of Congress Cataloging-in-Publication Data

Making government work : lessons from America's governors and mayors / edited by
Paul Andrisani, Simon Hakim, and Eva Leeds.
    p. cm.
    Includes bibliographical references and index.
    ISBN 0-8476-9972-2 (alk. paper)
    1. Privatization—United States.   2. State governments—United States.
   3. Municipal government—United States. I. Andrisani, Paul J. II. Hakim, Simon.
III. Leeds, Eva, 1953–
HD3888.C58 2000
351.73—dc21   00-020507

Printed in the United States of America

∞ ™ The paper used in this publication meets the minimum requirements of American
National Standard for Information Sciences—Permanence of Paper for Printed Library
Materials, ANSI/NISO Z39.48–1992.

This volume is dedicated to the proposition of "making government work" for the benefit of its citizens.

.

Contents

Foreword

Thomas Ridge
Governor of Pennsylvania

A few years ago, using the words *change, innovation* and *entrepreneurial spirit* to describe government was considered an oxymoron. Traditionally, government was considered too slow, too burdensome and not very "customer friendly."

Today, in Pennsylvania and a few other states and local governments, that is not the case. In fact, these concepts now are commonplace. The very ideas many in government avoided—change, innovation and entrepreneurial spirit—are the same ideas we have embraced to pioneer positive change across Pennsylvania state government. Why?

Because our customers demand change—fundamental change in the way government does business and provides services. Families, employers and nonprofits all have been forced to take a look at themselves, tighten their belts and change their ways. Citizens demand that government do the same.

The world is changing rapidly. Now, states not only compete with neighboring states, but with nations across the planet. This means that state and local governments must become more competitive and deliver services faster, more effectively and more cost-efficiently than ever before. To accomplish this requires creativity, innovative thinking and, yes, some risk taking.

In government, these concepts have had a difficult time gaining a foothold. They turn upside down the traditional command-and-control bureaucracy—the one that stifles innovation and change. We must replace this *culture of bureaucracy* with the *culture of innovation* if we are to succeed in this ever-changing and competitive global marketplace—and because our customers demand it. This is not easy, but it can be done. And Pennsylvania's Privatize, Retain, Innovate, Modify and Eliminate (PRIME) effort is a clear example of success.

By creating *"employee-driven change,"* we opened the process to our employ-ees and proved that frontline employees have countless ideas for improvement and innovation. We found that once employees become excited about change, ideas turn into actions with very positive results.

Changing from nineteenth-century bureaucracies to twenty-first-century, tech-nology-based governments is not easy and does not happen overnight. Change and innovation efforts hit constant roadblocks, and the map to guide these efforts for the most part is nonexistent. Persistence, communication and recognition that change is core-function government work—not only from the top down, but also from the bottom up—are vital to completing the job. The examples and insights provided by the other change leaders in this book will help you build your own roads that can lead your organization on the path to positive change—permanently.

Introduction

Paul J. Andrisani and Simon Hakim

This book provides insights from some of America's most innovative governors and mayors as to how to make state and local government more efficient and competitive. Although their experiences and ideas differ, on one thing they agree: the days of "Big Government" are forever over, and new ways of managing government must be developed to make government more efficient and more competitive, especially at the state and local levels. These are not typical stories of state and local governments. The writers featured are executives active during the 1990s who, in the jargon of the popular management literature, were "first movers"[1]—in this case, those who fought the tide of public-sector expansion to bring restructuring and a new efficiency to their governments.

The distinction between the experiences recounted here and those typically observed at the state and local levels throughout the country during the 1990s is shown in a January 1995 *Business Week* cover story, which is aptly titled "Downsizing Government."[2] The lengthy article captures well the sentiment of the country at the time. There was a growing realization of the need for restructuring, privatizing, and downsizing government, particularly at the state and local levels.

The *Business Week* data show clearly that while federal government employment grew from about 2 to 3 million (50 percent) from 1960 to 1994, state and local government jobs grew from 6 to 17 million (nearly tripling). Despite the burgeoning employment in the public sector during the period, and at the state and local levels in particular, public services had neither expanded nor improved commensurately.

More recent data from government sources (table 1) show that public-sector employment rose nearly 20 percent from 1980 to 1996, with all the gains at the state and local levels.[3] During the 1990s, government employment at the state and local levels rose 10 percent by 1996, while federal government employment actually declined by nearly 11 percent during this same period. Thus, the case studies of restructuring efforts reported upon herein are not typical of what has been happening at the state and local levels during the 1990s. They are apparently the exceptions and not the rule.[4]

Table 1   Government Employment (in millions): 1980–1996

	1980	1990	1996
Local	9,765	10,914	12,059
State	3,610	4,305	4,645
Federal	2,866	3,085	2,757
Total	16,241	18,304	19,461

In discussing the obstacles to downsizing government, a 1996 *Wall Street Journal* article reported that government restructurings, privatizations, and downsizings are difficult to implement because they are a "two-edged sword."[5] Quoting Indianapolis Mayor Steve Goldsmith, for instance, the article argued that public-sector efforts to restructure, downsize, and privatize "are in large part emulating private businesses" that have successfully reduced costs and improved the quality and efficiency of service delivery. They also note, however, that, just as with corporate outsourcing, big savings inevitably result from reductions in payroll and wages. This poses a major threat to a largely unionized public-sector workforce. Government workers are four times more likely to be unionized than private-sector workers, with 40 percent of all union workers in the United States working for the government.[6]

State and local government restructuring efforts highlighted in this volume do not imply that overall employment must decline as a result of outsourcing or that labor peace must inevitably be threatened. In fact, a recent U.S. Department of Labor study of displaced workers with three or more years of seniority reported that, of the 272,000 public-sector displaced workers who lost their jobs between January 1995 and December 1997, only 6.2 percent remained unemployed when surveyed in February 1998.[7] Furthermore, it is likely that most of those still unemployed were displaced later in the three-year period and may have found reemployment within a brief time after job loss.

These data and conclusions are also consistent with other studies of the displacement effects of public-sector outsourcing and privatizations. Johnson and Walzer (1996), for example, also found virtually no employment effects of privatization on municipal payrolls.[8] Still further, a study by Kikeri, "Privatization and Labor: What Happens to Workers When Governments Divest?" reports:

> Fearing unemployment and the loss of benefits, labor unions and state enterprise workers are often among the most vocal and organized opponents of privatization, taking action to block reform. . . . Given the crucial importance of privatization, it is important that governments find ways to develop a labor strategy that wins labor support for privatization and creates a social safety net for laidoff workers.[9]

Thus, in a nearly 20-million-person public employment workforce in 1996, job losses due to restructurings, privatizations, and downsizings within state and local governments have not been appreciable. This is consistent with the case studies reported in this book, wherein governors and mayors have typically made clear efforts and found unique ways to preserve employment through such means as reassignments within the public sector, shifting employment from public to private-sector payrolls, mitigating job losses through normal attrition without worker replacements, establishing mutual trust and cooperation with public-sector unions, and so forth. In a number of chapters in this volume, governors and mayors from both political parties recount the steps they took to ameliorate the concerns of their public-sector workers in the process of restructuring, privatizing, or downsizing state and local government. The progress in restructuring, despite the strong resistance to job loss, is reflected in the increased share of public services handled by contract workers since 1987 (table 2).

Table 2   Privatized Jobs: Share of Public Services Handled by Contract Workers, 1987–1995

Waste collection	30% to 50%
Building maintenance	32% to 42%
Bill collection	10% to 20%
Data processing	16% to 31%
Health/medical	15% to 27%
Street cleaning	9% to 18%
Street repair	19% to 37%

In the seventeen case studies of this volume, elected officials at the state and local levels present the dilemmas they faced and the processes they pursued to make government at their levels more competitive and efficient. In all, these cases represent eight turnaround situations recounted by governors and nine by mayors.

In chapter 1, Dr. Keon Chi of the Council of State Governments and Georgetown College sets the stage for all the case studies in the book by providing an overview of the trends and options facing government in terms of restructuring, quality management, and privatization. His remarks pertain mainly to the state level, but most are applicable to all levels of government where concerns about restructuring, quality management, and privatization are of relevance.

In chapter 2, Governor George Allen of Virginia discusses his state's restructuring efforts, the results of which he termed "The Virginia Renaissance." Cost comparisons between public- and private-sector delivery of services were shown to result in substantial savings that could only be realized through a change in the culture of government. The Virginia experience, in Governor Allen's view, clearly explains how the private sector can often deliver better service at lower costs, even when it must comply with public-sector policies and procedures and use the same state-required systems: through better management and greater economies of scale. In chapter 3, Governor Terry Branstad of Iowa describes his "Business Case for Decision Making." He spells out the "Iowa Competition Guidelines" process that his state developed for assessing the wisdom of outsourcing or privatizing state services.

In chapter 4, Governor Jeb Bush of Florida describes the "Bush/Brogan A + Plan for Education" in Florida. The plan has three major parts: (1) addressing accountability and improving student learning, (2) raising standards and improving training for educators, and (3) improving school safety and reducing truancy. The clear thrust of the program is to make education the paramount duty of state government.

In chapter 5, Governor Arne Carlson of Minnesota details his state's efforts to make Minnesota more competitive through welfare reform. Reform was conducted through various forms of partnerships with the private sector, including pilot programs and a professionally prepared evaluation study in implementing welfare reform.

In chapter 6, Governor John Engler of Michigan discusses his state's "Strategic Approach to Privatization." In this chapter, a theory of privatization is developed based on historical experiences throughout the world. It is then applied to a "strategic privatization plan" that examined most state functions and assets, evaluating which would be better performed by, or sold to, the private sector.

In chapter 7, Governor Zell Miller of Georgia discusses his state's privatization of the Lake Lanier Resort. Governor Miller also recounts how his administration reduced taxes by more than $500 million per year while simultaneously revising the State Merit System to make it more competitive. In the process of this turnaround, 2,100 state jobs were eliminated or outsourced, administrative services were streamlined, more than $600 million was redirected from low-priority to high-priority needs, all state services were thoroughly scrutinized, and many state services were ultimately privatized.

In chapter 8, Governor Tom Ridge of Pennsylvania discusses his state's efforts to develop a "Culture of Innovation" to make state government more competitive, "cost-effective, user friendly and customer-focused." A bipartisan and independent task force was established by legislation to "benchmark" Pennsylvania against all other states in "an effort to propose changes, which will reduce costs, increase accountability and improve service . . . (and which) could impact almost $7.3 billion over a five-year period."

In chapter 9, Governor William Donald Schaefer of Maryland discusses "Public–Private Partnerships" as a basis for improving delivery of government services. His experiences both as mayor of Baltimore during its turnaround and as the state's governor show the importance of involving both the business community and the citizenry in restructuring efforts.

In chapter 10, Mayor Dennis Archer of Detroit details the major role that his privatization strategy played in the turnaround of his city. Facing serious problems, Detroit began by carefully evaluating what it could and could not do well. The city sought to provide services only where they could "add value" and to sell or outsource those services that could be better delivered by the private sector. Broader in many ways than most privatization strategies, this is a story of government restructuring to pursue a consensus vision and focus. As a result, Mayor Archer recounts how nearly $10 billion in private funds for development and investment were attracted to the city, property values rose nearly 50 percent, and the city's bond rating was improved to "investment grade status" by all three bond rating agencies.

In chapter 11, Mayor Bill Campbell of Atlanta describes "How Atlanta Entered into the Largest Privatization Contract in North America," awarding a 20-year full operations and maintenance contract to United Water Services (UWS). Although Atlanta retained ownership of the system, operations costs were cut almost by half, and UWS now manages the workforce and all operations and coordinates all capital improvements. The contract saves ratepayers $400 million over its 20-year life—"money that can be directly invested in upgrades to the water system." In chapter 12, Mayor Richard Daley of Chicago describes his "Chicago Alternative Policing Strategy," built on the landmark academic study "Broken Windows" by James Q. Wilson and George Kelling (also prominently cited by New York's Mayor Giuliani in chapter 13). Mayor Daley presents Wilson and Kelling's main principles: "If a window in a building is broken and left unrepaired, all the rest of the windows will soon be broken. . . . One unrepaired, broken window is a signal that no one cares, and so breaking more windows costs nothing." Although not a case study of privatization, this chapter details government restructuring of its management in partnership with the community and private service providers to solve crime and disorder problems.

In chapter 13, Mayor Rudolph Giuliani of New York City weaves a fascinating story of the turnaround of the nation's largest city. In essence, the turnaround followed the setting of a simple strategy: "Privatization and workfare programs, downsizing and reengineering all comprise a means toward our larger goal: to deliver quality service at a reasonable cost, and to eliminate functions better performed by the private sector." Like Chicago, New York based its restructuring on the Broken Windows theory and used crime statistics, including quality-of-life offenses, to address problems quickly, to heighten awareness, and to raise the standard of public behavior throughout the city.

In chapter 14, Mayor Susan Golding of San Diego describes how San Diego's Multiple Species Conservation Program (MSCP) worked as a road map for the preservation of thousands of acres throughout the country: "acres that would not be saved today if it were not for this historic agreement and partnership. . . . The challenge of good government is not to dictate, but to build coalitions to jointly solve the tough questions that have no easy answer."

Another mayor who faced serious fiscal obstacles, and as a result restructured local government to make it more competitive, is Indianapolis's Mayor Stephen Goldsmith. In chapter 15, Mayor Goldsmith recounts the phenomenal change his administration brought about by privatizing the delivery of services and making local government more competitive. The development of the theory of "marketization" for assessing which services can be better provided by the private rather than public sector and the development of an "activity-based costing (ABC)" method were innovative and generalizable approaches to restructuring. For Goldsmith, "competition is key," and the benefits of better-managed government to the poor are all too often neglected.

In chapter 16, Mayor Patrick McCrory of Charlotte discusses "Managed Competition." The mayor gives a detailed description of the issues and procedures that were followed to restructure government and privatize services. Managed competition there has been "systematic and institutionalized" and resulted in head-to-head competition between public-sector service providers and the private sector. The comprehensive guidelines he developed are a model for privatization evaluation and implementation.

In chapter 17, Mayor Marc Morial of New Orleans details the efforts of his city to privatize government services. Morial and Robert K. Whelan of the University of New Orleans explain a "contingency theory," wherein privatizations are neither viewed as all good or all bad. The decision as to which way to go on the issue depends on the particulars of each situation. In Mayor Morial's words: "Cities should not simply accept the widespread American myth that 'private is better,'" and the mayor draws seven generalizable conclusions to help officials determine whether to privatize, what to privatize, and how to privatize.

In chapter 18, Mayor Edward Rendell of Philadelphia discusses "Competitive Contracting: The Philadelphia Story." The chapter is another fascinating tale of a city on the edge of bankruptcy. Faced with fiscal disaster upon his assumption of office, Rendell and other city officials looked to the private sector and to a plethora of modern management theories for solutions. "Government should run more like a business," he notes, and restructuring government to reflect corporate best practices proved to be Philadelphia's best approach.

As a collection, the seventeen case studies in this volume, and the overview chapter by Dr. Keon Chi, show how dramatic and profound the transformation of management practices within the public sector has been during the 1990s. In less than a single decade, many of these "first movers" have moved their state and local governments from the verge of bankruptcy and seemingly inevitable decline to fiscal solvency at the very least and sustainable competitive advantage at best.[10]

The leaders of both political parties whose works are recounted here have drawn upon recent changes in management practices reflected in the popular management literature and in the private sector, where the transformation in management practices has been even more dramatic.[11] Since the early 1990s, in the view of many authors of this volume, revolutionary changes in private-sector management practices have turned around the American economy and made it the envy of the world, contradicting the model of decline that was assumed as recently as 1995. The restructuring of the private sector of the American economy during the 1990s, the dramatic downsizing of assets and employees, and a profound refocusing on core enterprises and functions have led to an American "renaissance" in managerial practices.[12] Perhaps the main question in the minds of many might revolve around how government has managed to remain insulated from market forces, and indeed from the wrath of a disgruntled electorate, for so long. The revolution of private-sector practices has its roots in the mid–twentieth century. At that time, large private-sector firms were similarly insulated by virtue of their sheer size, by the limited geographic scope of the product markets in which they competed, and by governmental assistance, as some states enacted protective legislation to insulate the management of firms incorporated in their jurisdictions from hostile takeovers and shareholder actions. In the 1980s and early 1990s, however, and as a direct result of globalization and stockholder activism, some of these corporate giants were brought to their knees, forced to downsize in order to turn themselves around, gain cash to repurchase their own stock and avoid a takeover by disgruntled shareholders or corporate raiders. For the first time in a century, CEOs of major corporations were turned out of office and replaced with little notice or warning. General Motors is but a single case in point.

As a result of this change, many large corporations refocused their energies on their "core" businesses, reversing diversification efforts and attempts at vertical integration that had begun many years before. Functions that were not essential or that diverted managerial attention were outsourced in efforts to reduce costs and improve efficiency and competitiveness. Outsourcing firms became "preferred suppliers" who were screened carefully and leveraged (i.e., played off against one another) to minimize transaction costs and assure competition in the provision of services that could more efficiently and competitively be delivered outside the firm than from within.

These strong winds of change swept through the private sector during the 1990s with phenomenal speed and ferocity. Globalization and the rush to reach emerging markets in Asia led to a dizzying array of managerial innovations to improve the quality of goods and services while simultaneously lowering costs, increasing efficiency, and reducing prices.

These economic and competitive pressures also produced tremendous changes in the way state and local governments conducted business. Business and personal taxpayers moved themselves, their businesses, and jobs to locations where they could realize greater performance from government for the tax dollars they paid; an economy based on service industries is far more mobile, cities and states learned, than the economies of yesterday based on manufacturing industries with large fixed assets in plant and equipment. State and local governments began to compete for taxpayer dollars and economic development on the basis of what they could deliver to their current and potential tax base. And governors and mayors began to face overwhelming voter and business resistance to any suggestion of raising existing taxes or user fees, or legislating any new taxes or user fees, even for needed public infrastructure and service delivery improvements. In addition, many state and local governments faced increased difficulty in issuing new debt because of the obvious difficulties that they would face in servicing the debt.

The governors and mayors featured here faced these challenges of fiscal austerity. Yet they, like public- and private-sector leaders at other crucial junctures in our nation's history, rose to the challenge and acted as "change agents," developing strategies to make the delivery of government services more efficient and competitive despite the scarcity of financial resources available for enacting significant managerial changes in government. These included "stretch" strategies to allow them to get more out of what they had, rather than just trimming services to match available resources; the use of industry standards and "best practices"—quantifiable benchmarks by which to measure success; the implementation of the "case-by-case approach" to privatization; and, perhaps most significantly, the increasing outsourcing of information technology in order to bring the best IT talent (and economies-of-scale savings) to government operations. In the process they often improved public infrastructure and service delivery while reducing taxes or holding them steady. The chapters herein paint a compelling picture of the process by which they did so.

There will doubtless be even more rapid change in the way private- and public-sector organizations do business in the coming decades. This is all the more reason why the lessons and visions of the public officials featured here will be valuable to all who are interested in improving the efficiency of service delivery provided by government. It is our hope that this book may be credited with achieving some small measure of success in the quest toward more competitive government. If so, it must be built upon by others who will continue the effort to identify the critical success factors that distinguish state and local governments that are growing their revenue bases, and achieving high marks for citizen satisfaction,[13] from those who continue to be mired in decline. We hope that the success stories shared in this book will help achieve this objective.

Notes

1. For a discussion of this literature, see a widely influential volume by G. Hamel and C. K. Prahalad, *Competing for the Future* (Cambridge: Harvard Business School Press, 1996).

2. "Downsizing Government," *Business Week*, January 23, 1995.

3. See, for example, 1997 *Statistical Abstract of the United States*, U.S. Bureau of the Census, table 662; U.S. Department of Labor Bureau of Labor Statistics, Bulletins 2445 and 2481; and U.S. Department of Labor Bureau of Labor Statistics, *Employment and Earnings*, March and June.

4. A more recent *Business Week* story on privatization projects a 50 percent increase (from $20 to $30 billion) in U.S. government information technology outsourcing from

1996 to 2001. See W. Zellner, "Government: The Promised Land for Outsourcing?" *Business Week*, July 6, 1998, p. 39.

5. G. P. Zachary, "Two Edged Sword: More Public Workers Lose Well-Paying Jobs as Outsourcing Grows," *The Wall Street Journal*, August 6, 1996, p. 1. See also The Reason Foundation, "Privatization 1996: Tenth Annual Report on Privatization," Los Angeles, 1996; R. Pouder, "Privatizing Services in Local Government," *Public Administration Quarterly*, Spring 1996.

6. "Union Members in 1998," U.S. Department of Labor Bureau of Labor Statistics, USDL 99–21, January 25, 1999.

7. "Worker Displacement, 1995–97," U.S. Department of Labor Bureau of Labor Statistics, USDL 98–347, August 19, 1998. An additional 172,000 workers also lost public jobs during the period, but they all had less than three years of seniority when laid off.

8. R. Johnson and N. Walzer, "Competition for City Services: Has the Time Arrived?" Office of the Controller, State of Illinois, 1996.

9. S. Kikeri, "Privatization and Labor: What Happens to Workers When Governments Divest?" World Bank Technical Paper No. 396, 1998, p. vii.

10. Y. Kodrzycki, "Fiscal Pressures and the Privatization of Local Services," *New England Economic Review*, January–February, 1998.

11. See, for example, Hamel and Prahalad's influential *Competing for the Future* (1996).

12. To others, a reliance on private-sector approaches to public-sector problems (e.g., restructuring, outsourcing, quality control, customer focusing, reengineering, downsizing, focusing on core issues, etc.) has been the wrong way to go. This view holds that the public sector always seems to embrace popular private-sector "management fads" just as they prove unworkable in the private sector. For a fuller discusssion of this view, see Donald F. Kettl, *Reinventing Government: A Fifth Year Report Card* (Washington: The Brookings Institution, September 1998), pp. 6–15; and Micklethwait and Wooldridge, *The Witch Doctors: Making Sense of the Management Gurus* (Times Books, 1996).

13. At the federal government level, there is some reason to believe that restructuring has led to positive changes in the eyes of the citizenry. A *Wall Street Journal* article of December 13, 1999, by Sarah Lueck (p. A2) shows that when "compared with the private sector, the federal scores were generally lower, but not substantially so."

References

Becker, G. "Good-Bye, Tollbooths and Traffic Jams?" *Business Week*, May 18, 1998, p. 26.

"Downsizing Government." *Business Week* (Cover Story), January 23, 1995.

Grosse, R., and J. Yanes. "Carrying Out a Successful Privatization: The YPF Case," *The Academy of Management Executive* 12, no. 2, May 1998, pp. 51–63.

Hamel, G., and C. K. Prahalad. *Competing for the Future*. Cambridge: Harvard Business School Press, 1996.

Johnson, R., and N. Walzer. "Competition for City Services: Has the Time Arrived?" Office of the Controller, State of Illinois, 1996.

Kettl, Donald F. *Reinventing Government: A Fifth Year Report Card*. Washington: The Brookings Institution, September, 1998.

Kikeri, S. "Privatization and Labor: What Happens to Workers When Governments Divest?" World Bank Technical Paper No. 396, 1998, p. vii.

Kodrzycki, Y. "Fiscal Pressures and the Privatization of Local Services," *New England Economic Review*, January–February, 1998.

Lueck, Sarah. "Survey Measures Satisfaction with Federal Services," *Wall Street Journal,* December 13, 1999, p. A2.

Micklethwait, John, and Adrian Wooldridge. *The Witch Doctors: Making Sense of the Management Gurus,* Times Books, 1996.

Pouder, R. "Privatizing Services in Local Government," *Public Administration Quarterly*, Spring 1996.

"Privatization: Lessons Learned by State and Local Governments," United States General Accounting Office, March 1997.

Reason Foundation, "Privatization 1996: Tenth Annual Report on Privatization," Los Angeles, 1996.

Statistical Abstract of the United States, 1997, U.S. Bureau of the Census.

Stevens, L. Nye. "Privatization and Competition," United States General Accounting Office, June 1997.

"The $7.7 Billion Mistake: Federal Barriers to State and Local Privatization," U.S. Congress Joint Economic Committee Staff Report, February, 1996.

"Union Members in 1998," U.S. Department of Labor Bureau of labor Statistics, USDL 99–21, January 25, 1999.

U.S. Department of Labor, Bureau of Labor Statistics, Bulletins 2445 and 2481.

U.S. Department of Labor, Bureau of Labor Statistics, *Employment and Earnings*.

Welch, D., and O. Fremond. "The Case by Case Approach to Privatization: Techniques and Examples," World Bank Technical Paper No. 403, 1998, p. v.

Winerip, M. "Schools For Sale," *New York Times Magazine,* June 14, 1998.

"Worker Displacement, 1995–97," U.S. Department of Labor Bureau of Labor Statistics, USDL 98–347, August 19, 1998.

Wright, M., R. Hoskisson, I. Filatochev, and T. Buck. "Revitalizing Privatized Russian Enterprises," *The Academy of Management Executive* 12, no. 2, May 1998, pp. 74–85.

Zachary, G. P. "Two Edged Sword: More Public Workers Lose Well-Paying Jobs as Outsourcing Grows," *The Wall Street Journal*, August 6, 1996, p. 1.

Zellner, W. "Government: The Promised Land for Outsourcing?" *Business Week*, July 6, 1998, p. 39.

CHAPTER ONE

Restructuring, Quality Management, and Privatization in State Government

An Overview of Trends and Options

Keon S. Chi
*Council of State Governments
and Georgetown College*

In recent years, privatization has been one of the most controversial issues in public management and the delivery of public services at all levels of government. State governments were not as quick to initiate privatization projects as were the federal or local governments, but over the past few years, the number of state agencies with such projects has rapidly increased. In the years ahead, as in the last decade, state leaders and managers are likely to face tough decisions on whether to privatize certain state services or programs at a greater rate in efforts to improve productivity and cost-efficiency in state government.

Traditionally, governors and state policymakers tried to improve state administration and service delivery by relying almost exclusively on structural reorganization and innovative in-house management techniques such as planning, budgeting, management by objectives and organizational development. Privatization was not contemplated as a practical management tool. This pattern has changed in the past two decades. According to the 1993 and 1997 surveys conducted by the Council of State Governments (CSG), for example, a majority of state agencies across the nation have privatized some of their programs or services. Six out of ten state officials who responded to the 1997 survey said privatization activity has expanded in their state or agency, while the rest said such activity has remained about the same in the previous five years.

The issue of privatization, however, may not be treated as an isolated topic when discussing trends and options in the improvement of state administration. In order to have a balanced assessment of privatization activities, we need to review other related activities, especially in the areas of organizational change and management and productivity improvement.

Restructuring

The past three decades were a time of state administrative growth. The growth is evidenced by the increase in state employment and proliferation of state agencies. The number of state employees increased from 2.7 million in 1970 to more than 5 million by mid-1990. On average, each state now has at least 150 separately administered agencies, many of which perform related functions. The policy and program areas with the highest rates of growth were corrections, health care, education and public welfare, while program areas with the lowest growth rates were public protection, natural resources and highways. Contributing factors in administrative growth are population growth and associated problems as well as "federal influence" on state administration. During the past 30 years, the federal government influenced states through interference in policymaking and allocation of resources. Many of the separately organized state administrative units in existence today have been created by states because of the federal influence. In some instances, states replicated federal models while in other cases states tried to take advantage of financial incentives offered by the federal government by complying with federal requirements regarding creation of separate agencies.

During the same period, many states began to reorganize their executive branches by mostly following the traditional principles of executive reorganization. The reorganization principles are: grouping agencies into broad functional areas, establishing relatively few departments to enhance the span of control and pinpoint accountability to the chief executive and legislatures, delineating single lines of authority to the top, administering departments by single heads, curtailing boards or commissions in performing administrative functions, reducing confusion in service delivery for the public, and cost savings and efficiency. Other reasons or objectives recently cited for restructuring include productivity improvement, businesslike management and responsibility.

Most reorganizations of the executive branch in recent years followed one of three models. In the "traditional" model, the reduction in the number of administrative agencies is accomplished within the existing structural pattern of agencies headed by elected or appointed officials, including boards and commissions. In the "cabinet" model, heads of reorganized agencies in most states are appointed by and responsible to the governor. And, in the "secretary-coordinator" model, the structure and authority of agencies remain unchanged, and the secretary, appointed by the governor, has primarily a coordinating function.

The recent trend in restructuring has been toward the cabinet approach, which is used by a majority of the states. Authorization mechanisms for adopting cabinet systems include constitutional and statutory provisions, gubernatorial executive orders, and tradition. Cabinets perform varied roles, and the perceived benefits are many, such as: helping identify priority issues, serving as a policymaking body, allowing the chief executive to maintain closer contact with the executive departments and giving visibility on decisions. Cabinet members also perform ceremonial functions and can help improve interagency coordination and accountability. However, the composition of a cabinet differs from state to state. In Florida, for example, the cabinet consists of a small group of popularly elected constitutional officers, while in other states it consists mostly of gubernatorial appointees.

The organizational structure of state government is provided by each state's constitutional and statutory provisions and often is supplemented by gubernatorial executive orders. Although governors in many states have "the supreme executive power," the chief executives cannot exercise "organizational power" without legislative approval and/or constitutional amendment. In fact, the governors in more than 30 states do not have the power to reorganize their executive branches. In some states, the legislative branch creates a variety of administrative agencies to implement laws and is free to abolish or change the duties of any of these agencies except constitutional offices.

When contemplating restructuring, state policymakers can consider one of two options: comprehensive or partial reorganization. The comprehensive reorganization involves an overhaul of executive branch agencies, on a statewide basis, and could be implemented under constitutional or statutory provisions. States may try to centralize lines of authority for governors or to decentralize the executive branch by transferring central authorities to line agencies. The partial reorganization option, also called functional reorganization, involves one or a few targeted agencies and can include the creation of new agencies or the abolition and consolidation of existing agencies.

In essence, centralization and decentralization, by whatever name or label, are the two basic approaches used in reorganizing executive branches either on a statewide or agencywide basis. The widely publicized South Carolina case illustrates the extent of restructuring toward further centralization, while the Florida case depicts an attempt to decentralize the executive branch based on "reinventing government" principles.

Under the leadership of former Governor Carroll A. Campbell and after many debates and legal and constitutional hurdles, South Carolina created 17 "executive" departments in 1993 by abolishing or consolidating most of the 140 previously autonomous organizations. The 17 departments are: Alcohol and Other Drugs; Commerce; Corrections; Disabilities and Special Needs; Juvenile Justice; Mental Health; Parks, Recreation and Tourism; Probation, Pardon and Parole; Public Safety; Revenue and Taxation; Social Services; Transportation; Labor, Licensing and Regulation; Health and Environmental Control; Natural Resources; Health and Human Services; and Insurance. In addition, there are 39 "independent agencies." As a result of this restructuring, the governor now has much broader appointment power within the executive branch. The majority of state agencies are run by agency heads appointed by and serve the governor. For the first time, the governor presides over a cabinet and makes policy and management decisions through it.

Before the recent comprehensive reorganization took place in 1993, South Carolina with its 59 regulatory agencies was known as the most decentralized state. At least 15 agencies with missions associated with environmental and natural resources issued permits for construction. There were more than nine agencies providing social services to specific groups. There were at least 18 different categories of methods for appointing members to the various governing boards and commissions in state government. The points of accountability in the executive branch were so diffused that no one was responsible. And because many boards appointed directors of executive branch agencies, these chief administrators had as few as four or as many as twenty bosses. A 1991 report by the State Reorganization Commission said, "Under the present, fragmented structured arrangement, state government cannot plan and strategically guide South Carolina's future. There is a need for effective, administrative accountability within the executive branch."

On the other hand, Florida once tried unsuccessfully to decentralize the executive branch by reversing much of what the state had created years earlier. In 1969, Florida underwent a major reorganization by consolidating 200 separate agencies into 22 departments. Since then, numerous functional reorganizations took place in order to "efficiently and effectively respond to the needs of the public." Former Governor Lawton Chiles established a commission to explore and provide guidance for "right-sizing" state government and then created the Governor's Commission for Government by the People. The commission's final report stated that in order to be more effective, Florida's government needed to "become more customer-responsive, performance-driven and subject to measurable post-audit." The commission recommended the budget, personnel and procurement functions within state government be revised to improve the delivery of government services. The commission pointed out that such services be decentralized and that managers be given more flexibility and control over the areas they manage. The report stated that "top-down, centralized bureaucracies simply cannot cope with the rapidly changing, technology-intensive, information-age society of the 1990s. They are too slow; they are too rigid; and they are too distant from the real problems our people experience in their day-to-day lives. . . . The challenge of transition from centralized, industrial-era bureaucracies to decentralized, entrepreneurial, information-age organizations faces virtually every government in America."

The Florida case warrants a closer examination as to why the state could not restructure its executive branch despite the much talked-about "reinventing government principles." The six organizational principles adopted by the Governor's Commission for Government by the People were as follows: (1) government by the people is catalytic: it steers more than it rows; (2) government by the people is community-oriented: it empowers more than it serves; (3) government by the people is customer-driven: it meets the customer's choice rather than the bureaucracy's; (4) government by the people is value-oriented: it stresses prevention rather than cure; (5) government by the people is result-oriented: it funds outcomes rather than inputs; and (6) government by the people is market-oriented: it uses competition rather than monopoly. Despite his concerted efforts and campaigns, Governor Lawton Chiles' restructuring plans did not succeed.

Quality Management

Over the years, state policymakers have experimented with a variety of approaches to improve management and service delivery without relying on privatization. In the late 1960s and 1970s, for example, many of them adopted the planning-programming-budgeting system as the most rational way of making decisions in government. In the 1980s, they promoted management by objectives and zero-based budgeting. In recent years, however, quality initiatives seem to have replaced these management approaches in most states. The quality manage-

ment movement in state government began in the late 1980s when workers in
Minnesota introduced quality initiatives and several agency directors in South
Carolina established their quality network to increase awareness of quality man-
agement and service principles. By mid-1999, more than 40 states had adopted
the quality management approach under various labels, such as Total Quality
Management and Quality through Participation.

Proponents of the quality movement say that traditional approaches are not
working. Quality management emphasizes decision making along horizontal, not
hierarchical, lines, employee participation and teamwork, customer-defined quality, and continued improvement. Traditional approaches are often characterized
by centralized and control-oriented decision making. Proponents of quality management also share the underlying assumption that systems created by management, not employees, hinder an organization's performance. Therefore it is up to
management to improve its policies, rules, procedures, training, rewards, information and financial systems so that employees perform well.

Some states with quality projects reported impressive success stories. For example, Iowa initiated six major civil service redesign projects, including those on
welfare-to-work, licensing and income maintenance. North Carolina's Partner-
ships-in-Education initiative has resulted in a number of positive results. Ohio
trained more than 54,000 workers under its Quality through Partnership program.
The quality initiative saved the state more than $96 million in six years. Washing-
ton state repealed more than 1,900 sections from its administrative codes and
completed more than 190 quality improvement projects in four years.

Governors and other state policymakers might want to check out quality initiatives in other states. In 1997, the Council of State Governments released *Managing for Success,* a report on management improvement. In 1998, the National
Governors' Association released two reports on quality initiatives. The All States
Quality Forum, a national group of state quality service directors, has held annual
meetings to further promote and refine quality projects. Indications are that quality initiatives, unlike other management approaches, are likely to stay in state
agencies across the country.

It is not easy to improvement quality practices, however. We can highlight five
critical factors for successful quality initiatives in state government. First, for successful quality initiatives, governors themselves, along with agency directors,
must "walk the talk" with organizational commitment and resources. They must
be involved personally in the quality process. Without high-level leadership commitment to achieve management and service excellence, it is unlikely that any
quality initiatives can realize measurable results.

Second, successful quality initiatives require greater emphasis on employee participation in decision making. Such initiatives should create a process that lets employees who are closest to the problem identify ways to improve continually the quality and productivity of their workplace. They must encourage teamwork involving every employee, including frontline workers. Active participation by employee associations and unions is essential.

Third, state policymakers need to streamline their work procedures by instituting a shorter chain of command and using less paperwork. Quality initiatives can be successful only when government systems, such as personnel, purchasing and information technology, are changed to have a quality emphasis. Decentralized, cross-agency and cross-functional thinking is critical to the development of such new systems.

Fourth, the overall management and service delivery system should be focused on results. Quality initiatives should be designed to change the culture of government to manage for results, not just processes or inputs. Planning and budgeting should be tied to desired program results. Continued improvement should provide specific tools to improve the effectiveness of work processes that lead to achieve results and should hold people accountable for results.

Fifth, the most important factor for a successful quality initiative is customer satisfaction. State policymakers must make greater efforts to satisfy customers—external customers, including program clients and constituents, and internal customers such as workers in other government agencies. The ultimate goal of quality initiatives is to close the gap between what customers expect to receive and what they get from state government. State agencies should function as efficient and effective entities that are responsive to their customers. State managers and employees must be convinced that quality government is not a fad. To carry out effective and successful quality efforts, governors and policymakers must overcome resistance from state agency executives, midlevel managers and often employee organizations that all tend to favor traditional management and service approaches or the status quo.

One major issue in quality management in state government is whether quality management has sustaining power. Some quality experts propose that state officials consider an ongoing external advisory board and career civil service buy-in. Additional strategies include: constituency support by client groups and unions; instituting quality process through statutes, rules and regulations; depoliticizing the quality process; conducting continuous training; and selling the quality process, not the label, such as Total Quality Management. Of these areas, however,

the attitudes and decisions of top-ranked civil servants and midlevel managers
may be the most crucial.

Privatization

The term *privatization* has been defined variously as the transfer of government
functions or assets to the private sector; the shifting of government management
and service delivery to private providers; a shift from publicly produced to privately produced goods and services; government reliance on the private sector to
satisfy the needs of society; and a movement from collective action to private
control. In essence, however, privatization means the use of the private sector in
government management and delivery of public services.

It is difficult to pinpoint a turning point in the recent privatization movement.
At the state and local level, privatization activities have mushroomed since 1978
when California voters passed Proposition 13, designed to roll back property
taxes, thus prompting cities and counties to consider alternative service delivery.
Since the mid-1980s, the number of state agencies initiating privatization increased sharply. Reasons for a trend toward privatization of public services in
state and local governments were several, but privatization was considered a policy of reducing the role of government in service delivery. Some early assessments of privatization, by both advocates and critics, cited reasons such as the
ever-increasing size of government, spending reductions to deal with deficit problems and division of labor, the shrinking of the welfare state, and the role of
government in regulating the economy and providing public services.

But the primary reason for using private vendors to deliver government services and programs has been cost savings. Michigan Governor John Engler
seemed to represent the prevailing opinion of state policymakers who have promoted privatization in state government:

> It is my belief that the private sector is often better at getting the job done than
> government. First, the competition promotes operating cost-effectively, and the
> greater accountability helps ensure quality products and services. The private sector
> also excels at using innovative technology to solve problems, while government
> agencies do not always have the same latitude to innovate or take risks. Finally, the
> private sector has vast resources in computer technology, high volume processing
> equipment, and specialized personnel, plus the flexibility to assign them wherever
> they are needed most.

Typical arguments for privatization include: privatization helps government
save money, privatization is necessary for speedy implementation of certain pro-

grams, privatization provides high-quality services in some areas, privatization is necessary when government lacks expertise or personnel to carry out certain functions, privatization helps dissolve unnecessary government monopolies, privatization slows the growth of government or downsizes government, privatization introduces competition between government employees and private providers, and privatization is an alternative to traditional ways of improving government productivity. Arguments against privatization include: privatization does not save government or taxpayers money, privatization does not guarantee market competition and can result in "private monopolies," privatization leads to corruption, policymakers and managers lose control over privatized services and functions, privatization diminishes accountability of government officials, privatization is not necessary because other productivity improvement approaches are available, the quality of privatized services and functions are compromised due to private providers' profit motives, privatization lowers state employee morale and brings fear of displacement to affected employees, and privatization destabilizes economically marginal communities and neighborhoods.

The level of privatized services and functions varies greatly among state agencies. Of those agency respondents to the 1997 CSG survey who provided an estimate, 43 percent had privatized less than 5 percent of agency programs and services, and 31 percent privatized more than 15 percent. According to the survey, state transportation agencies led other executive departments in the number of privatized programs and services. Fifty-seven percent of respondents to the survey said their agencies privatized more than 15 percent of their programs and services, and another 21 percent privatized between 6 percent and 10 percent. The privatized programs or services include highway designs, road and bridge construction, highway maintenance, grass mowing, road maintenance, architectural services and hazardous waste disposal. Most often, the agencies contracted with private providers of transportation services. Saving money was not the main goal of privatizing transportation functions. An average percentage of respondents cited cost savings as a reason to privatize, but cost savings estimates were not impressive. Instead, a lack of agency personnel and expertise led transportation agencies to privatize. The trend toward greater privatization in transportation appears to be leveling off. More than three-quarters of respondents increased privatization activity in the past five years, but 60 percent expected future increases. Transportation agencies tend not to privatize systematically. Rather, they privatize on a case-by-case basis using a process they created through trial and error.

The state department with the second highest number of privatized programs is general services and administration. Compared to other agencies, administration and general service agencies have tended to privatize more systematically, using a standard decision-making process to determine which activities will be privatized. All survey respondents reported that they either increased or maintained their levels of privatization activity in the past five years. Privatized services include custodial services, architectural services, asbestos removal, building construction, pest control, mowing services, computer maintenance and engineering services. They overwhelmingly cited cost savings as the motivation for privatizing administrative and general services. They expect to continue privatizing functions. More than half the respondents said that their privatization activity will increase in the next five years. Regarding methods of privatization, almost all privatized functions were contracted out to private vendors. Other methods used to privatize services included service shedding and public–private partnerships.

The third functional area with the highest number of privatized services is the corrections department. Many states have privatized medical services of institutions, health and dental care, alcohol and drug treatment, correctional facilities construction, prison operations and laboratory services. Slightly more than half of corrections agencies surveyed said that they used a standardized monitoring process to evaluate the effects of privatization. Like most executive agencies, however, department corrections reported modest cost savings from privatization. Of the less than two-thirds of responding corrections agencies that quantified their cost savings, 60 percent saved less than 5 percent through privatization. Another one in three respondents saved between 6 percent and 10 percent, and none saved more than 15 percent.

Agencies that have privatized more than 15 percent of their programs include general services, health care, juvenile rehabilitation, mental health, social services and transportation. State agencies with low numbers of privatized services and functions include education, labor and public safety. Florida led all states in privatizing the most services and functions. Following Florida are Colorado, California, Michigan, Iowa, Maryland, New Jersey, Connecticut, South Carolina, Illinois, Tennessee and Texas.

Overall, contracting-out is the most widely used method of privatizing functions and services, with eight out of ten activities using this method. States also use grants and subsidies and public and private partnership programs. Other methods of privatization include franchises, sale of assets, vouchers, deregulation, private donations, volunteerism and service shedding. State officials most often cite cost savings for expanding privatization activities. Other reasons include flexibility, speedy implementation and the lack of state personnel and expertise to perform the function.

Do all state agencies privatize certain services or functions? Conceptually, state policymakers may consider five broad options for privatization. First, they may decide not to privatize any function or service, believing that they can improve cost efficiency and productivity through structural reorganization and quality management techniques. However, it is important to note that the history of public administration reveals a huge array of such efforts, many of which have been short-lived. Privatization proponents contend that government monopoly of certain services and functions is one major problem. Therefore, any efforts to improve management without competition could revert to usual and monopolistic performance, with the result being the status quo.

The second option is to privatize only professional, administrative and support services that do not directly involve state service delivery. Examples include architectural services, engineering and legal services, tax collections, custodial services, printing, information services, data processing and the like. This option is less politically controversial and relatively nonthreatening to state employees. This option also gives management some flexibility in achieving cost efficiency, in quick turnaround of products and in improving quality assurance. However, cost savings may be achieved only if privatization initiatives are carefully planned and managed.

The third option is privatizing selected public works and infrastructure projects such as construction and maintenance of highways, roads and bridges. This option has not been implemented as quickly as proponents hoped, however. Several reasons may have contributed to the slow progress in toll road privatization. The lack of private funding and the 1986 tax reform legislation that discontinued the investment tax credit significantly decreased private interest in owning public facilities.

The fourth option is to privatize selected state services and functions for specific clients and customers, such as health, mental health and mental retardation, social services, corrections and education. State policymakers and managers might want to consult with constituent groups to ensure their satisfaction. If client groups are involved in planning the new service and state employees are allowed sufficient input, then better, more cost-effective services may result. There is a greater risk of negative backlash if constituent groups are not satisfied with newly provided services or when an alternative plan is first proposed.

The fifth option is introducing the concept of competition into the administration and delivery of state services. Here, competition means breaking up the government's monopoly on public services. To implement this option, state policy-makers need to establish a centralized state agency with authority to make impartial decisions on whether and what to privatize to manage and deliver state services more efficiently and effectively. Such an agency should be nonpartisan and guided by a joint legislative–executive commission. Examples of this option are the PERM (Privatize, Eliminate, Retain or Modify) approach adopted by Michigan, the Council of Competitive Government created by Texas and the Commonwealth Competition Council of Virginia.

The key issues in privatizing state functions and services are decision-making procedures, cost analysis, constitutional or legal barriers to privatization and em-ployee concerns. State policymakers need clear policies and procedures to guide decision making for successful implementation of privatization. The CSG survey showed that some states and agencies use a formal decision-making process for privatization projects. Overall, however, they have initiated privatization projects without a standard decision-making or evaluation process. Such policies and proce-dures should range from initiating a privatization project, to the delineation of the services and functions allowed to be privatized to the availability of private provid-ers, risk and cost overruns, legal monitoring, and performance measurement.

State officials have considered cost savings the most important factor in deter-mining whether to privatize a service, function or program. To make good deci-sions, state policymakers should compare state employee and contractor costs based on objective and realistic criteria and methods. Agencies have been criti-cized for using techniques to increase contract costs or decrease in-house cost estimates to deny privatization opportunities to private providers.

Before initiating major privatization projects, policymakers should determine if constitutional, statutory, federal or internal regulatory barriers exist. Policy-makers should be aware of possible lawsuits by state employees. In Colorado, for example, the state employees' union filed lawsuits against the state. The result was that the existing law could not be used as the basis for privatization. Re-cently, many states have enacted privatization laws to revise civil service sys-tems, which tend to protect state workers and prohibit contracting out functions or services.

The recent CSG survey showed that proponents of privatization in state gov-ernment are governors and their staff, agency managers and legislative agency staff. Outside parties, such as interest groups and private consultants, also sup-port privatization. Typical opponents of privatization include state employee as-sociations and elected officials. The challenge for policymakers is to better com-municate with and involve opponents in the privatization process. State employees share many concerns about privatization initiatives. Some states address those concerns by reassigning personnel within government, allowing them to compete with private vendors and consulting with private organizations.

Specifically, policymakers may consider the following suggestions to ease the impact of privatization on state employees: (1) allow state employee associations/ unions to have representation in the privatization decision making; (2) prepare an "employee impact plan" when more than a few state employees will be affected; (3) develop an education plan about options for employees to be moved to the private sector, be retrained or be reassigned; (4) offer enhanced severance packages such as job placement services and career transition counseling; (5) provide displaced state employees with preferential treatment in hiring; (6) award bonus points to bidders offering employee accommodation plans; (7) use competitive contracting and help employees compete with private vendors; (8) reject offers in which employees will be moved to lower-grade positions; and (9) offer affected employees an early retirement option.

Conclusion

It is fair to say that privatization has been used as a practical tool for improving government productivity in state government. The success or failure of privatized functions and services depends on how the tool is used by state officials and private vendors. By educating themselves, officials improve their ability to guide the privatization process. Officials can learn lessons from the privatization experience of other agencies or states. Good advice is crucial for policymakers who decide on issues such as achieving cost savings, handling employee concerns, delegating authority and monitoring providers.

State policymakers should develop cost analysis formats for agencies to use. Only through accurate and reliable cost comparisons can states determine if privatization is likely to save money. Experience indicates that cost savings may result only when several qualified private providers compete to deliver services, or when carefully structured competitive bidding takes place among agencies and private vendors. Agency managers have to plan, manage and monitor privatization activities. Privatization does not mean the delegation of state authority or responsibility. Policymakers are ultimately accountable to clients and taxpayers for privatized services. From planning to monitoring privatization activities, policymakers should be aware of the dangers of corruption, service interruption and mismanagement or unfair labor practices by private firms. Private providers should be held accountable for both their service performance and management practices.

References

Allen, Joan, et al. *The Private Sector in State Service Delivery: Examples of Innovative Practices.* Washington, D.C.: The Urban Institute Press, 1989.

Butler, Stuart, ed. *The Privatization Option.* Washington, D.C.: The Heritage Foundation, 1985.

Chi, Keon S. "Total Quality Management," in *State Trends & Forecasts.* Lexington, Ky.: The Council of State Governments, October 1994.

———. "Organizational Changes in State Government: 1975–95," State Government Organizational Chart. Lexington, Ky.: The Council of State Governments, 1995.

———. *Privatization in State Government: Options for the Future.* Lexington, Ky.: The Council of State Governments, 1993.

Chi, Keon S., and Cindy Jasper. *Private Practices: A Review of Privatization in State Government.* Lexington, Ky.: The Council of State Governments, 1998.

Donahue, John D. *The Privatization Decision.* New York: Basic Books, 1989.

Engler, John. "Privatization: Heed the Call," ASI Solutions. Bala Cynwyd, Pa.: Assessment Systems, Winter 1996.

Kolderie, Ted. "The Different Concepts of Privatization." *Public Administration Review,* July/August 1986, pp. 285–291.

Osborne, David, and Ted Gaebler. *Reinventing Government.* Reading, Mass.: Addison-Wesley Publishing Company, 1992.

Reason Foundation. *Privatization 1999.* Santa Monica, Calif.: 1999.

Savas, E. S. *Privatization: The Key to Better Government.* Chatham, N.J.: Chatham House Publishers, 1987.

Sclar, Elliott. *The Privatization of Public Service.* Washington, D.C.: Economic Policy Institute, 1997.

U.S. General Accounting Office. *Privatization: Lessons Learned by State and Local Governments.* Washington, D.C.: U.S. Government Printing Office, 1997.

Restructuring Government

The Virginia Renaissance

George Allen
Governor of Virginia

In his first presidential inaugural address in 1801, the great Virginian, Thomas Jefferson, said that good government is "a wise and frugal government, which shall restrain men from injuring one another, which shall leave them otherwise free to regulate their own pursuits of industry and improvement, and shall not take from the mouth of labor the bread that it has earned." This was the sum of good government more than 200 years ago. It remains the objective of good government today, although there have been a lot of changes and ideas during the intervening years. An evolution in state government is taking place. Many of the changes are just beginning. The effects will be felt primarily in the future and thus will have a profound impact on life in Virginia throughout this century.

Essential to the economic vitality of Virginia is providing the services Virginians normally expect from their government by using the most efficient and cost-effective methods available. As my first act in office I began the Virginia renaissance by appointing a Blue Ribbon Strike Force—the Governor's Commission on Government Reform—to determine ways government can be revitalized and, more important, to provide the expected services at a reasonable cost to Virginia's taxpayers. The major focus was on value and customer service "satisfaction" rather than just customer service delivery. The commission members were prominent business and community leaders as well as elder statesmen from across the state. This membership was to assure significant public input and review.

Another area I specifically asked the commission members to investigate was

the way certain state functions were provided to the citizens. My specific charge
to them was to identify any program or service now offered by a state agency
that can be eliminated or transferred to the private sector without injury to the
public good and well-being. The charge also included a complete review of all
state regulations and elimination of any unnecessary rule.

Just like a business, state government must recognize its customers, the citizens of Virginia. It is time for state government to help satisfy its customers by
encouraging healthy competition and by ensuring that the government services
are needed and are provided by the most efficient and cost-effective organization—whether private, public or joint public/private partnerships. Entrepreneur-
ial-style government has its place in leading the coming government evolution
and accurately assessing the various options for service delivery.

Our system of free enterprise nourishes competition, which creates efficiencies. State government monopolies have been insulated from the rigors of the marketplace, and government employees neither were forced nor had the opportunity
to compete for their work. It has always been okay just doing it the "same old
way." No one challenged the status quo or took risks. There were no incentives
to become more efficient or to look for money-saving methods. The main objective was to spend all your budgets so you could demand an increase in the next
biennium. I, and the Blue Ribbon Strike Force, know the people of Virginia deserve and demand better from their state government.

Consequently, this has led to a multipronged attack on how to improve customer service and satisfaction and to identify areas of waste and inefficiency in
state government. It begins with the transition from thinking "government regulation" to thinking "what adds value." Government must become more innovative and pursue competitive approaches to providing services and increasing citizen satisfaction.

Core Philosophies

A series of core philosophies evolved from the work of the Blue Ribbon Strike
Force. These guiding principles form the basis for good Virginia government:

- *Competition* in government is good and will enhance performance among competing interests. Organizations that must compete for funding keep their costs

down, respond quickly to changing demands and strive to satisfy their customers.

- *Citizen ownership* of government is the only way to wrestle control of individual fate from the bureaucracy and restore it to the people. Expansion of government control through unnecessary and overburdensome regulatory and administrative edicts not only must stop, but must be reversed.
- *Customer service*–oriented government will help refocus the efforts of the state toward meeting citizens' needs with value rather than setting up roadblocks with rules, regulations and bureaucratic requirements.
- *Changing the culture* of government service will recognize and break down barriers that are prohibiting the public and most state employees from getting what they want . . . a reinvigorated, high-performance workforce. This will establish a principle of stewardship, the deep conviction that government must affirm the choice for service over the pursuit of self-interest.

Fundamental Premises

As with any dynamic enterprise, these four core philosophies of state government must emulate from the top and be understood, embraced and implemented by the workforce. This requires high-powered leadership and someone at the top of the organization who is committed to change. "Sacred cows" are just not permitted in challenging the status quo of state government. The process of change started early in my administration and continues today with key implementation elements in progress.

Crucial to change is implementation. The task of implementation has two fundamental premises. First, internal state management must improve. But before that can happen, government must have a strategic plan and the means to measure accomplishment. This is accomplished by expanding Virginia's performance budgeting process as discussed in the following case study. Second, as a general principle, we must introduce competition into the administration and delivery of state service. This must be on a regular and statewide basis. It must be a fair process between private business and public agencies with due regard for the quality of the services and the concerns of current state employees.

Internal state management improvement can only happen if government can accurately measure its cost of performance. Hence, the following case study details Virginia's performance budgeting process.

Internal State Management Improvement

Virginia's Performance Budgeting Process

Virginia's performance budgeting process significantly expands the Commonwealth's previous efforts in strategic planning and performance measurement by fully integrating strategic planning, performance measurement and budgeting. This integrated system of performance budgeting was designed to bring agency missions, program priorities, anticipated results, strategies for achieving the desired results, and budgeting together in a single cohesive process. Implementation of this fully integrated process in Virginia by executive memorandum in 1995 clearly places the Commonwealth in a leadership position. Several states have undertaken various components of this process, but Virginia is one of the first to comprehensively integrate all components and require every executive branch agency to comply. The 1996–1998 biennial budget was developed using the performance budgeting process.

The performance budgeting process was designed to focus on customers and results. Agencies are required to identify the various customers of each service, program or process and assess the expectations that these customers have. This understanding of expectations then guides the agency in specifying the desired results. Once these two tasks have been completed, the agency is in a better position to determine the resources needed to achieve these results and to develop a measurement system to monitor accomplishment.

Each agency is required to conduct an issue assessment, which is a strategic planning exercise that requires agencies to examine the fundamentals of what it is they do. For the assessment, agencies examine their recent accomplishments, strengths, weaknesses, opportunities and threats; identify their customers and their expectations; and determine what critical issues they face for the upcoming biennium. Each agency head presents the results of the assessment to a team consisting of personnel from the governor's Policy Office, the cabinet secretaries, and the Department of Planning and Budget, after which each agency develops goals, objectives, and strategies reflecting the governor's priorities and the agency customer needs.

Agencies complete the process with the development and subsequent submission of activity-based budgets, decision packages, and performance measures. Each agency develops and submits several performance measures that relate to the agency's highest priority activities, its mission, and its largest budgeted items. Performance measures were published in July 1996 and provide an invaluable internal management tool for agencies to monitor program performance and take corrective action for improving service to customers. In the future, performance measurement may potentially be used to benchmark agency activities against the best practices in other agencies, states, or private entities.

Baseline data have been developed along with established targets for each measure. Agencies are better able to prioritize activities and to determine what opportunities exist to consolidate programs, privatize functions, or eliminate activities entirely, freeing up limited dollars to be put to use for higher priority activities. As a result of this activity-by-activity analysis, actual funding reductions were achieved in 55 agencies. In addition, 26 agencies identified 47 activities for privatization, with an annual savings of $122 million. Moreover, the Virginia Department of Transportation was able to privatize more than $100 million in multiyear transportation road maintenance projects. Savings will be measured on an ongoing basis through the budget process, and progress toward each measure will be reported and available to the public in December of each year with the governor's budget document.

Regulatory Reform

A second area where Virginia is working to improve state management and its impact on Virginia citizens is regulatory reform. If citizen ownership of government is to become a reality, one of the first steps must be to eliminate unnecessary, costly, or burdensome regulations. Regulations developed to address a particular problem are not designed to offer the least intrusive mechanism for solving the problem. And, unfortunately, once promulgated, regulations are rarely repealed.

Virginia government recognizes that burdensome regulations involve government intervention that often lacks flexibility. This adversely affects individual entrepreneurial initiative, innovation, and creativity. When a regulation is promulgated, there should be a presumption in favor of freedom and against government intervention.

Hence, one clear way to return ownership of government is to reform the process of promulgating regulations. Successful reform of this scale requires a dramatic increase in the opportunities for all Virginians to participate in the rule-making processes. State regulators had become all too accustomed with the practices of excluding such opportunities for public comment by declaring their proposed regulations as emergencies. In 1993, the Joint Legislative Audit and Review Commission (JLARC) reviewed Virginia's regulatory process and

concluded that, although nearly 38 percent of Virginia's regulations were promulgated as emergencies, many were not associated with or in reaction to any
emergency at all. These appear to have been based largely on the regulator's desire to avoid public discussion and comment concerning the proposed regulations.

Executive Order 14(95) dealt directly with this abuse and mandated the nar-
rowly defined conditions upon which a regulation could be deemed an emergency. Additionally, every emergency regulation must now be replaced within
one year by a permanent regulation that has benefited from public comment. This
policy has been quite successful and has produced marked results. The number
of emergency regulations has plummeted to just over 16 percent of all regulations
promulgated.

Regulations must be designed cautiously and openly. Further, as regulations
are in review, Virginians must be given the chance to participate in the process.
After all, poorly conceived regulations steal energy from market forces that have
created a fivefold increase in the state's standard of living over the past century.
Every agency under authority of the governor is required to conduct a comprehensive review of all current regulations and mandates using these guiding principles:

• Regulations should have the least possible interference in the lives of Virgin-
  ians.
• No regulation should be promulgated if there is a less costly alternative that
  achieves the purpose for which the regulatory action was proposed.
• Regulations should be reviewed periodically based on measurable goals.
• Regulations should be clearly written and easily understandable.
• Public participation should be encouraged and guidelines for citizen involve-
  ment strictly followed.

After increasing the opportunities for citizens to shape new regulations, it is
essential to ensure informed public discussion of the proposed changes. The new
regulatory policy, bolstered by amendments to the state's Administrative Process
Act, focused upon making full disclosure to the public regarding all new regulations. Effective public participation in rule making requires that the public be
aware of how a new regulation is likely to impact the state's economy, its budget,
its citizens and their private property.

At the heart of the regulatory reform effort is the statutory requirement that
requires the economic impact analyses of proposed regulations to include, but
need not be limited to, "the projected number of businesses or entities affected

by the regulation, the localities and businesses particularly affected by the regulation, the number of persons and jobs affected, and the projected costs to affected
businesses to comply with the regulations." The economic impact analysis will
identify the benefits of a proposed rule and describe the costs, while seeking to
identify alternative approaches that may achieve substantially the same regulatory goal, but at a lower cost.

The result of work to review Virginia's regulations during the recent past reveals
that of the more than 1,600 regulations reviewed, 27 percent were terminated,
40 percent were amended, and only 33 percent were retained in their original form.
This represents more than 1,200 regulations whose impact on the citizens was reduced or eliminated entirely.

Competitive Government

The second major implementation step was started on July 1, 1995, when the
Commonwealth Competition Council was created in the Code of Virginia. The
council is unique. It is to provide an institutional framework for a statewide competitive program designed to encourage innovation and competition. The bipartisan council has members from the executive and legislative branches of government as well as citizen members.

The council monitors the products and services of state agencies to act as a
catalyst to bring competition and entrepreneurship to state government. Governments inherently are monopolies that do not compete within their own borders.
The lack of competition has insulated government workers from the rigors of the
marketplace. Profit may be the bottom line in the private sector but citizen service
and cost-effective quality are the bottom line in the public sector.

Competition must be introduced into the administration and delivery of state
services on a routine and statewide basis. This must be through a fair bidding
process between private business and public agencies with due regard for the concerns of current state employees. This managed competition means breaking up
the government's monopoly on public services. The public agency shrinks in size
if it fails to win contracts when competing against qualified private firms. This
dynamic process keeps both organizations permanently on their toes, protects
government from possible collusion by private firms, and rescues the citizens
from the grasp of public monopolies.

It is interesting to note that public employees are not against privatization or
competition of public services, but they are concerned. As one employee put it,

"We are taxpayers and as public employees we observe inefficient practices with our agencies." The employee concern is that privatization may not correct those inefficiencies, improve services, or cost less in the long run. Consequently, the decision process must be scrutinized and a variety of alternatives carefully considered. The private sector has also expressed concern that it may not be playing on a level playing field. The council recognizes the validity of these issues and has developed a process to answer the concerns and to guide Virginia government along the continuum of options. Figure 2.1 outlines the analytical process to assure that decisions to retain services as government, privatize, or compete will withstand public scrutiny.

Various automation tools have been developed to assist government agencies in completing all the steps in the process. The cost comparison program assists state managers in determining the fully allocated costs for the services they pro-

Figure 2.1   Commonwealth Competition Council Process

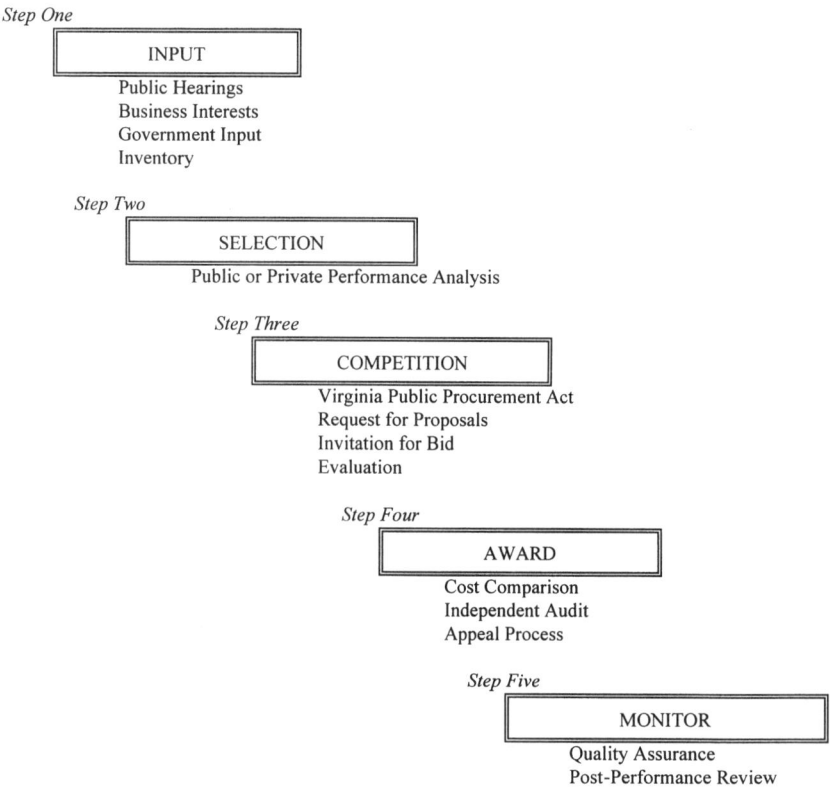

Step One

INPUT

Public Hearings
Business Interests
Government Input
Inventory

Step Two

SELECTION

Public or Private Performance Analysis

Step Three

COMPETITION

Virginia Public Procurement Act
Request for Proposals
Invitation for Bid
Evaluation

Step Four

AWARD

Cost Comparison
Independent Audit
Appeal Process

Step Five

MONITOR

Quality Assurance
Post-Performance Review

vide. The automated program uses the same accounting principles as used in the private sector. The state managers are also called upon to develop a range of options to remain competitive in the coming biennium. Lastly, a competition forum is conducted for state managers to provide the skills needed for entrepreneurial government.

It is a trailblazing effort to explore the boundless competition opportunities that are available within Virginia's state government. The structure and work of the Competition Council also are good for economic development in Virginia. Business comes to Virginia because Virginia government says we value the private sector. We're building a system of responsive government and a friendly, regulatory environment for business. The Competition Council is structured to review and respond expeditiously to business' unsolicited proposals to provide a particular government service. The unsolicited proposal process will fuel the competitive spirit and keep both business and government looking for ways to innovate and improve services.

An example of privatization where the private sector is in competition with government is discussed in the second case study.

Case Study: Competition Results

An example of where privatization has demonstrated capability to respond to needs of Virginia citizens is in the area of child-support enforcement programs, where the number of cases had increased by 52,382 in two years. The considerations of improving the child-support services immediately, the needs to serve the soaring caseloads and the ability to deploy additional child-support staff were some of the reasons privatization was considered.

Virginia Department of Social Services elected to solicit business to provide two private child-support offices in the Hampton Roads area in early 1994 in addition to the two existing state offices. This would split the case load four ways to establish a "friendly" competition among the four offices.

The following compares the privately run office in Hampton, Virginia, and a similar public office in Portsmouth, Virginia. These offices serve similar client populations in suburban and rural areas in the same region in Tidewater, Virginia. It is clear from the comparative statistics in table 2.1 that the private Hampton office established paternities and support orders and made collections for higher proportions of the cases than did the Portsmouth office during an 18-month review period.

The cost-effectiveness of the two offices was also documented. The private

Table 2.1 Virginia Performance Outcomes Compared

	Those Needing Service, Percent with Successful Outcome	
Services Needed	Private Office (Hampton)	Public Office (Portsmouth)
Location	73.9	58.5
Paternity Establishment	40.0	19.2
Support Order Establishment	35.7	16.8
Collection	40.8	22.3

Hampton office cost to collect one dollar of child support was 63 percent lower than that of the Portsmouth office during the 18-month period. As table 2.2 shows, the contractor was paid 11.5 cents for each dollar collected, while the public office spent 18.4 cents for each dollar collected. Of note is that according to the private contract, the contractor's payment will decline to 9.5 cents per dollar collected in the final year of the five-year contract period. The financial analysis is summarized in table 2.2.

Additionally, to determine whether privatization resulted in disproportionate increases in total state costs, we compared administrative costs before and after privatization. The privatized office's administrative costs did not increase dramatically after privatization. In state fiscal year 1994, the first year of privatization, the privatized office's administrative costs grew by less than 1 percent over the previous years imputed costs. In the second year after privatization, the privatized office's administrative costs increased by about 22 percent, a growth rate similar to the public office's 21 percent increase. The private office also has been able to hire several community work experience employees in support of the Virginia Welfare Reform Program, which the public office has not been able to do.

The question is, Why can the private provider afford to offer better services at a lower cost? Both state-run and private offices must comply with policy and procedures and use state-required systems; however, it is how the operation is managed, practices are used, and technology is implemented that can make the

Table 2.2 Total Administrative Costs Compared to Total Collections

	Private (Hampton)	Public (Portsmouth)
Total Administrative Costs	$1,791,733	$2,238,482
Total Collections	$15,553,480	$12,197,214
Cost to Collect One Dollar	11.5 cents	18.4 cents

difference. The net effect is found in the private office outputs and results noted above. These are the most accurate measure of the full benefits of the private office.

The public sector can learn from this example. The key point is to be innovative and evaluate the approach for the long-run return on investment. Something may be more expensive initially (e.g., initial cost for the private sector to develop bar coding of case files) but cheaper in the long term compared to hiring a file clerk at each office.

Resistance to Change

There will be resistance even to this type of change in government by those who favor the status quo. However, there are recognized strategies to overcome resistance to competition and privatization in state government. First, focus initially where competition is likely to produce dramatic results. Second, improve performance measures and cost accounting systems as is being done in Virginia. Third, emphasize competition. Private firms are not inherently efficient. It is competition that produces results. Government is no different. Lastly, defuse controversy by maintaining an open communication environment and by incorporating policies to reduce impacts to state employees.

Everyone in Virginia does not embrace change. The same was true when Thomas Jefferson was governor in 1779 and he proposed that the legislature move the capital to Richmond, "which was more safe and central than any other town situated on navigable water." Virginia is at a crossroads of change again. Our charge is to lead the renaissance in government by the actions I have described, which are focused to achieve our core philosophies. Outstanding customer service "satisfaction" is the standard for our citizen owners and customers of government. We rank our government programs based on outcomes rather than intentions.

Competition in government is at the cutting edge of government's evolution in the information age. Virginia is poised to ask the tough questions about what government should be doing. Is it the right mission? Is it still worth doing? These questions set the stage for more competition and choice in government services. It leads to a tremendous increase in performance, quality and service to the citizens. The main result, however, will be a change in the basic approach of government—a change in the culture of government and the way we do business.

Privatization in Iowa

A Business Case for Decision Making

Terry Branstad
Governor of Iowa

Privatization is not new to Iowa government. From the origins of the primary road system in the mid-1920s, the Iowa State Highway Commission (now the Iowa Department of Transportation) outsourced almost all highway and bridge construction. The College Student Aid Commission contracted out student loan disbursement, preclaim, and database services beginning in the mid-1960s. Since 1981, the state has contracted with Correctional Medical Services for medical services at a state prison. Retail liquor and wine sales were privatized in the mid-1980s.

More recently, however, privatization has expanded beyond these areas. Iowa state government decision makers now regularly ask themselves: From both quality and cost perspectives, who can most effectively provide a service for the taxpayers and citizens of Iowa?

Recent Privatization in Iowa

Iowa began to systematically pursue new privatization opportunities in 1991. Each agency director received "A Guide to Privatization in Iowa," which outlined general guidelines and principles. Suggestions for new privatization projects came from many sources: private companies, agency directors and other state administrators, citizen commissions, and the state's Department of Management.

From the outset, we based privatization decisions on business grounds, not ideology. Can the private sector provide the desired level of service at less cost than government? Who is best positioned to provide the service most effectively and efficiently? Brief snapshots of Iowa's major privatization efforts in the 1990s are presented below.

Alcohol Beverage Division

When a private-sector provider approached the state's Alcohol Beverage Division (ABD) in 1991 with a proposal to handle the division's receipts, warehousing, and delivery operations, we bid the work, compared costs, and found that the private sector could indeed save the state money for the receipt, warehousing, and delivery of alcoholic beverages. Privatizing these functions saved the taxpayers $800,000 in each of the five years of the contract. That contract was recently renewed for an additional five years at annual savings of $1 million per year.

Our analysis also showed, however, that the data processing activities in support of the ABD receipt, warehousing, and delivery functions were competitive with the private sector, and, therefore, data processing functions continue to be provided by state employees.

Veterans' Home

Similarly, at the state veterans' home, an analysis prompted by a citizen commission led to savings of $1,100,000 per year and the reduction of 125 FTEs by privatizing food service and housekeeping. These savings were matched with federal funds, which allowed the home to open 102 more beds and hire approximately 135 new staff members to meet the increased patient levels.

At the same time, cost comparisons showed the state's provision of laundry/linen services to be in line with private-sector costs. Therefore, laundry/linen services were kept in-house.

Public Defenders

As should be clear from the first two examples, a business analysis does not always lead to privatization. In the case of indigent defense, our analysis meant just the opposite. In 1991, we compared the cost of private versus state attorneys in providing legal representation to indigent defendants in criminal cases. Full-time public defenders employed by the state did the work for about $220 per case. The average cost per case assigned to a private attorney was more than double that amount, at $450. Based on this differential, 65 additional state public defenders have been hired since 1991, more than doubling the number of state defense attorneys. Given that state attorneys handled 57,000 cases last year (private attorneys handled 27,000), these new hires have saved the state about $7 million in the last year alone.

Because of conflicts of interest, continued overloading, and a lack of state public defender presence in some rural areas, private attorneys still represent indigent defendants in many cases. Our cost containment (and privatization) strategy in these cases has been to retain selected attorneys at a competitive contract rate. Typical contract rates are $55/hour for Class A felonies, $50/hour for Class B felonies, and $45/hour for other cases. The contract lawyers receive a preference in case assignments in return for the lower rate. During a six-county pilot of this approach in 1992, the cost per case dropped from $450 to $350. Following this successful pilot, the General Assembly authorized the state public defender to contract wherever it is cost advantageous to do so. We now contract in about 30 counties, with more than 900 contracts in place.

The State Public Defender's Office tracks the average cost per case in each county, and in those counties where the cost per case is high enough to show savings through contracting, we attempt to contract with local lawyers.

Women's Correctional Facility

Iowa's Fifth Judicial District Community Services Program constructed a new 48-bed women's correctional facility on the campus of Broadlawns Hospital in Des Moines, coming on-line in 1993. The facility was unusual because it sought to provide a secure environment in which inmate mothers could spend more time with their children. (Eight of the forty-eight beds are for women with children under five.) Because this prison population differed—it was less violent—we were seeking the opportunity to pursue a different strategy. In that setting and before a decision was made about who should actually operate the facility, we conducted a private versus public analysis. This analysis led to a management contract with a private firm, DTH, for a sum $100,000 under the projected budget. These savings enabled the facility to offer child rearing and domestic abuse prevention programs, which had earlier been cut from the plans for lack of funds.

Not only were cost savings achieved, but through a three-year contract (then renewed for another three years) with capped cost increase provisions, we have cost predictability, which eases budgeting pressure. The contract serves as an on-going "cost containment" function as well as a source of initial cost savings.

While potential cost savings were the primary motivation behind the contract with DTH, other important benefits also emerged. DTH proved more willing to work with state officials to tailor programming; local providers had relied too heavily on canned programs. DTH's entry into the Des Moines market prompted other treatment providers to be more responsive. Perhaps less entrenched in local turf patterns, DTH was able to cultivate new coalitions with other providers in the community, for example, in-home Headstart programming with Drake University.

Interstate Rest Area Maintenance

The Iowa Department of Transportation (IDOT) privatized interstate rest area maintenance in 1993, achieving significant savings in the initial statewide contract with an out-of-state firm. That contractor, however, proved incapable of delivering the desired level of service, and the relationship was terminated. IDOT then took a different tack. By splitting the rest areas into individual contracts and prohibiting vendors from servicing more than two rest areas, the contracts were won by local contractors who took a much greater interest in performing up to the expected standards of cleanliness and service.

For a variety of reasons, the level of service at the rest areas was also substantially upgraded at the time. While that change prevents direct pre- and post-privatization cost comparisons, IDOT projects that the current contracts save $950,000 annually over the amount it would cost IDOT to provide the current level of service. Also noteworthy, no state employees were laid off as a result of this privatization; IDOT placed them in other positions.

An earlier "make or buy" business analysis at IDOT resulted in work being done in-house. When 33 speed monitoring sites were installed in 1980, outside contractor estimates came in at $30,000 per site. IDOT installed them for $16,000 per site.

Department of Employment Services

Iowa continued to move toward even more business-oriented models for privatization. The Department of Employment Services sought to cut costs in four service areas: janitorial; heating, ventilation, and air conditioning; grounds maintenance; and refuse removal. Rather than only seeking bids from the private sector, the department also sought cost estimates from the existing provider, the state's Department of General Services. As a result, three of the four functions stayed with General Services, but at lower rates. One, janitorial services, was determined to be more effectively provided by the private sector. Combined annual savings for the four activities total $158,000.

Lessons Learned

Iowa's experiences point to the following keys for success:

- Agency cooperation and "buy in," based upon an ability to use privatization to achieve savings and preserve service.
- Full understanding of the function under analysis, including all associated costs.
- Importance of permanent, ongoing contract management by state government employees.
- Long-term contracts, generally of three to five years, with cost increases limited through a tie to a price index.
- Full disclosure of financial information on current state costs to perform the activity.
- "The little things": paying attention to detail, seeking and responding to input from all concerned, providing full information, and anticipating problems.

Toward Competitive Provision of Services

In the spring of 1996, the evolution of privatization in Iowa state government took another significant step. An interagency working group investigated others' successes and proposed guidelines for a competitive delivery of services initiative in Iowa. "Competition" was launched in May 1996, and two pilot projects were identified in the IDOT a few weeks later (sign shop and pavement markings). These projects are being implemented at this writing. By "competition," we mean issuing a request for proposal for the provision of a government service and accepting proposals from both the state work unit currently providing the service and potential private-sector providers.

In addition to the two DOT projects, the state's data processing centers, currently undergoing reorganization, may also present opportunities for competitive processes. Similarly, management of a proposed statewide network of workforce development centers may be competitively let. To complete the current agenda, consolidated state government debt collection is being evaluated.

Iowa is moving toward the competitive model because it makes sense. It makes sense because from a customer point of view the issue is not public versus private; it is monopoly versus competition. Taxpayers want the same value for their tax dollars as they demand for their other consumer dollars. Rightly or wrongly, they often perceive government as inefficient and unresponsive.

Government workers are just as fed up with this reputation and the systems that created it. Public-sector workers are every bit as smart and productive as private-sector workers, but they too often feel trapped in systems that stifle initiative, efficiency, creativity, and productivity. By putting the engine of competition to work for all concerned, public employees share the incentives that drive performance in the private sector. Government costs will go down and service levels will go up.

Every morning, businesses wake up to the reality check of the marketplace. All day they respond and consumers benefit. For those government activities with private sector counterparts, the marketplace can deliver the same potent reality check. Government will have to listen and taxpayers and citizens will benefit.

To help ensure a level playing field for competing state workers—and on a case-by-case basis—we provide the employees currently doing the work with assistance in understanding their current cost structure, streamlining their operations, and preparing a bid. We give the employees latitude in reengineering their unit, operations, and budget.

To further minimize disruption and treat public employees fairly, we will try to find other state positions for those who are displaced. Other placement services will also be available. Another key feature of our competition initiative is that state workers can propose pay and performance incentive features that will both benefit them and taxpayers.

Not every government function should be competed. Competition is not appropriate where considerable policy discretion is exercised in the function or where there is no competitive market for the service. Conversely, the most likely areas to be competed are those where little policy discretion is involved and where there are many potential providers of the service.

Allowing state employees to bid has also opened the door to a less confrontational relationship between state government and AFSCME, the principal public employee union in Iowa. Management's inclusion of AFSCME in the competition initiative has improved communications and led to a more constructive atmosphere for implementation.

We will continue to learn from ongoing privatization efforts, exploring the benefits business-oriented decision making can bring to Iowa citizens. The public demands—and deserves—no less.

Appendix

The following are other examples of privatization in Iowa State government:

- Collection of Defaulted Student Loans. In fiscal year 1995, the College Student Aid Commission paid $1,568,328 in commissions to four private vendors. The average cost to the vendors was approximately 20 percent of the amount collected; the cost to collect internally was almost 23 percent.
- Mail Services. The Department of General Services contracts for about half of total lettershop services required by state agencies in the Capitol Complex.
- Data Processing for Child Support Recovery Software Development. The Department of Human Services projected a net savings of $2.6 million from outsourcing this activity in fiscal years 1993–1999.
- University Farm Services. Iowa State University eliminated internal farm production operations and used private operators beginning in the 1995 crop season. This change resulted in one-time savings of more than $1 million and ongoing savings of $200,000/year, eliminating about ten full-time equivalents.

Bush/Brogan A+ Plan for Education

Jeb Bush
Governor of Florida

While there is no magic bullet that will solve every problem facing our education system, we are working to make education the paramount duty of our state. The fundamental premise at the core of Florida's education policy should be unequivocal: every child can learn and no child should be left behind. We will

- Set high standards and provide adequate funding, and then hold schools and educators accountable for the performance of the students they are entrusted to educate.
- Provide rewards for success and consequences for failure.
- Give families more educational choices, including more magnet schools and more charter schools.
- Improve school safety and classroom discipline through better teacher preparation and more alternative schools for disruptive students.
- Increase total funding for K–12 public schools (state and local funds) by 7.1 percent, or $750 million, in 1999, so that schools have adequate resources to accomplish these goals.

The A+ plan for education has three major parts—one addressing accountability and improving student learning, one to raise standards and improve training for educators, and one to improve school safety and reduce truancy. Improving student learning will become the test by which we should measure education policy. The Bush/Brogan administration challenges the status quo and everyone in the public school system to do better.

The Bush/Brogan Commitment to Accountability and Improving Student Learning

Revise State Education Goals

If we are to expect dramatic efforts to improve Florida's schools, we must challenge our schools to ensure that all children gain at least a year's learning for each year in school. The first step is to make sure that Florida has a state education goal that expresses this challenge. The state goals addressing readiness, teacher quality, high school graduation, and family literacy must reinforce the overall goal to improve student learning from readiness to adult education.

Measure Annual Student Learning

We cannot expect our system to meet the challenge to improve without a way to measure progress and know when we succeed and when we fail. The current Florida Comprehensive Assessment Test is a beginning, but it only addresses reading, writing and mathematics performance in grades four, five (mathematics only), eight and ten. To better track student learning, the state testing program will be expanded to all grades from three through ten. The new tests will measure student learning from year to year and become the backbone of the state's accountability system. The new tests will be implemented in the 2000–2001 school year.

Close the Education Gap in Our Public School System

We will never be able to claim excellence as long as children are left behind to fail or drop out, unable to compete successfully in our society. We must move beyond labeling and lowering expectations for large numbers of children to find innovative ways to boost their learning and their success. The Bush/Brogan plan includes funding for close-the-gap training, expanded mentoring programs, intensive reading programs, challenge college scholarship programs and supplemental instruction to increase educational opportunities for all students regardless of their race, background, or socioeconomic status.

Grade Schools and Report Progress

Once progress is measured, it must be reported to the students, parents and communities the schools serve. Given reliable and easy-to-understand information on the quality of their schools, parents can become better partners in the effort to improve. The release of the first list of critically failing schools was the first step toward informing parents of school performance and holding schools accountable for their performance. Those schools improved quickly and in some cases dramatically. The Bush/Brogan plan requires all schools to receive a report card on how well they perform. They will receive grades from A to F and will receive rewards or sanctions depending on their performance. School performance includes more than overall student achievement. Schools will also be measured on how well the lowest performing students learn. Schools will not receive passing marks if the lowest performing students are left behind. Schools having excellent performance or making significant improvement will be recognized. Parents will receive report cards on how well their child's school performs each year. Report cards are valuable tools for assessing the progress of our children and can serve the same function for our schools.

Eliminate Social Promotion

Sadly, the percentage of our students who read below basic levels increases as they move through school. It is well documented that young children with learning deficits fall farther behind with each passing year. This occurs largely because children's learning problems are not corrected early and they are passed to the next grade without being expected to master the basic subjects of reading, mathematics and writing. The policy of social promotion (being promoted without demonstrating achievement) will be eliminated in Florida's public schools. Students will be required to meet standards in order to be promoted to the next grade. A total of $527 million was appropriated in 1999 for school districts to use on intensive instruction designed to help students meet promotion and graduation standards. Schools will have maximum freedom to use these funds to support innovative programs to improve students' reading, writing and mathematics skills. Schools may use funds for such strategies as summer school, after-school instruction, tutoring, home reading programs, mentoring and extended day programs to help students master academic skills.

Reward Schools for Achievement and Improvement

The private sector has long used incentives to improve performance. It works! The public sector, however, sometimes confuses uniformity with fairness. The true measure of fairness is when compensation matches the quality of work. Beginning next year, schools that receive an A and those that improve at least one grade based on student achievement, attendance, dropout rate, discipline and college readiness will be rewarded with up to $100 per student. The budget includes $15 million for the school recognition and reward program. The highest performing and improving schools will also be deregulated and given the freedom to manage their own budgets and use innovative strategies to produce even more dramatic improvement.

Help Failing Schools and Give Parents More Choice if They Do Not Improve

Schools with added challenges need our help and attention. They need our best teachers, our strongest partnerships, and our most determined parents. Schools performing at a failing level will be given two years to improve during which they will receive assistance from the school district and the Department of Education. If the school fails to improve beyond an F in the second year, it will be subject to State Board of Education sanctions currently provided in law. The Bush/Brogan A+ plan gives parents an opportunity to send their children to a higher performing public school or private school of their choice. Opportunity scholarships to higher performing public schools or private schools will be revenue neutral or result in a cost savings for the school district and the state. We owe our children a quality education. If the schools they are required to attend cannot provide one, then they should be free to choose another school. To participate in the program, private schools must agree to accept all eligible students. All students utilizing opportunity scholarships must continue to participate in the state testing program.

The Bush/Brogan Commitment to Higher Professional Standards for Educators

Raise Standards for Professional Educators

Florida's standards for educators have been too low. We require only a tenth-grade mastery of reading and mathematics to become certified to teach our children. Applicants who cannot meet these low standards are allowed alternatives that are even less rigorous. How can a system demand higher expectations of students while it continually dilutes standards for the adults who teach them? The

Bush/Brogan A+ plan increases standards for education professionals at every level, entry to colleges of education, initial certification to teach, and recertification. With the exception of qualified applicants with disabilities, alternatives to passing general knowledge examinations will be eliminated. The State Board of Education is directed to reassess and reset passing scores on teacher examinations to ensure that entering teachers have mastery of college-level skills in reading, writing and mathematics.

Rate Colleges of Education on Performance

Currently there is little accountability for teacher preparation programs in Florida. The Bush/Brogan legislation requires that colleges of education be rated on their performance. Factors such as the percentage of students who complete the program, the percentage who pass teacher examinations and gain employment, and the satisfaction of employers will be included in their rating. Each school's rating will be published in the college or university catalog and included in the institution's performance reports.

Raise Standards for Admission to Colleges of Education

Standards for admission of students into colleges of education will be raised. All applicants will be required to pass a test of general knowledge to be admitted as a teacher candidate. We expect our K–12 students to pass tests to be promoted and to graduate. We should not expect less of teacher candidates and teachers.

Reward High-Performing Educators

What incentives does the system now have for improving teacher performance? How do we recognize excellence? Excellence has disappeared from some school district teacher evaluation systems. How would we react if no student were allowed to make an A in a subject? If we want A+ schools, we have to identify and reward excellent educators. The Excellent Teaching Program provides an incentive for teachers who attain National Board Certification. The Bush/Brogan A+ plan requires that high-performing teachers be rewarded annually within the school district salary structure. The plan requires that school district employee salary plans devote at least 5 percent of each educator's base pay to annual performance evaluations by the year 2002. These evaluations must have provisions for assessing excellence in teaching and must be based largely on student learning gains.

Focus and Improve Teacher Training

Currently, there is no coherent state policy for the use of professional development dollars. There is little or no evaluation conducted to determine if the training is effective. What we do have is widespread testimony of teachers that teacher training is often a waste of time. The A + legislation sets state policy for the use of teacher training funds. State funds allocated to teacher training will first be used to improve teacher performance in the classroom. Additionally, the appropriations act includes $10 million to establish highly focused teacher training institutes and expanded technology-based training such as distance learning and Internet-based assistance. Training must become more market-driven and result-oriented, requiring customer satisfaction to be continued.

The Bush/Brogan Commitment to Safer Schools

Invest More in School Safety

Florida has the premier school violence and crime electronic data reporting system. The state is investing resources into improving the quality of information by training more school personnel. This information is useless if it is not used to guide school safety efforts. The Bush/Brogan plan requires all schools to develop school improvement plans that include specific measures for improving school discipline and safety. The appropriations act provides $70 million, an increase of $20 million, to support these safety plans.

Expand Second-Chance Schools for Disruptive and Violent Youth

Florida has a chronic dropout problem. We devote hundreds of millions of dollars to support dropout prevention programs throughout the state. With more and more students reporting that they are afraid to go to school, our first priority must be to ensure a safe, secure learning environment. The Bush/Brogan A + legislation frees up funds for school districts to direct a greater portion of dropout prevention funds to support second-chance schools and other alternatives for disruptive students. The plan also creates an incentive program for public–private partnerships in operating off-campus, second-chance schools.

Prepare Teachers to Handle Classroom Discipline

Teachers consistently rate classroom management as the weakest area of preparation for the job of teaching. Today's students offer greater challenges to experienced teachers as well as those just entering the workforce. The A+ plan responds to the need to better prepare teachers to handle discipline in the classroom by adding it to the list of skills required for certification and by holding colleges of education accountable for doing a better job in this area. Teacher candidates should work with our best teachers through internships to gain hands-on experience in this critical area. Teacher training funds and school safety funds may be used to support these efforts and provide effective teacher training in managing student discipline.

Reduce Absenteeism and Truancy

High rates of school absenteeism and truancy lead to lower student performance and increased daytime juvenile crime. Truancy has been identified by law enforcement agencies and the Department of Juvenile Justice as being a chronic problem in Florida. Before a school can take legal action, it must go through lengthy and often expensive steps. For example, students must receive a comprehensive evaluation before the student or parent can be held accountable. Bureaucratic requirements for enforcing school attendance laws will be reduced and schools will be expected to rigorously enforce school attendance. Students have to be in school to benefit from programs funded by the state and local taxpayers. In addition to enforcing school attendance, the plan establishes a pilot program to raise the compulsory school attendance age from 16 to 18. This pilot will be evaluated for possible statewide adoption.

Through all of these initiatives, we can ensure that children in Florida's educational system learn a year's worth of knowledge in a year's worth of time.

The Minnesota Family Investment Program (MFIP)

A Thorough Restructuring of Welfare

Arne Carlson
Governor of Minnesota

Minnesota has become a national model for its implementation of an innovative welfare reform effort known as the Minnesota Family Investment Program (MFIP). This program began as a seven-county pilot program in 1994. After eighteen months, 52 percent of MFIP participants had moved off of assistance and into jobs. As governor, I led the fight to implement this program. I believe that the most important element to reforming welfare is to create an environment for children where work is a way of life. I saw too many children growing up in homes where parents had never worked and where the concept of work had no value. I saw MFIP as a program that would transform the welfare system from one that discourages families from working to one that expects, supports, and rewards work. After the initial success in the pilot program, I pushed hard to make this a statewide initiative. My efforts came to fruition on April 30, 1997, when I signed into law a landmark welfare reform bill, making MFIP the state-wide welfare reform initiative, effective January 1, 1998. What follows is a closer look at the details of the MFIP and how it came into existence.

Minnesota's innovative approach to welfare reform began in response to a move in 1986 by the state legislature to cut welfare benefits. At the time, Minnesota provided cash benefits to low-income families with children under the Aid to Families with Dependent Children (AFDC) program. Minnesota's benefit lev-

els for the AFDC program, $528 per month for a parent and two children, were
the fifth-highest payment standard in the nation.[1] Legislators argued that families
receiving AFDC, and the benefits that usually accompany it such as food stamps
and Medicaid, were better off than families with a full-time earner making minimum wage. The minimum wage at the time was $3.35 per hour.

The issue of benefit levels was not resolved during the 1986 session. Legislators reached an impasse over a proposal to cut benefit levels for AFDC recipients.
The impasse was averted by the governor appointing a bipartisan commission on
welfare reform. The Minnesota Commission on Welfare Reform included county
officials, nonprofit providers and advocates for the poor. The ten-member commission was cochaired by the director of Catholic Charities, a nonprofit organization serving the poor, and a county commissioner from Hennepin County, Minnesota's largest, urban county. The commission's mandate was to submit
recommendations for improving the welfare system to the Legislature by December 1986.

MFIP Grew from Frustration with AFDC

Although the impetus for forming the commission was a debate about benefit
levels, the commission undertook a much broader task of studying the AFDC
program and identifying ways to improve how government responds to families
in crises. Key findings included in the commission's report were instrumental in
shaping the objectives for restructuring welfare in Minnesota.

The commission found that most single parents left AFDC after temporary
help.[2] In fact, 57 percent of the recipients were on AFDC less than 24 months.
However, AFDC did not appear to be working for a small number of recipients,
roughly 10 percent of the total caseload, who remained on the program for an
extended period. Over time, this small group collected between one-third to one-
half of all AFDC benefits.

The commission also found that federal laws and rules governing AFDC dis-
couraged work. A single parent receiving AFDC was usually better off not working because her benefits were reduced by almost a dollar for every dollar she
earned. Since federal AFDC rules about earned income and work expense disre-
gards changed following enactment of the Omnibus Reconciliation Act (OBRA)
of 1981, the percentage of AFDC recipients reporting earned income dropped
from a pre-OBRA experience of 28–32 percent to a post-OBRA experience of

about 14 percent according to information collected in Minnesota for quality control purposes.

Supports, such as subsidized child care for low-income working families, were not readily available to people trying to transition off of cash assistance. In Minnesota, state funding of a subsidized child-care program for low-income families was first authorized in 1985.

Finally, the commission found that recipients, eligibility workers and program administrators found it increasingly difficult to understand and administer welfare programs. More than 80 percent of Minnesota's AFDC families also received food stamps.[3] Rules were not consistent between the two programs. For example, the AFDC program allowed families to exempt a vehicle worth $1,500 from the asset limit used to calculate eligibility. Under the food stamp program families were allowed to exempt a vehicle with a value up to $4,500 from the asset limit.

This dissatisfaction with AFDC prompted the commission to recommend shifting the focus of AFDC in Minnesota from an income maintenance program to a transitional program to enable long-term recipients to move toward self-sufficiency.

Development of the MFIP Model

Responsibility for carrying out the commission's recommendations was initially assigned to a newly created Office of Jobs Policy. This office was charged with pulling together a working group of staff from the state's education, jobs and training, human services, planning and finance agencies. The work group set out to explore how Minnesota might reform welfare if there were no federal restrictions. After much deliberation, the group came out with a product referred to as the cosmic waiver because it sought federal law changes and administrative waivers necessary to create incentives for recipients to exit the welfare program. The cosmic waiver was put out on the street for reaction from recipients, county staff, job training staff, advocates and educators. After incorporating suggestions from the various constituencies, the cosmic waiver evolved into the Minnesota Family Investment Program (MFIP), and the Minnesota Department of Human Services took over responsibility for carrying out the plan.

Development of MFIP was centered around two goals: moving families out of poverty and reducing their dependency on welfare. Inclusion of a goal to reduce poverty set MFIP apart from welfare reform efforts in other states. MFIP is also one of the few state welfare reform efforts to combine mandated work-focused activities with financial incentives for families that work. Under the program:

- Families receive income supplements as they work their way out of poverty. They leave public assistance when their income is roughly 20 percent above the 1996 federal poverty level.
- Parents are expected to begin supporting their families within strict time limits or their benefits will be reduced.
- Working families receive help with subsidized child and health care and job placement.
- By replacing AFDC, Family General Assistance (a state cash-assistance program for families that do not qualify for AFDC), food stamps, and employment and training programs with MFIP, program administration is simplified. Streamlining program administration allows staff resources to be directed toward the principal goals of MFIP—moving people into work and out of poverty.

MFIP is a thorough restructuring of welfare. With MFIP, assistance is redefined. It is no longer something government "provides" and a family "receives." Instead, the relationship between government and the family emphasizes mutual responsibility for both parties. The focus of the program is on outcomes for families, assisting families to achieve greater independence by increasing their income. Parents are expected to take responsibility for their families' well-being by going to work (or beginning work-related activities) within a specified period of time or they will face tough financial sanctions. Government supports working parents by providing access to subsidized child care, low-cost health care coverage, and tax credits and by aggressively pursuing child-support collections.

Testing MFIP and Evaluating Its Effectiveness

State legislation authorizing MFIP to move forward was first enacted in 1989. Later that year, Congress passed federal legislation to allow Minnesota to test MFIP. MFIP began as a demonstration project in 1994. Seven field trial counties were selected for the test. Based upon an analysis of 41 variables, a cluster of four central Minnesota counties was selected to represent rural Minnesota. Hennepin County, which includes Minneapolis, and two suburban counties represented the urban environment. Random assignment of applicants and recipients to MFIP and AFDC (the control group) was used to ensure that differences in outcomes between MFIP and the control group could reliably be attributed to the MFIP program rather than to other factors, such as changes in the economy and the employment rate. The Manpower Demonstration Research Corporation (MDRC) was hired to evaluate the field trials.

MDRC issued a report in October 1997, reviewing the impacts of the MFIP field trials after the first 18 months of operation (see table 5.1).[4] The report showed that MFIP is meeting its two principal goals of moving families out of poverty and reducing their dependency on welfare. In fact, it is one of the most effective efforts in the country at moving long-term, urban welfare recipients into

Table 5.1 Eighteen-Month Impacts of MFIP for Single-Parent Long-Term Recipients in Urban Counties

Outcome	MFIP Group	AFDC Group (Impact)	Difference Change	Percentage
During 18 months after random assignment				
Percent employed	76.0%	59.0%	17.0%	28.8
Earnings	$4,912	$3,871	$1,041	26.9
Welfare benefits received*	$11,074	$10,256	$ 818	8.0
Total income**	$15,986	$14,127	$1,859	13.2
Percent below 1994 poverty level***	71.4%	85.2%	− 13.8%	− 16.2
During months 16–18 after random assignment				
Percent employed	52.1%	37.6%	14.5%	38.7
Receiving welfare benefits*	80.6%	76.9%	3.7%	4.8

Source: Manpower Demonstration Research Corporation, *Making Welfare Work and Work Pay: Implementation and 18-Month Impacts of the Minnesota Family Investment Program,* October 1997.

Notes: The sample includes 676 single parents assigned to the MFIP group and 687 single parents assigned to the AFDC group.

*"Welfare benefits" are defined as receipt of food stamp coupons or cash benefits from AFDC, Family General Assistance, or MFIP.

**"Total income" includes earnings plus welfare benefits, both based on administrative records.

***Since the measure of income used here includes earnings, cash, welfare, and food stamp benefits but does not include income from other sources, the poverty rate reported here is not comparable with the official poverty rate.

work and out of poverty. After 18 months on the program, 52 percent of long-term, urban MFIP recipients were working, an increase of almost 40 percent over the control group. Poverty among these families was reduced by 16 percent.

Preliminary results from the report show it was the combination of financial incentives and mandatory employment activities that produced the increased employment and earnings and reduced poverty among long-term, urban welfare recipients. It is unusual for a welfare reform effort to achieve simultaneous goals of increasing employment among the recipient population and making families better off financially. Offering either the financial incentives or the mandatory employment activity component alone would not have achieved gains of this magnitude in both areas simultaneously.

The preliminary results also show that a different intervention strategy may work better with new applicants for MFIP who reside in urban areas. In the field trials, the MFIP model did not mandate work activity until the twenty-fourth month of assistance. Thus, new applicants were offered only financial incentives to work, which produced a modest (less than 5 percent) increase in employment and no increase in earnings. This finding led to a modification for statewide implementation of intervening earlier with mandated work activities.

The first 18 months demonstrated successful implementation of a mandatory, work-focused employment and training component of MFIP. Previously, Minnesota's participation in employment and training programs was voluntary and the emphasis had been on education.

Case managers, under contract with the county to provide direct services to recipients in MFIP field trial counties, reported that they found it easier to encourage recipients to work because MFIP is designed to guarantee that work will increase income. Under the old AFDC program, recipients often found themselves financially worse off when they reported earned income. Because of this uncertainty about whether work would be rewarded, case managers and county eligibility staff had been reluctant to encourage recipients to get a job.

The MFIP field trials ended June 30, 1998. MDRC is scheduled to issue a final report about the field trials during calendar year 2000.

In addition to preliminary results directly attributable to the program design of MFIP, successes in other areas are contributing to a decline in Minnesota's welfare caseloads. The local economy has been relatively strong the last few years, and state unemployment rates have consistently been below the national average. Aggressive child-support efforts have more than doubled the amount of state support collected over the past six years; collections grew to $363 million in state fiscal year 1997. MinnesotaCare, a program that allows low-income families to buy health insurance at reduced rates, is responsible for keeping 4,600 families off welfare and is estimated to save taxpayers $2.5 million a month in welfare and related medical assistance costs.[5] Substantial increases in state funding for child care have expanded access to child care subsidies for working families trying to avoid welfare.

Expanding MFIP Statewide

During the 1997 legislative session, policymakers decided to expand MFIP statewide, as Minnesota's response to the federal welfare reform changes in the Personal Responsibility and Work Opportunity Reconciliation Act (PRWORA) of 1996. Statewide MFIP incorporates the demonstration project's most successful features and maintains the dual goals of reducing poverty and dependency on welfare. Some changes were made to the program design to contain costs such as calibrating the assistance standard and work incentives to produce an exit from MFIP at 120 percent of poverty rather than the 137 percent of poverty level used in the field trials. Other changes were made in response to MDRC's 18-month impact report such as intervening earlier with employment mandates: two-parent families are expected to engage in employment activities right away; and intervention for single-parent families begins after six months on the program. A 60-month time limit on receipt of cash assistance was also adopted for statewide MFIP to conform with federal law.

When reviewing Minnesota's efforts to restructure welfare and assessing how it fits in with federal welfare reform, it is important for states to consider that Minnesota received waivers to implement MFIP prior to PRWORA.

Lessons for Others

The concept for MFIP has endured the test of time. The durability of MFIP can be attributed to the soundness of the program's basic principles. The goals and design of MFIP were shaped by the research and findings of the Commission on Welfare Reform. Support for the MFIP model was garnered by seeking input into the design from a broad set of stakeholders both inside and outside of government. Plans for rigorous testing of MFIP added credibility to the welfare reform effort.

MFIP's survival, and now statewide implementation, is also a result of a loyal cadre of state agency staff who were instrumental in the development of the program and have remained committed to the effort through implementation; the investment and hard work of county staff and employment and training providers under contract with counties; and the strong, bipartisan support MFIP has received at both the state and local levels of government.

Conclusion

Minnesota has shown that it is possible to achieve dual goals of reducing dependency on welfare and alleviating poverty among families by changing the content and structure of welfare. By pairing financial incentives with mandatory work requirements, MFIP has been able to reduce poverty among families participating in the program by 16 percent. While time and care have been required to get reform right, Minnesota has succeeded in transforming its welfare system into one that expects, supports and rewards work.

Notes

1. Sam Newlund, "State AFDC Payments Are Nation's 5th Highest," *Minneapolis Star and Tribune*, May 25, 1986, p. 8B.

2. Commission on Welfare Reform, *Report of the Minnesota Commission on Welfare Reform, Aid to Families with Dependent Children Program,* December 1, 1986.

3. Mark Kleczewski, *Low Income Single Parents: Disposable Income*, Minnesota Department of Human Services, February 25, 1997.

4. Manpower Demonstration Research Corporation, *Making Welfare Work and Work Pay: Implementation and 18-Month Impacts of the Minnesota Family Investment Program*, October 1997.

5. Gestur Davidson, Shawn Welch, and George Hoffman, "Does Subsidizing Health Insurance Reduce Welfare Caseloads? The Case of MinnesotaCare," unpublished manuscript, Minnesota Department of Human Services, June 1997.

The Strategic Approach to Privatization

John Engler
Governor of Michigan

The Privatization Context

Privatization has become a buzzword of the 1990s whose meaning and intent are often ambiguous. But in Michigan, my administration has viewed privatization as a means of improving the quality of services for our citizens while reducing the cost of providing these services for our taxpayers. When Americans work 184.6 out of 365 days (or until July 3, 1996) to pay for government services and regulations before earning actual take-home pay, the government should instead look to the private sector for the provision of necessary services.[1] Privatization enables the government to benchmark its performance and analyze its ability to meet the needs of its citizens more effectively.

Some governments use privatization as part of a larger effort to fundamentally redefine the role of government. For people in eastern European nations who have gained freedom from central government oppression, privatization describes a complete change in the nation's economic structure. To varying degrees, government leaders and citizens in these nations realize that government's role has been too pervasive, that markets have a legitimate role, and that private citizens have the capability and motivation to make decisions formerly made by the government. In short, privatization is a means of economic improvement, even survival.

In western European nations, especially the United Kingdom, privatization is used to reinvigorate local economies and restore citizen participation in economic decision making. Margaret Thatcher's government used privatization not only to balance government budgets, but also to reduce the role of government in privately owned functions that operated in other countries. More importantly, Thatcher expanded citizen ownership of state departments by allowing public employees to purchase assets in state-owned companies in order to encourage employee support and prevent the return to an ever-expanding welfare state that had occurred prior to her administration. In short, privatization reflects a major change in the relationship between government and the market.

In small cities throughout the world and especially in the United States, privatization is not simply an ideology but an obvious and practical means of providing fundamental services to citizens. Political decision makers often lack the resources and the desire to build large government institutions that provide services as basic as trash collection, road repair, and transportation. Rather than expand government bureaucracies, these decision makers choose the obvious alternative and contract out. While there is currently a profound interest in privatization among many states, it is difficult to achieve without careful planning and a methodical approach.

The Strategic Approach

For privatization to be accomplished successfully, the following elements must exist:

1. Opportunity: Privatization can occur only when the public sector currently owns an asset or provides a service AND when the private sector is capable of operating an asset and providing a service.
2. Ability: Government processes and systems often represent virtually insurmountable obstacles to privatization.
3. Desire: Government decision makers must have the willingness and the motivation (including public understanding and support) to privatize.

In Michigan, we have developed a strategic privatization plan that examines many state government functions and assets and that determines which can be better performed by or sold to the private sector. The plan, designed to work in tandem with other reform activities of government, decentralizes much of the decision making throughout state government and involves the private sector in the planning process.

Developed over several months in cooperation with the agencies of state government, the plan also provides a general set of criteria under which privatization should be considered. Privatization is given the broadest possible meaning, exemplified by our description of 11 different kinds of privatization. More importantly, the plan includes an exhaustive list of activities and assets of state government to be evaluated for privatization. However, the list does not insist that everything be privatized; privatization may be inappropriate for reasons as simple as the absence of private sector competition to provide a service.

Opportunity

In compiling our list of activities and assets, we have encouraged introspection and creativity. We have asked our managers to consider not only how best to provide a service, but whether state government even should be in the business of providing certain services. The plan then requires each department to conduct an analysis of each item on its respective list. The analysis will determine if a function or asset is a candidate for privatization, both in terms of policy and cost benefit to taxpayers. If appropriate, providers will be sought and selected through competitive bidding to provide these services for the people of Michigan.

Sometimes even the threat of privatization makes state and city employees more efficient. Woodrow Stanley, mayor of Flint, Michigan, announced that the annual garbage collection bill of $6.2 million was too expensive. After soliciting bids from five companies, Stanley discovered that private companies could provide the service for $2 million less. Flint's city employees quickly sliced $1.4 million from their budget, required workers to work full eight-hour days instead of allowing them to leave early, decreased the sanitation staff from 47 workers to 35, and increased the stops on each route from 665 to 775. Although Mayor Stanley decided not to privatize, he saved taxpayers money and encouraged more efficient service.[2]

The private sector has a terrific opportunity to participate in the privatization effort. First, firms interested in doing business with the state should consider the areas of opportunities. Second, firms should develop creative ways to provide a service either better or less expensively than state government. Finally, firms should submit their ideas to agency heads either informally or through formal bids.

Ability

Government must ensure that privatization gives citizens services of equal or higher quality through careful contract management. As a prelude to privatization in Michigan, a task force carefully reviewed the state's contract management procedures. It found that our procurement system did not guarantee that the state acquires the best value for taxpayer money. The adage "You get what you pay for" is equally applicable in government procurement.

Rather than always seeking the lowest price, the task force recommended that a greater emphasis be placed on value to assure that our privatization efforts provide good quality services for our citizens. We have begun to achieve this by undertaking a reform of the state's procurement procedures and rules. Services are provided in a competitive environment where vendors must operate as efficiently as possible. The bottom line is that our citizens deserve and receive better services and products delivered more efficiently and at lower cost.

Desire

Like individuals and businesses, states work in a competitive, global environment. State government must wisely and efficiently provide resources to citizens that will help rather than inhibit their ability to compete. Until a competitive spirit is instilled within the operations of state government, we can never be fully competitive in enabling our people to prosper in the world economy.

Elected decision makers in Michigan are like those of every other government: we have an agenda for change that requires action. In Michigan, however, changing state government itself is part of the agenda. State government is too expensive and too unwieldy to provide services at a competitive cost. Regardless of the individual objectives of any elected official, all objectives require some reprioritization of resources. Accomplishing these objectives usually requires a more efficient management and utilization of resources. By giving citizens, consumers of government services, businesses, and elected officials a stake in a better outcome, all parties will enhance their desire for privatization. Privatization is not a right-wing ideological movement, but a means of improving the quality of services to citizens, receiving the best value, and eliminating services that are of no value.

While many states approach privatization with a narrow list of projects (and an almost identical list of failures), our strategic approach is to make privatization analysis routine for virtually every program and asset of state government. All agency directors are brought into a process that assumes privatization as the rule rather than the exception. We view privatization as synonymous with competition. Individuals and businesses must compete, and government is not immune from the need or failure to be competitive. Privatization is thus essential for us to meet the needs of our citizens more effectively.

Implementation

Bringing competition to government has been a key tenet of our strategy to right-size government. From privatizing campground reservations, travel information and Medicaid patient inquiries to outsourcing lottery products, desktop computing and seasonal data entry, we have strived to reduce bureaucracy, the unnecessary use of taxpayer money, and inefficient services. This section describes and analyzes four examples of privatization in Michigan that provided more effective and cost-efficient services.

Example 1. Accident Fund of Michigan

In 1912 private-sector employees established the Accident Fund of Michigan, a public state agency that provided coverage for injured workers. Although it was then uncertain whether private insurers would enter the marketplace, state agencies eventually were competing with more than 200 private-sector businesses to provide workers' compensation insurance. What was wrong with this picture? When I took office in 1991, the Accident Fund was essentially operating as a tax-exempt, state-run insurance monopoly. I believed that state government did not belong in the insurance business, and in October 1993 I signed a six-bill package that authorized the sale of the Accident Fund.

Employees of the Accident Fund were encouraged to match the most favorable bid and buy the insurance company. A group of employees raised money through the newly created Accident Fund Management Corporation, but their bid fell about $400,000 short. The employee bid is something I was very excited about, and I would have liked for them to have succeeded. Although they were unable to purchase the company, the 450 employees of the Accident Fund were assisted throughout the transition. The legislation authorizing the sale required bidders to guarantee current workers one year of employment; the winner of the bid, Blue

Cross and Blue Shield, sweetened their proposal by retaining 75 percent of the employees for five years.

Accident Fund employees also received retirement benefits. Those who had vested in the state retirement system before the transfer occurred received employee retirement benefits in addition to health coverage from the private owner without regard to preexisting conditions. The sale included an early-out retirement plan for employees under 55 who had accumulated enough service years. It also allowed employees who had worked for the state at least five (but less than ten) years to buy up to five years of service time and vest.

When the Michigan Treasury accepted a $225 million check from Blue Cross and Blue Shield for the purchase of the business in June 1995, Michigan set a record for the largest privatization transaction ever in the United States. We distributed the money into three funds: $195 million was deposited into the state's Rainy Day Fund to help protect against potential economic declines, making the $1 billion plus Rainy Day Fund the largest balance in Michigan history and one of the largest in the nation; $40 million went to the newly created State Parks Endowment Fund; and $20 million helped create the Civilian Corps Endowment Fund to train at-risk youth and improve Michigan's natural resources. By returning the Accident Fund to the private sector and allowing it to operate within a free market, everyone benefited—Michigan taxpayers, the Accident Fund's policyholders, injured workers. And it helped the business climate.

Example 2. Department of Transportation

My administration has increasingly hired private contractors to do road work traditionally performed by state employees. Part of the need for outsourcing results from the Michigan Department of Transportation's (MDOT's) reduction of employees. Since 1977, MDOT has reduced full-time employees from 4,992 to 3,687—a 24 percent decrease. MDOT cuts from 1991 to 1995 alone saved nearly $20 million in wages and fringe benefits per year. MDOT plans to reduce full-time employees by an additional 560 by September 1999 and estimates savings of $34 million annually.[3]

In 1991, MDOT began "MDOT Tomorrow," a program designed to cut expenditures by $115 million and move dollars from bureaucracy into road building. In addition to reducing personnel and management, MDOT privatized numerous services. Through the Adopt-A-Highway program, volunteers pick up roadside litter and save the state $3 million. In 1995, MDOT paid private companies $5.4 million to maintain roadside rest areas. Paying state employees under the old system would have cost an additional 4 percent.[4] MDOT also hired private companies to mow state-owned land along highways for $23.60 per acre, significantly cheaper than the $35 an acre charged by state employees. [5] A clear example of the cost-effectiveness of privatization is MDOT's contract with Wayne County to provide road maintenance services along a 27-mile strip of I-94. Over two years, the savings of caring for less than 30 miles of the state's highway are estimated to be $50,604.[6] MDOT reports annual savings of $5.7 million from privatizing the maintenance of rest areas, mowing, and other activities.[7]

MDOT has used privatization more than any other state agency, and consideration of further privatization is ongoing. All actual construction is now done through the private sector, and maintenance of state highways traditionally has included outsourcing to local governments. Outsourcing not only makes use of private-sector expertise so that MDOT can concentrate on its core functions, but also supplements department staff in periods when the workload exceeds capacity.

Example 3. Families First

A study by the Mackinac Center for Public Policy reported that since 1981 the number of Michigan children removed from their homes due to neglect and abuse has doubled, while the number of these children cared for by private agencies has risen from less than half to two-thirds. The study also found that state-run intervention services were not providing the most cost-effective, beneficial services. Although national child care accreditation agencies recommend child-to-worker ratios of 25:1, the Michigan Department of Social Services (MDSS) was 159 employees short as recently as November 1992 with a target rate of only 30:1. MDSS-supervised foster care was also expensive, as the tab reached $21.80 a day per child.[8]

Michigan's Families First program was implemented by MDSS in 1988 as an alternative to traditional yet more expensive protective services such as foster care. After a caseworker determines that there is no immediate threat to a child's safety, Families First aims to provide safe, intensive emergency services in a family's home. The program's goal is safely to remove risks, not children, and help families make positive, lasting changes. The program is time limited (maximum of six weeks), intense (minimum of eight to ten hours of service in the home per week), accessible (caseworkers are on call twenty-four hours a day and seven days a week), practical (families are trained to solve their own problems), and linked with other resources.[9]

University Associates, a Lansing-based research firm, evaluated the Families First program in 1995. The study spanned five years and compared a group of 225 children who participated in Families First with 225 children who received foster care services. During the six-month evaluation period, 626 children were referred to Families First; 96 percent of these children would have required placement in foster care without the intervention of Families First.

The study found that avoiding foster care for 96 percent of the children referred to Families First over the program's six-year period could have saved the state of Michigan over $219,343,000 for the first year after intervention. If foster care had been averted for only 85 percent of the children placed by Families First, the state still would have saved $185,000,000 for the first year after intervention.[10] Families First has calculated that its cost per family averages $3,930; these costs cover the initial four- to six-week intervention period and the three-, six-, and twelve-month follow-ups. These expenses are minimal compared with $11,000 a year per child in foster care and $86,000 a year per child in juvenile detention centers.[11]

More important than the financial benefits are the personal benefits. Social workers enjoy caseloads of only one to two families at a time, decreasing burnout and increasing the personalized attention they can provide. The survey found that 100 percent of referring workers said they would use Families First again, and over 90 percent of the staff rate the program as effective.[12] Families benefit from in-home services such as help with parenting skills and financial management, job placement, and transportation. Their caseworker is available whenever needed, and most importantly the child remains in his home. Eighty-two percent of the families who participated in Families First reported behavioral changes such as improved communication, appropriate discipline, and better care of children. Ninety-two percent were very satisfied with the interaction with their caseworker, and 98 percent said they would recommend Families First to others in similar situations.[13] Families First also reports that of the families who have completed the program since 1988, more than 80 percent were still together a year later.[14]

Example 4. Office Supplies

Historically, the Department of Management and Budget operated state warehouses that bought bulk quantities of office supplies at cheap rates due to economies of scale. State departments would order supplies from the warehouse through interoffice billing and then purchase special supplies from small local businesses. Although the actual supplies were inexpensive, the overhead costs of the warehouse and the side contracts made distribution inefficient and the supplies more expensive.

The changing market created additional complications. Small businesses, often surviving only because of state contracts, began to consolidate or to go out of business as they lost their ability to compete against larger suppliers. Today there are only 6,500 office supply dealers throughout the United States, half the total of six years ago.[15]

In March 1996, we began implementing a new process, called Just In Time, that allowed departments to order office supplies directly from an approved vendor, Boise Cascade. Eighty percent of orders submitted to the vendor by 5 P.M. are received the following day, with the remaining 20 percent received within two days. The process, used by the private sector for many years, enables us to eliminate our central warehouse and receive a higher discount on noncontracted items. We save additional funds by reducing inventory, warehousing costs, side contracts with small businesses, and the storage of large quantities of supplies.

After testing the program and utilizing the remaining stock in the state warehouses, all state departments began using Just In Time before October 1, 1996. In addition to providing goods more efficiently, the Just In Time contract is projected to save the state approximately $1.5 million annually over the current office supply system.[16]

Conclusion

Privatization in Michigan has been successful—saving our citizens money and providing more efficient services. By rightsizing Michigan state government, we have decreased the bureaucracy and placed more control back where it belongs—in the hands of citizens and local industries. When we focus on the things government should do and stop doing the things the private sector can do better, Michigan citizens and taxpayers are better off.

Notes

1. Michael Kamburowski and Joseph G. Lehman, "Cost of Government Day," in *Michigan Privatization Report* (Mackinac Center for Public Policy: Summer 1996), p. 5.

2. Lawrence W. Reed, "Privatization and American Business," in *Champions of Free-dom* (Hillsdale, Mich.: Hillsdale College Press, 1996), pp. 168–169.

3. "State Transportation Spending in Michigan" (Prepared for Michigan Road Build-ers Association by Public Sector Consultants: October 1996), p. 1.

4. "State Transportation," p. 1.

5. Michigan Department of Transportation.

6. Michigan Department of Transportation.

7. "State Transportation," p. 3.

8. Mark G. Michaelsen, "Privatized Child Foster Care Works for Michigan," in *View-point* (Mackinac Center for Public Policy: August 2, 1993), pp. 1–2.

9. Families First, Michigan Department of Social Services.

10. "Evaluation of Michigan's Families First Program: Executive Summary" (pre-pared by University Associates: June 1995), p. 3.

11. Families First.

12. "Evaluation of Michigan's Families First Program," p. 1.

13. "Evaluation of Michigan's Families First Program," p. 1.

14. Families First.

15. Department of Management and Budget press release, March 4, 1996.

16. Department of Management and Budget press release, March 4, 1996.

Reforming Georgia State Government

Lake Lanier Islands Resort and Water Park

Zell Miller
Governor of Georgia

This nation was founded on a belief in limited government. Over the past several generations, however, government has been increasingly called upon to intervene in more and more social and economic problems, and the size of government has increased dramatically. Too little thought is given to the question of what role government ought to play, or to the long-term costs and consequences of a growing government. Many have come to see government as the problem and not the solution, as they observe waste and inefficiency.

As a result, our citizens want better service from state government. They are not willing to pay more to get those services because they are not convinced that they have been getting value for their tax dollars.

My job as governor is to identify the important responsibilities that government should undertake and to deliver those vital services efficiently and effectively. I have four initiatives directed toward reforming state government.

First, private business is cost-efficient because it has someone looking over its shoulder who has a direct financial stake in it. Analogously, in state government, I am trying to cultivate a stronger sense of financial responsibility to the taxpayers. My goal is to collect enough tax revenue to do our job efficiently. We have enacted the third tax cut of my administration in the form of removing the state sales tax from groceries. It is the largest tax cut in state history at $500 million a year. A sales-tax reduction was chosen over other tax-reduction methods because this form of tax reduction is automatic and will benefit all Georgians.

My second major initiative is a significant revision of the state Merit System to make our state workforce more efficient and effective. Despite its name, the Merit System is not about merit. Instead of rewarding good workers, it provides cover for bad ones. When it was established more than 50 years ago, we needed a professional workforce, free from patronage. Today, however, the Merit System hamstrings state government by slowing the hiring of essential employees and by making it nearly impossible to fire bad employees. It can take six to eight weeks to fill a critical position in state government. It takes a year to a year and a half to fire a bad worker because of mounds of paperwork, hearings, and appeals.

On July 1, 1996, an "employment at will" system took effect. All new hires by the state are to be in the unclassified, unprotected service. New state workers will serve on an "employment at will" basis just like in the private sector in Georgia. This personnel system will have minimum impact on existing state workers and will avoid the potential liability associated with any legal obligations that the state may have to existing workers. Because this "employment at will" system applies to all new positions as well as new hires for future vacancies, however, transformation to this new personnel system will occur at a rate of about 15 percent annually.

The third initiative is government review and budget redirection. There is a familiar old proverb: "Give a man a fish, and he eats for a day. Teach a man to fish, and he eats for a lifetime." This captures the primary goal of budget redirection. Every single state agency is working to cut administrative costs and programs that are out-of-date or nonproductive. It is not enough simply to make state government trim and lean. It is more important to redirect the money that is freed up to the top-priority programs of the citizens and taxpayers, such as education and crime prevention. Georgia's fiscal year 1997 budget redirected more than $627 million in existing funds away from lower priorities and puts it into higher priorities. In the process of streamlining the state's administrative operations, the state payroll is reduced by a net of 902 jobs. In fiscal year 1997, privatization eliminated an additional 1,200 state jobs. Government has to establish some overriding priorities and live by them in its budget. In Georgia, the priority is to teach fishing rather than to hand out fish.

The fourth initiative is privatization. I have created a public–private, bipartisan commission that will look at every single state agency with two questions in mind. First, where can the state make more efficient use of our resources by outsourcing administrative support functions? This means that we compare the core functions of each state agency with the actual activities of these agencies in order to select areas for outsourcing, such as food and janitorial services, building maintenance, and other administrative support services.

The second question when privatizing is: What functions belong in the private sector and ought not to be in state government? For example, government has no business operating resort hotels and water parks that compete with the private sector. The state has leased the 1,200-acre Lake Lanier Islands Resort and Water Park. Under the terms of the 50-year lease, the state will make no further capital investment in the park, and it will earn $340 million during the lease term. The case is considered in more detail below. Prior to privatization, the state treasury had never received any income from the property. The successful private bidder has employed all but five of the six hundred state workers at this facility. Other resort parks, lodges, and golf courses are being reviewed for their privatization potential.

Privatization makes it possible for the government to compare its cost-effectiveness with the private sector. For example, we are privatizing a 500-bed state veterans home after comparing it to a privately managed facility that has 169 fewer employees and spends 50 percent of our cost. Under direct state operation, skilled nursing care at this war-veterans home costs $163 per day per bed as compared to the successful private sector bid of $92. State funding requirements for this facility will be reduced by nearly 50 percent.

The state will also privatize three new state prisons, providing the opportunity to see how the operating costs of state-run prisons stack up against the private sector. These three new 500-bed prisons will be financed, constructed, and operated by the private sector. The state will only rent the bed space. Studies have indicated that the private sector can provide prison space at a cost savings of 20 to 30 percent. Other privatization projects that are under study include welcome centers, motor vehicle tag and title operations, hospitals, nursing homes, revenue collections, delinquent tax collections, college dorms, and building security.

There are three essential elements to successful privatization or outsourcing. The first is competition through a request-for-proposal (RFP) basis. Single-source negotiations should be avoided except in rare circumstances. The contract must specify in detail what the state expects to receive from the private contractor. Finally, good contract administration is required to ensure that the public interest is well served. In this regard, Georgia acquired the services of a major law firm to assist in the development of model RFPs and contracts. In the cases of the war-veterans nursing home and the Lake Lanier Islands project, full-time state contract compliance officers are located on-site to protect the interest of the state.

The Lake Lanier project has a long history. In the early fall of 1995, a task force was assembled to study the potential for privatization of the state of Georgia's Lake Lanier Islands Resort and Water Park. On May 16, 1996, a private

company took over the operation of this recreation complex. The case chronicles
how we accomplished this privatization goal over a nine-month period.

Lake Lanier Islands consist of approximately 1,200 acres of lakefront property
located on the south end of Lake Sidney Lanier. The series of land masses that
comprise Lake Lanier Islands is owned by the federal government U.S. Army
Corps of Engineers and is leased to the state of Georgia (Lake Lanier Islands
Development Authority, or LLIDA) for development and operation. Lake Lanier,
located approximately 45 minutes from downtown Atlanta, is a 38,000 acre lake
with 520 miles of shoreline. It is one of the most visited Corps of Engineers'
lakes in the United States with more than seven million visitors annually.

The state initiated the development of the islands in the early 1960s to stimulate the economy in and around Hall County and to enhance the recreational resources available to the citizens of Georgia. The state, through the auspices of
the LLIDA, invested the capital needed to build the infrastructure of the islands.
From fiscal year 1968 forward, the state began to subsidize LLIDA's operations
and to invest, through bond financing, additional monies into the islands. Today,
developments on the islands include a 250-room privately owned resort hotel, a
225-room state-owned resort hotel, two championship 18-hole golf courses, a
major water park, beach, campground, and related facilities.

My Commission on Privatization of Government Services established a task
force to review the possibility of privatizing the operation of Lake Lanier Islands.
The study group included representatives from the Lake Lanier Islands Development Authority, the Privatization Commission, Department of Natural Resources,
the Attorney General's Office, the Army Corps of Engineers, and a private-sector
participant with experience in hotel and resort management.

Following the policies and procedures established by the Privatization Commission, the team looked at the history of Lake Lanier Islands and the current
operation of the facilities. They studied the financial performance and the financial potential of the islands under state control, as opposed to the potential under
private operation. The evaluation criteria required answers to the following two
questions:

1. Should state government be in this business?
2. Would outside organizations provide the associated services without the
   involvement of state government?

The task force concluded that once the state has fulfilled its initial economic
stimulation objectives, the state should no longer be in the business of owning

and operating resort hotels and water parks that compete with the private sector. With the exception of the water park feature, private-sector entities owed and managed competing facilities in and around Lake Lanier. Most notably, the state-owned and operated resort hotel is in direct competition with the privately owned resort at Lake Lanier Islands. Therefore, the state should not be in this business.

Concerning the second question, there were numerous private-sector entities that possessed the management expertise and financial resources necessary to provide the services currently offered at Lake Lanier Islands. With the exceptions of administration of the lease with the private sector and issuing of alcoholic beverage licenses, the involvement of the state could be significantly reduced.

The task force also found that the LLIDA was well managed, but it could not generate sufficient funds to pay from revenues the cost of future capital expansion necessary to keep the islands competitive. Additionally, the state's initial investment of some $17 million could not be repaid by the LLIDA.

The task force recommended that the LLIDA proceed with the privatization of Lake Lanier Islands through a long-term lease arrangement. The following suggestions were offered in structuring the request for proposals:

- Ideally, lease all of Lake Lanier Islands to a single entity as opposed to entering into agreements with several different parties.
- Provide for vendors to propose a tiered annual rental amount with a minimum, guaranteed payment amount that will enable the LLIDA to cover its ongoing operating costs and debt service obligations. The state should recover its investment in the property as quickly as possible.
- Structure a lease arrangement that requires an up-front payment sufficient to retire any outstanding debt obligations related to the improvements of Lake Lanier Islands.
- The LLIDA should establish performance criteria for the operation and physical plant maintenance such that the integrity of the state's investment in the islands is preserved until such time as the state's investment has been recovered. To this end, the LLIDA should mandate that a reserve for the replacement of fixed assets, equal to 5 percent of annual revenues, be funded on a yearly basis.
- The LLIDA must ensure that requirements mandated by the lease with the Army Corps of Engineers are addressed in any lease with the private sector.

On November 21, 1995, the Privatization Commission adopted a resolution and recommended to me that the management of the Lake Lanier Islands Resort and Water Park be privatized as soon as possible. Through the competitive bid process, the LLIDA should enter into a long-term lease with the private sector that would pay the state sufficient revenues for the state to recapture its total investment in the Lake Lanier Islands. These funds and certain reserves of the LLIDA would flow to the state treasury.

The request for proposal was issued on December 16, 1995, with responses due by February 16, 1996. The state received nine proposals. A nine-member evaluation team was established, consisting of the executive director of my Privatization Commission, executive director of the LLIDA, two members of the LLIDA Board, a representative from both my Office of Planning and Budget and the State Law Department, a private-sector representative retired from hotel and resort management, a private-sector representative working in the property acquisition and development field, and a representative from the Real Estate Division of the Army Corps of Engineers.

The following three proposers were selected for oral presentations to the evaluation team: Delaware North Parks Service, KSL Recreation Corporation (KSL), and Silver Dollar City, Inc./Tishman Hotel Corporation/Willowbend Development Corporation (SDC). After the oral presentations, the team selected KSL and SDC as the two finalists and called them in to clarify a number of issues contained within their proposals.

On Monday, March 25, 1996, the evaluation team selected KSL Recreation Corporation as the "apparent successful proposing group." The negotiation team, led by the head of my Privatization Commission, Mr. Joe Tanner, began immediately to negotiate with KSL to finalize a long-term lease. We engaged the services of the accounting firm Price Waterhouse and of the law firm Troutman Sanders.

The RFP called for a minimum return to the state of $7.6 million cash up front, a minimum annual guaranteed payment of $2 million, and a percentage of the gross annual sales that exceed $20 million. The KSL response was $9 million cash up front and a $3 million guaranteed annual minimum, with an additional annual guarantee of $100,000 for years one through five, an additional annual guarantee of $200,000 for years six through fifty, and 3.5 percent of gross annual revenues that exceed $20 million.

KSL proposed to make significant improvements and additions to the Lake Lanier Islands facility. Some of the ideas in the conceptual master plan presented by KSL include: an additional 18-hole championship golf course with a world-class golf learning center, because KSL hopes to attract professional, nationally televised golf tournaments with the addition of the golf facility; expansions to the hotel facilities including additional hotel rooms, a larger ballroom and more dining facilities, as KSL hopes to attract more corporate and convention business with these improvements; a family area of the islands including vacation villas, children's activities, and a "Treehouse Village on Robinson Crusoe Island"; additions and improvements to the existing water park facilities; and new dining facilities, concert facilities and boat access from the lake to various parts of the islands.

KSL took over the operation of the islands on May 16, 1996. Price Waterhouse projects that, under the terms of the 50-year lease, the state will receive payments in excess of $315 million. Until privatization of the islands, the state treasury had never received any income from this property. In the unlikely event of a default by KSL, all existing, as well as new, improvements will revert to the state. All improvements revert to the state at the end of the lease term as well.

In summary, the state will no longer be in competition with the private sector at Lake Lanier Islands. Improvements on this property are returned to the local tax digest. For the first time in more than 25 years of operation and investment, the state treasury will begin to receive a return on this investment.

.

CHAPTER EIGHT

Creating a Culture of Innovation

Pennsylvania's PRIME Initiative

Thomas Ridge
Governor of Pennsylvania

When Lieutenant Governor Mark Schweiker and I took office in January 1995, we committed ourselves to making sure Pennsylvania state government is cost-effective, user friendly and customer focused.

We worked with the General Assembly to establish the Improve Management Performance and Cost Control Task Force (IMPACCT) to study state government operations and the successes of other states to reduce costs, increase accountability and improve service. The IMPACCT Commission also looked for ways to increase efficiency and effectiveness, consolidate similar functions, return functions to the private sector, and make Pennsylvania more competitive and entrepreneurial in the world economy. This was the first time in more than 20 years that an independent task force challenged the mindset of Pennsylvania state government and created a far-reaching agenda for change.

The 17-member, bipartisan IMPACCT Commission performed a top-to-bottom review of virtually every agency within the executive branch. Staffed by more than 250 volunteers, there were 16 IMPACCT task forces targeting major areas of government operations. The task forces focused on the following:

- Administration
- Banking and Insurance
- Bureaucracy, Organization and Staffing
- Community and Economic Development
- Department of State and Historical Museum Commission

- Environmental Management
- Fiscal Management
- General Services
- Health-Care Delivery and Social
  Services
- Information Technology
- Labor and Industry
- Liquor Control Board
- Performance-Based Budgeting
- Productivity and Quality
  Improvement
- Public Safety
- Transportation

The IMPACCT report puts the dimensions of this undertaking in perspective: "Pennsylvania is the fourth-largest state government in the nation. If it were compared to the private sector, our government could rank in the top 20 companies of the Fortune 500."

The commitment of this civic-minded group exceeded my highest expectations. The 10,000 hours they donated to this reform effort could easily be valued at more than $2 million. For many years to come, the taxpayers of Pennsylvania will reap the benefits of this tremendous effort.

The IMPACCT Commission was very thorough, not only in its methodology, but also in its quest to determine the needs and expectations of Pennsylvanians. Many families know what it's like to tighten their belts and learn how to do more with less. Today, they are expecting no less from their state government.

On February 29, 1996, the IMPACCT Commission issued its landmark report, *Making Government Make Sense*. The 159-page report identified hundreds of cost-saving opportunities. The IMPACCT report said that Pennsylvania state government needed to become less bureaucratic and more entrepreneurial, and it needed to work to increase the value of all state services. The general framework for IMPACCT included:

- Making Pennsylvania more globally
  competitive
- Reducing regulation and inspection
- Streamlining government services
- Focusing on customer service
- Investing in information technology
- Simplifying financial management
- Managing the environment
- Enhancing our transportation system
- Improving health care and social
  services
- Fostering labor-management
  cooperation

Laying the Groundwork with Employee "I-Teams"

The foundation for implementing the IMPACCT report and for establishing a reengineering plan to go beyond the IMPACCT recommendations began the day after the report was issued. At my direction, Lieutenant Governor Schweiker instructed each state agency under our jurisdiction to form an Innovation Team (I-Team) of talented employees from all levels of the organization. Because successful change efforts of this kind are employee driven, we recognized early on that the I-Teams were the catalyst for change and were really the most important element in this reform effort. Now, throughout state government, we have more than 300 employees from 22 different state agencies serving on I-Teams.

We recognized the critical importance of leadership and of having management commitment "out front" and visible at the highest levels of our state government. Because of the lieutenant governor's "hands-on" management style, the PRIME initiative (see below) not only has stayed on track, but has continued to gain momentum over the last three years.

In sharp contrast to the traditional hierarchical, command-and-control model, each agency I-Team is empowered to set the priorities, action plans and time lines for implementing change initiatives. The I-Teams examined the IMPACCT recommendations and made suggestions for improvements. The I-Teams prioritized the proposed changes and developed innovative ways to implement them. The I-Teams also planned the action steps to implement the recommendations.

Launching the PRIME Initiative

The formal start of our reengineering effort began on April 19, 1996, with my executive order establishing the **P**rivatize, **R**etain, **I**nnovate, **M**odify and **E**liminate (PRIME) initiative.

- *Privatize* is about competition. It's about producing breakthroughs in performance by introducing alternatives in providing state services.
- *Retain* is about keeping and nurturing what works. We want to support successful efforts and work to make them even more cost-effective and results oriented.
- *Innovate* is about unleashing the creative talents of employees to find new ways to make state government less cumbersome and more user friendly.
- *Modify* in the broadest sense is about changing the core values and culture of state government. The PRIME initiative is about moving away from the bureaucratic command-and-control model to a team approach that favors flexibility and employee participation.

- *Eliminate* is about rooting out waste, mismanagement and inefficiency. It's about getting rid of all unnecessary and duplicative work.

The objective of PRIME is to overturn the traditional paradigm of state government—making it more customer centered, efficient and globally competitive through employee-driven change.

My executive order also established the PRIME Council, chaired by Lieutenant Governor Schweiker, to oversee PRIME. Composed of 13 exceptional individuals from the private and public sectors, the council offers advice and assistance to the PRIME effort generally and help on specific change initiatives.

Under the terms of my executive order, council members serve one-year terms and receive no compensation for their services.

Using Information Technology to Break through Barriers

In many respects, the strategic use of information technology is the key to accomplishing our PRIME reform agenda. Our strategic uses follow:

- **Transmitting Disaster Relief Money Electronically.** Instead of using conventional mail to distribute disaster relief funds, the Pennsylvania Emergency Management Agency now can transfer the funds electronically through the state treasurer. This saves time and money and gets the funds to those who need them more quickly.
- **Pennsylvania as a National Leader in Campaign Finance Reform**. Answering the question of how a political campaign is funded now is only a click away. The Pennsylvania Department of State has fulfilled my promise to allow easy access to public information by developing the campaign finance web page. Anyone with access to the Internet, either at a library, at school or at home, may access campaign finance reports twenty-four hours a day, seven days a week at www.dos.state.pa.us/campaign.htm.
- **Modernizing the Insurance Department**. The department has significantly upgraded its operations through technology. These improvements include the department's first e-mail system, a new phone system, access to voice mail, CD-ROM technology and the development of the Insurance Department web page. These positive changes to the department allow the employees to serve their customers quicker and more efficiently.

Making Pennsylvania More Competitive

From the first day of my administration, it was clear that Pennsylvania must have the resources and jobs climate to excel and compete with other states for jobs for our workers. Now, the Commonwealth is carrying out an ambitious economic agenda—with the help of its customers, the taxpayers. Our guiding principles include taking care of the employers who call Pennsylvania home, recruiting employers and increasing the opportunities for family-sustaining jobs, revitalizing our communities, enhancing the delivery of community and economic development services, and lowering the cost of doing business in Pennsylvania. These initiatives, plus many more, are playing a key role in sharpening the Commonwealth's competitive edge. Our initiatives follow:

- **Reforming Workers' Compensation**. After decades of escalating costs, we completed a comprehensive overhaul of the state's workers' compensation system. The outcome, Act 57 of 1996, was one of the most important pieces of jobs legislation ever enacted in Pennsylvania. It protects and ensures benefits to legitimately injured workers, while dramatically lowering the costs incurred by insurers. This reform has resulted in an average reduction of nearly 50 percent in workers' compensation rates and has paved the way for more than $1.5 billion in savings, much of which has been reinvested in Pennsylvania's workforce.
- **Establishing Job Creation Tax Credit and Opportunity Grant Programs**. The Governor's Action Team uses these two new initiatives to create or retain more than 100,000 jobs by partnering with communities and many world-class companies in every region of the state. The Job Creation Tax Credit allows companies to receive $1,000 in tax credits for each full-time job created. The program is open to both small and large companies. Opportunity Grants provide the Commonwealth with the flexibility to customize assistance to create jobs.

Reducing Unnecessary Regulation and Inspection

Over three years, steps were taken to make better sense of who and how we regulate and inspect to ensure public health and safety.

- **Inspecting Seasonal Farms**. Typically, three agencies—the departments of Environmental Protection, Labor and Industry, and Agriculture—conducted three separate visits of these farms to ensure compliance in safety, clean water and produce preparation. Now, as a result of cross-training, the farm operator receives one visit from the Department of Agriculture inspector, who, by addressing all three areas, saves time and money—precious commodities for the farm owner.

- **Doing Better with Less**. As part of its continuing effort to streamline operations and improve services, the Department of State has cross-trained legal staff to handle cases among their 27 professional licensure boards. By cross-training the legal team, the agency can make one lawyer responsible for more than one type of prosecution, increasing the number of cases investigated. This has enabled the department to rapidly resolve complaints and bring cases involving unprofessional or unethical conduct to a faster resolution. In the first year alone, the agency was able to prosecute 40 percent more cases.

- **Speeding Up Workers' Compensation Decisions**. The Department of Labor and Industry is responsible for ensuring that workers' compensation insurance coverage is delivered and that benefits are distributed properly. The department undertook an initiative to entirely restructure the workload, performance and accountability of the worker's compensation judges responsible for resolving disputes over benefits. The new system significantly speeds up workers' compensation decisions. The average length of time to produce a decision in 1997 was 12.7 months. That time was reduced by workers' compensation judges to 9.7 months during the second quarter of 1999.

Streamlining Government Services

State government touches the lives of every Pennsylvanian. Whether it is repairing roads and bridges, educating our youth, protecting property and persons, or promoting economic development, government has a major affect on our lives. One of the cornerstones of PRIME is the belief that government should have a positive effect on the lives of Pennsylvanians and that it should be done with less taxpayer money. State agencies should make every effort to eliminate duplication, consolidate and streamline operations, and ensure that public services are delivered in the most cost-effective and efficient way possible.

- **Establishing a New Center for Local Government Services**. The center is a one-stop shop for all local government needs. It administers such programs as technical assistance and statistics. One of the center's most important accomplishments was the outsourcing of the Commonwealth's municipal training program, which saved taxpayers $850,000 without reducing the quantity or quality of training offered.

- **Consolidating Contracts with Area Agencies on Aging**. In response to the call to reduce paperwork and streamline administrative requirements, employees of the Department of Aging implemented a PRIME initiative that reduced the number of contracts that need to be processed each year from 312 to 52. The team leader on the project said that "consolidating the contracts wasn't rocket science, but when one considers the staff time saved at both the local and state level, the savings are at least $217,000 annually."

- **Instituting a Single Application**. The Department of Community and Economic Development has developed a single application form for assistance. The idea is simple. Through one form, applicants can apply for financial assistance from the department's various funding sources. It is a symbol of our new approach to economic and community development that features effective service and personal attention to the needs of the customer.

Focusing on Customer Service

Pennsylvanians are our customers, and the goal of PRIME is to meet or exceed *their* expectations, not the expectations of the bureaucracy. In ways almost too numerous to mention, Pennsylvania state government has gone from being "customer blind" to being "customer driven":

- **School Profiles**. We now have an educational CD-ROM for use by parents, educators and taxpayers. The Department of Education has compiled statistical profiles of the public schools that include information on school enrollment and attendance, intended pursuits for high school graduates, school financial information, dropout rates, class size, staffing, programs available, vocational programs, technology, and library resources. The CD-ROM was distributed to each school and more than 600 community libraries and will be available through the department's web site.

- **Telephone Reservation System**. The Department of Conservation and Natural Resources instituted a new customer-focused, visitor-friendly telephone reservation system for Pennsylvania's 116 state parks. The new toll-free number, (888) PA-PARKS, is available Monday through Saturday, 7 A.M. to 5 P.M. The customer-service representatives have access to a database linking all state parks and can easily make a reservation for a caller anywhere in Pennsylvania. In the past, visitors would be forced to call each park individually to check for availability of campsites and to learn about special activities. More than 100,000 people used Pennsylvania's new customer-focused, user-friendly telephone system since June 1998 to make reservations or receive information about Pennsylvania's state parks.

- **Establishing Customer Work Groups**. The Department of General Services is fundamentally changing how the Commonwealth does business by providing customers the opportunity to tell the agency how well it is doing and to recommend how it can improve. Through its customer work groups, the department aims to establish long-term partnerships, simplify policies and procedures, reduce regulatory burdens, increase quality and competition, and improve operational efficiency.

- **Making State Forms Available by Fax and on the Internet**. Taxpayers now can reach the Department of Revenue twenty-four hours a day, seven days a week—toll free. For the first time, taxpayers get the information they need when they need it.

Simplifying Financial Management

One year ago, the Commonwealth managed and accounted for its finances and operations in much the same way it did half a century ago—a way that is simply unacceptable in today's world. It became evident upon close inspection that opportunities existed to make simple fiscal management changes that would lead to immediate and tangible results, and we've made many changes in the way we now manage taxpayer dollars. Some of these changes follow:

- **Filing Tax Forms Electronically**. In meeting today's business needs, the Department of Revenue has developed and made available free software for the electronic filing of PA Sales and Use Tax returns. PA TIDES or PA Tax Information Data Exchange System is software that is easy to use and guides taxpayers through the process of completing and filing the forms electronically. The taxpayer saves time and postage while the department saves in printing and processing costs.

- **Converting the Toll-Free Lottery Line**. Changes at the Pennsylvania Lottery demonstrate its commitment to ensuring that lottery funds are efficiently managed. The Lottery operated a toll-free service for players to verify if they had a winning number. Realizing that this toll-free service was not needed with other information sources available, the 800 number was changed to a 900 number that charges the user for the information. Consequently, the $250,000 expense item became a $250,000 income generator for the Lottery fund, which provides benefits to older Pennsylvanians.

- **Consolidating Statewide Service Contracts**. Under the leadership of the Office of the Budget, statewide contracts for a variety of services have been established. Two examples include contracts for local area network services and consultant services for the year 2000 computer challenge. By creating statewide service contracts, the contracting process became simplified and more economical. By combining the business requirements of all state agencies needing similar service, volume-pricing discounts can be earned and less time is needed for contract preparation and approvals.

- **Imaging State Tax Returns**. With millions of tax returns entering the Department of Revenue's processing center each year, new technology will allow information that previously was keypunched to be photographed and stored electronically. The imaged tax return can be processed 400 percent faster than the old method and with 95 percent accuracy. The stored electronic image will be more readily available than a return stored in an off-site warehouse. When assisting a taxpayer in the past, it could take three days or more to get historical information. Now it takes minutes.

Managing the Environment

Pennsylvania is blessed with natural beauty and rich resources. Our river network, vast forests and fertile lands are renowned nationwide. It is important to strike a balance between managing and protecting our natural resources while ensuring we do not create barriers to our economic growth. To this end, our Department of Environmental Protection and Department of Conservation and Natural Resources have designed creative changes to ensure that both coexist:

- **Adopting a Regulatory Basics Initiative**. Through this initiative, the Department of Environmental Protection has involved individuals, the regulated community, and citizen and environmental groups to help identify regulations or policies that should be changed. This has resulted in the elimination of more than 1,300 sections of regulations and more than 1,700 pages of policies.

- **Putting Inmates to Work**. The Department of Conservation and Natural Resources and the Department of Corrections teamed up to implement the Community Work Program. Faced with millions of dollars in continuing maintenance to state parks, staffs now use inmates to tackle immediate problems. The low-security inmates trim trees, clear brush, paint buildings, plant trees, install drainage devices and help fight forest fires. By employing inmates, the parks and forests not only are enhanced for our customers, but budget dollars can go toward larger maintenance and upgrade projects.

• **Expanding the Timber Harvest**. For a variety of reasons, including insufficient staffing, for years the Commonwealth has not been harvesting the amount of timber from state forests as recommended in the forest-management plan. An IMPACCT recommendation was to develop a long-term plan to rectify this situation. The plan was to harvest the optimum amount of trees to provide more material for the timber industry, generate more revenue for the Department of Conservation and Natural Resources and ensure the health of the state forests. The $2 million in revenue generated each year from this program will be applied to protecting new vegetation, tree planting and herbicide applications. This revenue also will fund 21 new foresters to conduct the expanded harvesting program.

• **Creating a Money-Back-Guarantee Program**. The Department of Environmental Protection now requires itself to make timely decisions about permit approvals. If the department doesn't meet its deadline, the customer's permit fee is refunded. More than 120 different permit types are included in this program. In the first four years, more than 40,000 applications were processed, with few deadlines missed.

Enhancing Our Transportation System

Pennsylvania has one of the largest transportation systems in the nation. The Department of Transportation (PennDOT) has worked tirelessly to become more customer friendly. Examples include:

• **Using Computers to Process Drivers' Licenses**. PennDOT eliminated the written skills test for people from other states with valid licenses and decreased the test time from 120 minutes to 75 minutes, allowing more tests to be given per day. Additionally, the old paper system for applying for a driver's license has been replaced. Applicants now use a computer screen to request a license that saves people time and improves customer satisfaction.

• **Registering Drivers and Vehicles Online**. Many Pennsylvanians are making use of a new online messenger service to help Pennsylvanians renew their drivers' licenses and vehicle registrations; change their address; and receive license plates, registration cards and registration stickers. Prior to this new service, messengers would drive to Harrisburg, conduct business and return home. There now are more than 100 online messaging locations across the state, where these messenger services are conducted via computer with PennDOT. Transactions that used to take weeks can be accomplished in minutes.

Improving Health-Care Delivery and Social Services

The Commonwealth carries out its responsibility to provide health care and social services through three departments: Public Welfare, Health, and Aging. Together, these agencies employ 29,700 people—more than one-third of the state's 78,000 employees.

- **Eliminating Duplication in the Renal Pharmacy Program**. The departments of Health and Aging worked together to eliminate duplication of efforts in administering pharmacy services to more than 10,000 renal patients. Under the new arrangement the Department of Aging's PACE Program will be the sole administrator. This will, for the first time, create a uniform method of delivering this vital service. This new process will significantly reduce the process time and will save approximately $200,000 a year.
- **Reporting Birth Information Electronically.** The Department of Health has made available to all birthing hospitals an electronic system to report birth information. The system creates an electronic file of all births that is automatically transmitted to the Department of Health. This enables parents to receive a free certified copy of their newborn's birth certificate within two weeks. Before this system was implemented, parents sometimes waited several months for a birth certificate.
- **Helping Older Pennsylvanians**. The Department of Aging implemented the Volunteer Ombudsman Program. This innovation provides free and confidential assistance to older Pennsylvanians who express concerns about their long-term care services. Additionally, trained and certified ombudsmen visit long-term care facilities and advocate for those who cannot do so on their own behalf by resolving problems and acting as their voice. This program has provided a cost savings of $174,000 by relying on volunteers rather than paid staff.

Fostering Interagency Cooperation

With 21 state agencies sharing the goal of serving their constituencies to the best of their ability, sometimes the lines become blurred as to where one agency's services end and another agency's services begin. Therefore, there can be a benefit to having two or more agencies working together to provide better customer service to the customers of the Commonwealth. Through the PRIME effort, the lines of communication have opened up—leading to positive changes for Pennsylvanians:

- **Pump and Tank Inspection**. Until recently, inspection of certain types of underground storage tanks and pumps was the sole responsibility of the State Police Fire Marshals. Creative thinking led to the transfer of this duty to the Department of Labor and Industry whose inspectors already were on the same sites. Now, more than 18,000 personnel hours per year have been freed up, allowing the State Police additional resources to conduct arson investigations.
- **Welfare and Inmate Matching**. In a cooperative effort, the departments of Public Welfare and Corrections worked to eliminate welfare benefits in violation of state law. A computerized match was completed of state prison inmates and individuals receiving cash assistance, medical assistance and food stamps. Terminating open cases saved taxpayers more than $2.9 million.

PRIME Time Performance Measurement

We decided from day one of PRIME that the process of change had to be "opened up" to employees—or the entire effort would be doomed to failure. We learned that in practice this was very true. Frontline employees have countless ideas for improvement and innovation. We found that, once employees get excited about the change effort, ideas get turned into action that have very measurable performance. We learned that employees will not only put forth innovative ideas, but will, when asked, design very creative methods to measure performance.

Through PRIME, we learned that to create accountability and to measure agency performance over time, a reporting process was necessary. It occurred to us that we should ask the people held accountable to help set up the process. The result was surprisingly simple. With the help of several agency staff, we created a short one-page electronic template that could be submitted each month. The template contained all the information that was necessary to track progress and measure performance over time.

Through this plan, agencies reviewed all recommendations specific to their agency, and, with some basic parameters to guide them, they determined their own priorities and timetables for accomplishing these recommendations. Each I-Team took very seriously the responsibility to create their own timetables and priorities. This "freedom" led each agency to submit conservative, but realistic, timeframes for implementing recommendations.

This process also had an additional side benefit. We found that by having some ownership in their performance measurement, members of each agency I-Team became more concerned about performing up to expectations.

Another important lesson we learned was to publish the results of our performance measurement regularly and to make them part of an important event. We created what we now call the *Innovator's Briefing* as a way to easily and quickly portray how each agency performs. The *Innovator's Briefing* consists of nine simple and easy-to-understand charts that graphically illustrate each agency's performance. The *Innovator's Briefing* uses the timetables and progress reported by the agencies each month.

Recognizing Achievements

One other important component of our PRIME performance measurement is to recognize outstanding performance. This stimulates others to rise to the occasion and demonstrate how they, too, "measure up." We created a mechanism where a portion of the savings resulting from an innovation is retained by the agency or agency work group. This has led to an incentive-based system that allows employees to clearly measure their performance and to see the value of performance measurement. The Innovation Bank recognizes outstanding innovations that have associated with them a real dollar savings. Not only must the innovation perform in terms of its intended results, but it must result in a tangible dollar savings for taxpayers.

The agency work group spearheading the innovation then can retain a portion of the savings (10 percent of the total savings). For example, employees in the departments of Public Welfare and Corrections, working together, designed a method that identified inmates receiving welfare benefits in violation of state law. This led to a savings of more than $3 million per year. The employee work group in Public Welfare returned $260,000 for the department's use. The Department of Corrections staff assisting on the project received a prorated percentage of the savings as well. The employees, through the Innovation Bank, clearly see the value of their performance.

Promoting Communication and Participation

The PRIME initiative now is on solid ground throughout state government. This is evidenced by its more than 360 change initiatives, saving Pennsylvania taxpayers more than $315 million. While we still have work to do, we can draw several conclusions with regard to the idea of employee-driven change and performance management. First, as managers and leaders, you cannot overstate the importance of two-way communication. Second, you must gain the trust, support and participation of employees at every level of the organization. Third, you must put into place methods to measure performance. And fourth, you must recognize outstanding achievement.

During a major organizational change, the challenge of leadership is to continually explain the purpose and impact of change to stakeholders inside and outside the system. Leaders who embrace positive change must persevere in the face of organizational resistance and make sure that their actions are consistent with their professed goals. They also must seek out every opportunity to engage in personal, face-to-face communication.

Part of our strategy for accomplishing this direct connection in Pennsylvania has been initiated by our lieutenant governor, who has conducted a number of "town meetings" with state agencies. These meetings have played an important role in motivating the workforce, making them "change ready," and giving them an opportunity to voice their ideas and concerns. Our town meetings with state agencies also have benefited the cause of employee participation.

As Pennsylvania prepares for the future, our overriding commitment will be to institutionalize PRIME, so that it will not end with the implementation of the IMPACCT report recommendations. Our restructuring plan is designed to continually generate new cost-saving ideas, and it requires a long-term commitment to reach its full potential. Replacing the traditional *culture of bureaucracy* with a *culture of innovation and fiscal restraint* is a daunting, multigenerational responsibility, and I believe Pennsylvania is ready for the challenge.

By continuing to improve our business climate, by working to reduce costs, by investing in the professional development of our employees and by keeping an open mind to alternative methods of delivering public services, PRIME will play a key role in enabling our Commonwealth to become a leader among states and a competitor among nations.

CHAPTER NINE

Public–Private Partnerships

One Sector

William Donald Schaefer
Governor of Maryland

Page Boinest
Research and Public Relations

Three years of an economic slowdown triggered a revolution of sorts in states. Government's role, growing comfortably into the niche of being everything to everybody, collided with the economic realities of the early 1990s, a period punctuated in many areas by declining revenues and skyrocketing bills for welfare, Medicaid, and unemployment services. When people began to lose their jobs, saw their salaries freeze, and watched their benefits evaporate, they became a lot less charitable about the scope of services state, local and federal governments should be providing. The battle cries in hallways of statehouses all across the country—and certainly in Annapolis, Maryland—were "Downsize!" "Restructure!" and, finally, "Privatize!" Government, according to the "downsizer's" refrain, should be run like a business, and services that could be turned over to the private sector should be turned over to the private sector.

The idea of privatizing, working with the private sector, is not new. Much of the renaissance of the city of Baltimore, which occurred during my years as the city's mayor, resulted from a partnership between the city and business community, a pooling of resources and a shared vision. The project that revitalized Baltimore's downtown, the development of the city's Inner Harbor for commercial, tourist, and convention business, grew out of a healthy respect cultivated between the public and private sectors. As the city's harbor was transformed from a rat-

infested eyesore to a gleaming recreational and business district, the spirit of revitalization spread into other neighborhoods. The city government, now working
side by side with businesses intent on developing the downtown, turned to a third
partner to share the project: the citizens.

It was a logical relationship: the city, which answered to the citizens, looked
to the business community for the capital investment and flexibility in procurement to undertake the revitalization. The business community needed the city for
the property, variances, and political blessings, while counting on the citizens to
patronize and support the end product. The citizens needed both the city and
business community, because without them, nothing would have changed positively. It took all three partners to make the project successful. By the time the
city's new downtown had flourished, the three partners in the successful ven-
ture—the public, private, and citizens' sector—were working as "one sector."

Scores of projects representing hundreds of millions of dollars have succeeded
in our state because the government, business, and citizens worked as one sector.
Projects such as contracting out to provide telecommunications for the deaf, the
operation and management of homes for the developmentally disabled, the development of a state park, the restoration of the beach at Ocean City, the operation
of Baltimore Port terminals, and the baseball stadium at Oriole Park at Camden
Yards rely on striking a balance between government, business, and citizen participation. This activity, this working out who does what, this—privatization—is
what we go through every day to determine whether the private, public, or citizen
sector should be involved in a particular function or responsibility. This allows
everybody to do what they do best.

It is not simple to figure out who should do what, let alone to get everybody
to agree. It is not easy transferring a function or duty and responsibility away
from government. By acknowledging the public's demands for a reassessment of
the services government provides, and by recognizing that getting people to work
together was becoming increasingly more difficult, I moved Maryland toward a
comprehensive privatization policy to breathe some new life into private–public
partnerships. A few questions had to be considered:

1. Should government be in the business of providing everything to everybody?
2. What factors do you use to determine what government should continue to do
   or to cede to the private sector?
3. Can we save money by privatizing?
4. Can the private sector perform the same service at a more reasonable rate?
5. If we save in the short term, will we pay in the long term?
6. How do we balance the demands of providing extensive services, at a savings,
   while ensuring the best quality of service?

7. How does privatization work, from a practical standpoint?

While crafting a policy for Maryland, we kept in mind a few "givens" that guide government in the delivery of services and that underscore the fundamental difference between the public and private sectors when it comes to caring for people. The private sector is driven by the bottom line: companies make money or they go out of business. By its nature, a business operates on the premise that it can discontinue an unprofitable line. But governments are not afforded the same luxury: if it is too expensive to take care of expanding prison populations, government cannot simply open the doors of the jails and let inmates walk away.

Out of concern for the bottom line, the private sector will not assume some of the problems for which government is the safety net. Government ends up with the problems no one wants, and it cannot always expect a return on the investment. Governments spend money on programs to help the homeless, without fully expecting that each person helped will repay those services by one day becoming a tax-paying citizen.

The private sector can afford to be selective about the services it may or may not want to provide. It can choose exactly what clientele it will service, while the state ends up caring for the severely disabled, the chronically ill, and the desperately poor among its citizenry. A private company can choose a hospital site, choose its patients and choose which ailments to treat.

Our policy had to be based on knowing what the private sector is willing to do and on understanding what government should do, before deciding how or what to privatize. We adopted a statewide policy to foster a higher degree of communication and cooperation between government, business, and the citizen. The policy had to reflect both the public and private sector roles. To accomplish both these goals we adopted a Policy on Privatization for government and created an Advisory Council on Privatization for the private sector.

The policy on privatization clarified the intent, identified the players and assigned general responsibilities for government. The role of the Advisory Council was to solicit ideas and resources from the citizens and work with government to implement them. The agency responsible for providing the oversight of the activities under the policy on privatization would be the same agency earmarked to staff the Advisory Council to ensure that both government and the citizen were exchanging and communicating the same information and following the same mission.

The policy was adopted based on four main points:

• The state should consider which sector, public or private, will be the more effective at increasing efficiency, improving quality, or reducing the cost of particular operations.

- Privatization can be used as a catalyst to promote quality management and economic development.
- Privatization should be a routine process whereby public managers first think about the feasibility of using private means to provide governmental services.
- Privatization opportunities should be evaluated on either an individual function/program basis or a statewide service basis.

The Department of Budget and Fiscal Planning was the agency designated to take the lead role. It is directed to evaluate privatization opportunities proposed by each agency, oversee cost comparison analysis used to determine privatization potential, ensure that there are adequate measures taken to assure full opportunity for public employees, and review specifications and evaluation criteria (as well as oversee the proposal process) when both the public and private sector compete. The Budget Department also provides the staff support and technical assistance to the Advisory Council.

The state agencies in the Executive Department are the ones with the major role in achieving the results of "one sector" participation through privatization assessments. Their responsibilities are simple and straightforward. They are to evaluate privatization as an alternative to continued budget appropriations for existing functions that can be performed competitively by the private sector as well as evaluate privatization as an alternative to a new budget appropriation for new initiatives that may be performed competitively by the private sector. I also asked each agency to consider competing with the private sector to perform certain duties.

Working in tandem with government is the Advisory Council on Privatization. The council was adopted on the premise that Maryland had experienced an increased demand for public services and increased costs for existing programs, resulting in the need for new revenue sources. Elected officials and governmental managers must have all available management tools to improve the efficiency and effectiveness of state programs and services. Privatization of select government programs and responsibilities is a viable alternative to conserve scarce public resources.

The council's duties are both to advise the governor and to assist the citizens in privatization. They are to review and evaluate unsolicited privatization proposals, provide information on privatization issues, and offer procedural and implementation assistance. The council provides independent oversight to ensure fair, comprehensive, and objective comparisons of privatization alternatives. It has the authority to request status reports from state agencies on implementation efforts of specific privatization opportunities as well as request new evaluations of specific privatization opportunities. Both the council and the state agencies have an ongoing responsibility to communicate their findings and educate each other on the complex roles and responsibilities of the government.

Now that we understand the genesis of a privatization policy, we need to recognize that privatization will not solve all of a government's budget problems. As we chart the best course toward privatizing some services, we are prepared for the sometime trial-and-error nature of our goals. The Hickey School, for example, Maryland's largest juvenile services facility, was a traditionally state-run entity ripe for privatization. Demands on staff, the ever-increasing size of the juvenile population, and the need for an innovative curriculum to reduce recidivism all promoted the state to seek a private operator in 1991.

A request for proposal (RFP) provided the broad guidelines for the type of operator the state was seeking. The company deemed to provide the best program for the money, with a track record in serving juvenile offenders, won the contract to operate Hickey. Because of security lapses and a less-than-focused curriculum, however, the state chose to step in and resume control of the facility until another vendor could take over.

Maryland's Department of Juvenile Services, willing to stand by the concept of privatization, rebid the Hickey contract. This time it outlined in the RFP specifically defined program requirements expected from the vendor that would operate the juvenile facility. The state learned from the first trial that it needed to spell out what types of programs it expected for Hickey, and the state turned over Hickey's operations to the new vendor in the spring of 1993. As of July 1997, the vendor has successfully operated the facility under a five-year contract. No significant charge orders were required. Some small issues have generally been resolved to the mutual satisfaction of the state and vendor.

The total value of the contract was $80,000,000, providing care for more than 300 youths. Prior to the expiration of the contract, the state is preparing to rebid the operation of the facility through competitive bid. The state is also considering the privatization of another juvenile facility, which may include construction and development along with the operational management.

Back in 1993, we were putting together our privatization initiative during this period of trial and tribulation. To help us avoid the same pitfalls, we adopted a methodology to guide us in making these determinations. This methodology relies on the competence of managers doing the assessments. We should encourage more involvement from business and the citizen in cases when they possess the optimum resources, not in cases when the government fails to do its job. In the latter cases, we should fix our own problem, not transfer the problem away.

Our methodology is based on the premise that our managers are as good, as competent, and as knowledgeable in their jobs as their counterparts in the private sector. Nonetheless, the process to determine whether we need to change our mode of operation can be difficult, and having a uniform and straightforward guide to making these assessments helps. Our methodology is based on four main steps:

1. Analyze the potential for privatization.
2. Examine the cost of the activity to the government.
3. Plan the necessary procedures.
4. Implement.

Step 1

The first step is to assess whether the specific activity lends itself to a higher degree of involvement from the private sector. It is a group of questions geared to focus on the public responsibilities and private capabilities in performing the particular function. We adopted 13 questions indicative of our concerns:

1. Is there more than one private vendor capable and interested in providing the activity to ensure competition?
2. Can the activity be specified in advance with clear objectives and goals?
3. Can the delivery of the activity be measured adequately to monitor performance?
4. Can the private vendor be easily replaced during the term of the contract?
5. Is the economical delivery of a service more important than control and accountability?
6. Can the contract provide for the transfer of liability or risk?
7. Is the public safety of citizens protected in case of default?
8. Would the funds and revenues presently available continue to be available if the private sector performs the activity?
9. Can the private sector implement and deliver the activity quicker?
10. Does government have the ability and resources to manage, control and regulate the contract?

11. Is the proposed privatization activity consistent with state law, rules and regulations?
12. Do elected officials and affected citizens support the proposed privatization activities?
13. Have strategies been developed to overcome or minimize short-term problems (employee reaction, service delivery) that could arise during the transfer of the activities?

These difficult questions frequently lead to many more questions. They are not roadblocks but roadways to help us find the right direction.

Step 2

The second step is to examine the cost to government. This has caused much consternation because most government agencies view their costs by comparing them to something else, rather than determining their cost on their own merit. Much of what we need to do in Maryland will be left to the government. We need to educate the public and ourselves of what it costs us to provide these services. And before we think of asking the private sector to bid on something (and spending their time and money) we should know what our bottom line is.

The objective of this analysis is to determine what it costs government to perform the activity, what it would cost government to monitor the activity, and what future costs government can avoid by transferring the activity to the private sector. This analysis should be done on each of these three categories, as a five-year plan, and should at a minimum include personnel costs, operating costs (maintenance, vehicles, equipment, office space), capital costs (present and anticipated), insurance and liability costs, allocated administrative costs, and management and supervision costs.

Step 3

Perhaps the most important point of our assessment is step three—plan the necessary procedure. This is truly a framework for agencies to decide what best works for them. There is no right or wrong approach. It is meant to emphasize that these opportunities must be evaluated on a case-by-case basis while considering how one is going to implement. It is meant as a safeguard against precipitous action. The evaluation should address many issues:

- Timing: Are there issues raised from Section I that need to be resolved prior to proceeding? Does the timing of the privatization effort affect potential cost savings? How long will it take to achieve the desired result?
- Personnel: What is the transition plan if the privatization will impact on state employees? Will current state employees have an opportunity to bid? Will the private vendor be required to absorb existing state employees? Can internal reorganization and different management techniques accomplish the same or similar goal?
- Cost: Is there a savings goal, short- and long-term, without which privatization will not be considered?
- Agency Impact: Does the privatization of this activity affect other programs and responsibilities for other state agencies and departments? Are there alternative public solutions? What is the best way to structure the deal (lease, contract, sale, partnership, pilot program)? What process will be put in place to take over the activity in case the privatization fails?

Step 4

The last and final step is implementation. By the time we get to this point we should be 99 percent clear on our objectives and how to obtain them. Although it may take some time to work out the mechanics of the procurement, the procedure should be fairly straightforward. We prepare a request for proposal and/or proposal specifications, conduct the procurement, review the responses including a final comparison of costs of private versus public and, if applicable, establish an oversight procedure and transfer the activity.

Our methodology can take an hour or two years, depending on the magnitude of the proposed privatizing activity. Projects that exemplify the "one sector" do not happen overnight. But there are many activities that can be identified and transferred, in whole or in part, out of government fairly quickly. We have adopted a methodology that works for the myriad of government functions. It is based on common sense, an articulation of what government does, what government should do in the future, and how to get there from here.

The methodology is amenable to making difficult decisions. Maryland has a procurement process that allows for competitive negotiation. Evaluations of proposals can carry varying weights for technical, programmatic, and price scoring. For fairly straightforward privatization proposals, it is relatively easy to specify the minimum standards regarding quality and to provide for cost to be the deciding factor.

For more complicated proposals, we use an array of methods:

1. Establishing a baseline requirement of standards and price and negotiating separately with the vendors that qualify.
2. Setting up separate evaluation teams, one for objective and quantitative aspects (technique, price) and another one for subjective and qualitative aspects (program and esthetics).
3. Holding a competition, judged by a panel, of the top three to five bidders after a minimum/maximum price range has been established.

Privatization proposals requested for the development of state assets for revenue purposes (e.g., the sale of a vacant hospital) are more outcome based, where the state measures the potential of income versus the furthering of state goals and initiatives. In these cases, the bidders are given general guidelines of what the state will accept, are asked to come up with their best ideas for a particular property, and delineate what the state can expect from the proposal. The state is under no obligation to accept any proposal and can decide to reject all or accept one based on what is believed to be in the state's best interest.

Conclusion

A final thought on the realities of privatization: Some of what Maryland hopes to accomplish in privatization requires legislative action. Legislatures can provide powerful allies or troublesome detractors, depending on which side wins the public relations battle.

One of the unavoidable factors in Maryland's legislative debate about privatization was the NIMBY (not in my backyard) phenomenon; even the most vocal proponents of downsizing, restructuring and privatization are not always enthusiastic about such changes if they affect their communities.

It sounds elementary, but consider this example from Maryland: A task force recommending legislation on areas of government that could be privatized met with limited success in its first General Assembly session. The task force proposed a series of bills to privatize services in Maryland, including the legislation intended to turn over two of Maryland's chronic-care hospitals to the private sector. The proposal died under heavy lobbying from the communities in which the hospitals were located; hospital employees feared they would lose their jobs, and opponents convinced legislators that privatization, at least in that case, would result in patients being abandoned without care. Privatization can be a good political buzzword, but it takes willing partners to implement it to enjoy the benefits.

For Maryland, the process of moving toward increased privatization continues, building on a long-standing tradition of public–private partnerships. Governments can certainly be the catalysts for public–private partnerships, but we cannot forget that businesses and citizens are the vital partners. When government, business, and the citizen work as one sector toward a goal, they can always succeed.

The Role of Privatization in the City of Detroit's Turnaround

Dennis W. Archer
Mayor of Detroit, Michigan

Geni Giannotti
Buildings and Safety Engineering Department

I recently read about a manager attempting organizational change. He envisioned a well-run, forward-moving enterprise—like a flock of geese flying swiftly toward their destination. Instead, he found his organization to be more like a herd of buffalo standing idle in a field—heads down, grazing contentedly, and going nowhere. Even when the fences were removed there was no sign of urgent movement and no alignment to move toward any destination. What the manager needed to do to get the operating results he wanted, he figured, was to first assemble the workers into a V formation, and then teach them to fly.

When I began my administration on January 1, 1994, I saw the same lack of vision, focus and sense of urgency. We were fortunate, though, that this lack of direction and leadership did not cause our employees to be any less enthusiastic about change or participation in change. This city government has a great asset in its workforce and we realized that, without organizing and leading our employees, we cannot accomplish our economic revitalization.

Background

The current administration took office in 1994, after more than 30 years of massive social and economic changes, including a deteriorating financial condition.

For a variety of reasons, Detroit lost one-third of its population between 1965 and 1990 and experienced the poorest economic growth of any of America's 76 largest cities. From 1980 to 1990, the city lost 80,000 jobs. By 1990, almost one-third of its population lived below the poverty level.

The city experienced 23 budget deficits in 30 years. Most noticeably, in fiscal years 1991 and 1992 deficits exceeded $100 million each. Continued financial and operational pressures resulted in reactive management, and the lack of financial resources left city employees without training, computers and other tools to work effectively.

During the last ten years, this economic decline directly affected Detroit's employees in the form of layoffs, pay cuts, pay freezes and increased workloads. Detroit lost many good employees through defection to private-sector positions that offered "greener pastures" or more secure futures. Those who stayed often did so at a sacrifice. An example of employee sacrifices inherited by my administration was "DOWOP" days—days off without pay. As an "equitable" solution to declining revenues and to avoid additional layoffs, the pay of nearly two-thirds of Detroit's city employees was reduced by 10 percent, ostensibly commensurate with reduced work hours. The flaw in this strategy became apparent when workloads, in fact, did not decrease by a related 10 percent. As a result, city government was generally understaffed and sometimes underpaid. Employees kept their heads down, trying to deliver 100 percent of the services, using 1980s tools and methods, in 90 percent of the hours.

Management struggled without adequate reporting capabilities, generally unable to ascertain operating results. Financial systems designed in the 1970s were incapable of providing anything except basic financial information. No tracking systems existed to determine cost or productivity of operations, further impairing management decision making.

The city's financial problems also undermined employee empowerment and participation in decision making. Many operational decisions were removed from the agencies responsible for making decisions and were given instead to higher fiscal authorities. For example, the decision to hire or train staff was often denied due to lack of funds, whether or not it adversely impacted on the agency's ability to operate.

The city was fortunate to have an employee base more productive than the "buffalo" described by the author I read. But, at the same time, the frustrating inability to influence decisions or effectuate change left workers poorly motivated to explore "beyond the fences."

Privatization

Given these conditions, there were strong calls throughout the community for drastic measures. Those outside the "fence" looking in were quite vocal in stating that success could not come from incremental changes and improvements. Privatization was the most commonly recommended solution, generally without any analysis of the underlying problem. Other municipalities had used it successfully, and it appeared to the outside world that Detroit was not internally capable of solving these problems itself. Privatization was promoted in two forms. One was to contract out certain public services to improve productivity, cut costs, or both. The second was to sell valuable city assets to generate cash and reduce the city's financial commitment to them.

During the 1994 campaign, I made a commitment to our employees and unions that they would be part of the revitalization of the city. A quick shift to privatization would seem to take opportunities away from our employees. It was my view that the city's service delivery issues are fundamental and can improve only by developing adequate and capable staff, equipping employees with the proper tools and then leading and motivating them to work effectively. Permanently transferring their work to outside enterprises, albeit an easier short-term remedy, would solve very little in the long run. Also, my policy is not to choose between competing constituencies or competing agendas, nor to choose from limited options, made in closed-door, backroom settings. I will always favor broad-based discussion and participation and inclusion, rather than exclusion, in decision making.

The city is no stranger to the practice of privatization. My administration inherited numerous major contracts that outsourced the support of various city operations. In many cases, these contracts were used to provide staffing as personnel levels declined. Most of the contracts signed by the previous administration exist to support *noncore* services, such as civic center event management, zoo concessions, golf course management, parking garage operations and incinerator management. These contracts were valued as high as $100 million and as long in duration as 20 years.

Currently, in city *support* agencies, such as Law and Technology, private contractors augment services when internal expertise is not available or special projects present special needs, such as stadium development or year 2000 programming. In *core* service areas, when efforts to recruit city employees or acquire equipment prove to be ineffective, the city will rely on private contracts to provide services. For instance, when qualified drivers and equipment are not available for summer grass cutting, peak-volume bulk-garbage pickup or excessive snow removal, noncity workers may be used. The current city policy, firmly stated, is that privatization will not be considered if it results in a loss of employee jobs. Rather, we prefer that employees come together to develop aggressive, competitive improvement plans that also help to ensure their job security.

The City of Detroit Perspective

In reviewing our experiences with privatization of city services, we know that contracting out services to private entities does not necessarily reduce costs. Moreover, privatization is potentially antithetical to the goal of increasing employment opportunities within the city, where unemployment was at 13 percent when I took office. Under a full privatization approach, there is no assurance that a private firm hires from the same urban labor pool. If a private contractor does provide services from this labor pool, to earn a profit it would have to either pay workers less than they could earn at city jobs, or charge the city more to maintain current wages. We have seen this in at least two areas where the city has contracted out for services. In the first instance (privatized service invoicing), the profits from the business do not appear to pass through to the employees, resulting in employee turnover, less effectiveness and higher cost than the previously city-provided services. In the other (parking ticket processing), we have found that the city paid more per unit for the service than most other major cities in the nation. Where the city can and does provide a service, we have seen very few cases where productivity of the contractor exceeds that which can be obtained from city employees or where the proposed cost to provide the service is less. As a typical example, when we requested proposals to augment streetlight repair due to tornado damage, we found that competitive pricing of $280 per light far exceeded the current city cost for the same services, at $100 per light.

Effective privatization can only occur if the city can manage its contracts diligently, and even so, dependence on outside parties will always contain risk. Shortly after I took office, we began spending more time overseeing the quality and progress of two of our largest outsourced contracts in our Water Department and at our resource recovery facility. Differences developed between city management and our contractors over "contract interpretations." Both contracts ultimately led to costly and time-consuming legal actions and operational disruption. If we have the information, personnel and tools to capably manage contracts with private firms to deliver efficient, cost-effective services, we should be able to utilize them to manage our own employees and resources with the same level of expectation.

When contracting out appears inevitable, this administration seeks first to contract with nonprofit organizations, if possible, or *establish a partnership* with other public or private organizations that allow the city to retain control. Many of our current city lot grass-cutting contracts have been granted to community organizations. In addition, the recently opened Museum of African American History (the largest in the world) is managed by contract by a nonprofit entity. An example of the type of partnership we commonly seek is our current public lighting upgrade, where we are working with a public utility to modernize the system while we maintain city ownership of it and jobs within the department. In our Income Tax Division, we have partnered with a private consulting firm, under a shared-risk contract, to launch a major collection program to provide funding for a new computer system. Once the system is in place, the staff will be trained on the collection programs, which will be permanently transferred in-house. This is a new approach for our collections contractor, which has, up until now, privatized income tax programs in Philadelphia and elsewhere.

Most advocates for privatization cite "bureaucracy" as a discouragement to productivity. I do not believe that we can solve our problems by merely privatizing existing bureaucracies. Although we have found that inherent "red tape" does inhibit service provision, we have been able to devise solutions that do not preclude our employees from being part of the solution. A recent example of this is the designation of our Housing Department as a Housing Commission. This agency continues to operate under the control of the administration, with the same employees and unions, but is moving toward decentralization, with greater flexibility in processes such as purchasing and hiring. As a result of these changes, and by partnering with the Department of Housing and Urban Development (HUD), backlogged requests for housing repairs have been reduced from 11,000 to only 400, without privatization, and the Housing Commission was removed from the HUD Troubled Housing List for the first time since 1979. Similarly, the Detroit Institute of Arts (the fifth largest in the nation) has struggled under its obligation to comply with city procedures and policy, although it is funded primarily by private sources. To alleviate this inefficiency we have transferred management responsibilities for the Institute to the nonprofit foundation that currently funds and oversees it. This transition allowed all current city employees the choice to continue to work with the institute or be transferred to other positions within city government without any reduction in pay, benefits or seniority.

We have found proposals that involve the sale of city assets to be similarly unfeasible. While a sale may result in a one-time cash influx, it would also mean the loss of the income-producing properties that are a critical part of our financial turnaround plan. The sale of Detroit's water and sewerage and public lighting operations is most commonly advocated. These operations enable the city to sell services to other municipalities and entities, thereby generating revenues. These assets carry long-term value to Detroit citizens, in addition to their cash-flow streams, which far outweigh the short-term cash infusion that their sale could justify. For instance, the Public Lighting Department status as a "municipal utility" reduces its cost of power to its customers, including city facilities and local schools, to about half that which the local public utility charges. The revenues from the city's sale of power fund the street lighting system, which is provided to citizens at no additional charge. The rates provided by our Water and Sewerage Department to our citizens, surrounding customers and communities are among the lowest in the nation. Many of Detroit's other assets—museums, zoo, airport, golf courses, civic center and arena—play an important role in attracting visitors to the city. By retaining these institutions, they will flourish as the city rebuilds, allowing our taxpayers and customers, rather than private firms, to reap the benefits.

This administration continues to maintain that outsourcing of major service areas, especially if it results in loss of city jobs, is not a practical alternative for this city. No one knows the customer, the market or the job better than the employee who has been providing those services for five, ten or thirty years. A better solution would be to, first, completely understand the factors inhibiting productivity and then take corrective action and provide training, equipment information and other tools to city employees to improve the level of service they can provide. The pride of ownership of our employees' services, and the productivity that follows ivthat pride, cannot be replaced by contractors.

Alternative Solutions

Government is the mechanism we use to make communal decisions about how we live. My priority with regard to restructuring the way the city does business has been to focus on a communal decision-making process for providing services. Rather than unilaterally pursue a course that may hold more costs than benefits, I decided instead to challenge Detroit's employees. They needed to help me develop alternatives to forestall the threat of privatization but allow us to meet our service obligations to the public. This challenge was met with enthusiasm and creativity. My administration took the following steps to accomplish that goal:

1. We began to peel back the strict budgetary controls that were driving our operational decisions. Department management was *empowered* to be decisive, take risks, and get results.
2. We provided the *vision* of the future—a glimpse of what is beyond the fences and may be beyond the horizon. The city's vision, mission and goals are included in appendix A.
3. We provided *alignment*—through a series of programs including our Goal-Based Governance System—to mobilize Detroit's workforce and set a direction and a common set of values. While we have not yet achieved that flying formation mentioned earlier, we are organizing the field for action.
4. We made a commitment to develop and encourage *leadership* skills and employee involvement through our quality improvement programs.

Some of the methods employed are described below.

Quality Improvement Programs

Many of these steps—developing vision, alignment, and leadership skills—are the focus of the city of Detroit's quality improvement programs, our version of Total Quality Management. Implemented during our first year in office in 30 or 40 incremental steps, many of these initiatives represent basic quality principles. The city's quality initiatives do not constitute a model or step-by-step program. Rather, they are foundation-building steps that form an umbrella or vehicle for the cultural transformation we seek and encourage. They focus on improving communication at all levels of the organization, seeking the input of our employees, managers, and unions, as well as community and business feedback. Here are a few examples of the numerous quality improvement programs implemented during the last four years:

- Biweekly department director meetings and written progress summaries, which bring together all top city leaders frequently to share information. Annual retreats with this group are conducted for planning and feedback purposes.

- Quarterly leadership conferences with all city managers to inform and educate on key issues and policies.
- Departmental diagonal slice meetings in which the mayor's office seeks employee feedback at all levels.
- Establishment of citywide employee newsletter and departmental newsletters and citywide e-mail.
- Addition of $1 million annually to the city's training budget and implementation of more than 40 training programs and seminars, made available to all city employees; regular offerings include Covey's "Seven Habits of Highly Effective People," Problem Solving, Exceptional Customer Service, Conflict Resolution, and a 40-hour mandatory supervisory training program.
- Establishment of Continuous Improvement Process (CIP), an employee-based, five-day process mapping and improvement model. An example of successful use of CIP exists in our Health Department, where the process was used to eliminate an eight-week backlog of birth and death record processing. In our Human Rights Department, processing time for applications for small or local business status was reduced by 50 percent using the CIP method. Our CIP method is similar to Louisville's "Cityworks" program but is highly structured to address process constraints in particular.
- Various community feedback forums, including quarterly town hall meetings, mayor's night-in and customer surveys; partnering with the citizenry on the Community Reinvestment Strategy, we can identify and incorporate their needs and desires into future neighborhood development initiatives. We also conduct annual public budget hearings, allowing taxpayers to communicate their priorities and provide input on city services and expenditures.
- A mayor's office organization structure based on "group executives" who divide responsibility for overseeing the operations of all city agencies. The five existing group executives provide policy, guidance and support to department management, while empowering them to perform without mandates, strict control or extreme oversight.

Some of the larger quality programs, as described below, involve city employees, unions and private firms working communally as a team, instead of pitting them against each other with the threat of private contracts. These programs allow the city to find internal solutions to minimize the need for privatization as a solution for our problems.

Working as Teams to Find Solutions:
Goal-Based Governance System

In February 1995, the city initiated its Goal-Based Governance System (GBGS), our primary mechanism for disseminating my vision for the city and aligning all agencies and employees to march toward the same outcomes. It translates city-wide goals into departmental actions, developing departmental missions, goals, measures and targets, developing supporting action plans for accomplishing the goals.

As a first step, I communicated my vision of the city: "To make Detroit a world-class city that successfully attracts people to live, work and visit, and business to invest, grow and prosper." Underlying this vision are four cornerstone goals:

1. Affirming Detroit as a safe city.
2. Providing essential, efficient, and user-friendly services.
3. Obtaining business expansion and growth.
4. Restoring financial solvency.

GBGS is helping us to identify and prioritize our essential services and determine where technical improvements, reengineering or resources are required to meet our goals. GBGS has defined our vision and aligned our employees' focus toward our goals. In addition, the administration has defined its core values, which helps to set the priorities and standard of behavior to be exhibited in striving toward our goals.

The development of GBGS was built throughout our first four-year term. During 1995, after a year of planning, all departments worked to develop their individual mission statements, goals, targets and initiatives, which support the four cornerstones. By 1996, the administration developed a quarterly reporting system to measure departmental progress against goals and understand impediments to progress. In 1997, GBGS was incorporated into the budget process to evaluate and prioritize goal-based programs for approval in the fiscal year budget. This new budget format allowed us to receive the Distinguished Budget Presentation Award from the Government Finance Officers Association for the last two years. In 1998, GBGS was tied to department managers' performance evaluations. To the greatest extent possible, this GBGS process is driven "bottom-up," with the direct involvement and input of our employees. The departments are encouraged to utilize any of the city's quality management programs to assist in achieving their goals and executing their initiatives. A summary of the process and a city agency's mission, goals, targets and initiatives taken from our recent annual budget document follow in appendix B.

Labor–Management Quality Improvement Partnership

During 1995, the city partnered with its unions and Federal Mediation Conciliation Services (FMCS) to initiate its Labor–Management/Quality Improvement partnership (LM/QI). The overall goal of this program is to improve service delivery and at the same time foster teamwork between management, unions, and employees. The basic approach is to develop effectively functioning labor–management committees within city departments, as a structure for enhanced communication and problem solving. Working together, the committees utilize the city's quality improvement principles and methods to improve processes, resolve issues, and evaluate alternatives for better service delivery. Training provided to the committees includes Problem Solving, Conflict Resolution and Team Building. CIP is also a tool which is made available for the committees to use.

One year of planning resulted in the establishment of an Executive Steering Committee in 1995, followed by implementation of two successful pilot agency committees in the Recreation Department and EMS during 1996. These committees consist of departmental managers and top union representatives who meet monthly to identify improvement projects, including those targeted by GBGS, and formulate plans. Involving the relevant employees, the Recreation Department LM/QI Committee was able to develop an improved supply requisition delivery system, and members of the EMS LM/QI Committee were asked by management, for the first time, to participate in an assessment of new emergency vehicles to ensure that the specifications meet the needs of the drivers.

During 1997, we streamlined our Turnaround Team concept, as described in the next section, to pilot employee involvement within the LM/QI structure. An LM/QI Committee was established in the Accounts Payable Department, and all employees were given the opportunity to be on one of five teams, which met over six months to recommend and then implement specific improvement initiatives. The Buildings and Safety Engineering Department has recently established six such teams responsible for developing and implementing programs in areas such as training, employee recognition, special events, internal communications, public awareness and work-area improvements. Since 1998 employees have worked under the LM/QI structure to engage in benchmarking research and travel to understand other cities' processes and to identify opportunities for improvement in Detroit's city government. All LM/QI committees are encouraged to solicit employee participation, with the option of shorter term teams, for ad hoc problems, or longer term teams for focused programs. In this way, interested employees at all levels within the agencies can provide their input and talents and participate in the improvement process. By the end of 1999, twelve LM/QI committees existed in the agencies, with further citywide implementation during 2000.

Turnaround Teams

In addition to Goal-Based Governance and LM/QI, the city of Detroit established employee involvement "Turnaround Teams" during 1994, comprised of 180 city employees and outside professionals formed to question the way Detroit does business. For nine months the teams met weekly and analyzed cross-departmental areas such as information systems, telecommunications, collections and accounts payable processes, debt management, grant management, and fleet and facilities management practices. One departmental team focused on rebuilding the Law Department. Their work encompassed best practice research, process improvements, "quick fixes" and other cost savings and productivity measures. Over the nine-month project term, most teams launched several improvement projects simultaneously by employing subcommittees and additional ad hoc team members. The focus of the teams was not only to recommend but specifically *to implement* solutions. Due to the lack of budgeted training funds, team training was limited to only a one-day orientation session, and the problem-solving methods employed by the teams were left to their discretion. Other than project guidelines and support offered by a mayor's office "coach" to each team, the teams were empowered to identify problems and seek solutions using their judgment and skills. The following sample of successes, resulting during 1994 alone, reflects the remarkable creativity and capabilities exhibited by our employees when the "fences" are removed.

- Saving over $1 million per year from owning, instead of leasing, telephone hardware. We found that city telephones were not only archaic, in some cases rotary dial, but that we continued for years to lease them on a monthly basis, beyond their useful lives. A nominal buyout for existing phones was executed and the savings invested in new equipment.

• During 1994, collecting $2.6 million of income and utility taxes, through teamwork of the city's Law and Income Tax Department and partnering with federal and state agencies, without outside collection agencies.

• Cost savings from negotiating master leases and using in-house space planning talents instead of utilizing a private contractor for a series of 22 agency moves and consolidations.

• Eliminating $1 million in late fees by reengineering the payment process for utility bills and partnering with local utility companies to streamline invoicing. Annually, we were receiving and processing 48,000 utility invoices. Through teamwork this number was reduced to less than 300, vastly improving processing and payment time.

The Turnaround Team issued almost 80 recommendations, and approximately 30, including those above, were implemented during the nine-month project. The remaining 46 recommendations continue to be analyzed and acted on by the city, resulting in even greater cost savings and efficiencies up to four years after the teams concluded their work. The teams' cost savings and positive financial impact were significant enough that they helped generate the city's first surplus in many years. This is another example of employees and other volunteers weighing in to help provide better city service more cost-effectively. Their work helped to save jobs of employees who might have been laid off if we had been forced to privatize some services that were questioned under the Turnaround Team process.

We have also established a number of other employee team projects that have helped us move together toward our goals. Using solely internal resources in 1995 we established "one stop" licensing and permitting centers, allowing citizens to go to only one location, instead of as many as 14 previously, to obtain services. A task force of public and private members who analyzed the situation during the previous year designed the centers. These streamlining efforts in the Buildings and Safety Engineering Department have been extremely successful, shortening the time it takes to issue a building permit. When I first took office, the city issued only 2,600 building permits. This year that number increased to more than 6,000, a 150 percent increase that has been met with no increase in staff over the last four years. Of those, almost 5,000 permits are issued on demand or within days. Ninety percent of all permits are issued within four weeks. We have received actual feedback from some residential builders indicating that they now receive permits faster in Detroit than in other surrounding communities.

A restructuring of this department is under way to finish implementing the task force report and allow us to continue to meet the rising demand brought on by record city development. The restructuring invites all departmental employees' involvement and utilizes internal resources exclusively to achieve its goals. Instead of privatizing permit and inspection services to keep up with demand, we will assess their value to the community and eliminate unnecessary requirements.

The Turnaround Teams initiated and planned another major project, our Detroit Resource Management System (DRMS). This project has brought together more than 300 city employees as well as private consultants to design and implement a state-of-the art financial management software. I strongly advocate the collaboration of creativity and commitment generated by our employees, the citizens, the unions and the business community. In this way we retain control over our mutual destinies and create solutions that we can all live with.

Conclusion

Detroit's city government, through our participative and team-oriented programs, has been able to evaluate what we do well and what we do not. We are looking at functions that add service value and those that do not. We work together to determine which of these functions and services can be provided more effectively by outside enterprises. While we may use privatization to provide certain services in some instances, we will continue our efforts to provide the vision, focus and resources that will strengthen and lead the city's workforce to our desired goals.

The most remarkable testimony to our restructuring approach has been this city's return to financial prosperity. After six months in office, our deficit for the fiscal year had decreased from a projection of $88 million to only $53 million. The next four fiscal years have evidenced surpluses of $19 million, $18.5 million, $12.4 million and $13 million, respectively. We have made the final payment on $82 million deficit funding bonds that we inherited and have achieved a $200 million turnaround without increasing taxes and without the use of privatization. By building partnerships and including our employees, the community, unions and businesses, there is a renewed faith in the city's future, as evidenced during our first term by these achievements:

- Attraction of more than $10 billion in private-sector development and investment within the city limits.

- Property value increases of about 50 percent ($2 billion) over the last four years.
- Upgrade by all three bond rating agencies to investment grade status, moving into the "A" category with two of the three agencies.
- Award of one of six federal Empowerment Zones, and related $100 million in federal funds for use in 89 projects.

Most violent-crime statistics have declined since 1994, deaths by fire are at a 15-year low, our garbage pickup is on time, and we have repaved more than 500 miles of road. This improved financial condition has allowed us to reduce our property tax rates and install more than 7,000 personal computers throughout city government. Our current goals now incorporate the phaseout of corporate income taxes and gradual reduction of individual income taxes.

We are now in the sixth year of removing fences and encouraging our employees to lift their heads and become involved in Detroit's revitalization. It is starting to appear that what the city of Detroit strives for is not a heard or a flock in any formation. It looks more like a team, with a playing field instead of a grazing field, where good coaching helps everyone to outperform the competition.

Appendix A: 1999–2000 Budget Executive Summary—City of Detroit's Long-Term Operational and Financial Policy

Operational Goals and Objectives

In the spring of 1995 the city began the process of implementing a new system of evaluating programs called Goal-Based Governance. This year's budget has linked the plans developed under GBG to financial resource allocations. This correlation will serve to better clarify and prioritize departments' activities and result in improved city service delivery.

A clearly stated vision and mission along with cornerstone objectives influencing each step of the decision-making process form the root of Mayor Dennis W. Archer's long-term strategic plan.

Vision of the Future Detroit

To make Detroit a world-class city that successfully attracts people to live, work and visit and business to invest, grow and prosper.

Mission of City Government

To provide timely, cost-effective and high-quality services, consistent with available resources, that are responsive to citizen needs for essential services and business needs for development and growth in the city.

The mayor's stated vision and mission translate into a clear challenge to elected officials and all city workers. That is:

TO MAKE DETROIT THE BEST-RUN CITY IN AMERICA

Cornerstone Goals

Every planning decision takes into account four cornerstone goals:

1. Affirm Detroit as a safe city.
2. Provide essential, efficient, and user-friendly services.
3. Restore financial solvency.
4. Obtain business expansion and growth.

The Process of Goal-Based Governance

What is Goal-Based Governance?

A method for translating the cornerstones of the Archer administration into specific missions, goals, measures and targets at a departmental level. The end result will be improved service activity throughout city government.

What Guidelines Were Given to Departments?

1. Build from a reality base.
2. All departments address all cornerstones.
3. Build goals within present budget provisions.
4. Goal-Based Governance is part of larger organizational and work-culture initiatives.

What Is the Departmental Process?

The process began with participation in each department of all levels of employees to build departmental goals, measures, and targets. The planning focused on operations improvements and included special projects. The final product was approved by the mayor's office in the summer of 1995, coordinated across departments and implemented. All employees have been encouraged to participate and commit to their departmental plans.

What Is a "Vision"?

A clear and compelling statement that defines what the unit must strive to become in order to contribute maximum value.

What Is a "Mission"?

A clear and compelling statement which explains why the unit exists and what value it provides to its customers and to the overall "vision."

What Is a "Goal"?

Operational goals are the set of primary objectives that a unit strives for on a day-to-day basis. Project goals are the set of special objectives associated with completion of a one-time task important to day-to-day operations improvement.

What Is a "Measure"?

Specific indicators of performance toward goal achievement; should be quantifiable.

What Is a "Target"?

Measurable, quantitative, time-limited standards of performance against which achievement of goals can be gauged.

During the 1995–1996 fiscal year the city began the Continuous Improvement Process as an extension of the Goal-Based Governance System. This is a systematic approach to identify and eliminate waste or nonvalue-added activities through continuous improvement in all products and services. The objectives are to optimize all resources to produce world-class quality products and services at the right time, in the right quantities, based on customer demand; to establish an efficient and effective business system based on continuous improvement; and to eliminate or manage constraints.

In March 1994, the mayor appointed 34 citizens to a Land Use Task Force and asked them to make recommendations regarding the objectives and policies that should be considered in making land-use decisions for the city. They produced a report that proposes a framework for land use. The report looks ahead several decades and makes recommendations designed to create more livable communities, more attractive areas for job development and a thriving central city. The recommendations provide a general guideline that can be used to evaluate land use and project development proposals.

After receiving additional community input, the Land Use Task Force recommended a follow-up community-based planning process in order to provide more detailed reinvestment recommendations. This is known as the Detroit Community Reinvestment Strategy (CRS).

CRS was designed by a group of twenty local neighborhood and community leaders that met over the course of four months in 1996 to design the general mission, goals, and objectives of the CRS process. The report developed by these community leaders provided the organizational structure followed throughout the CRS process and helped to solicit funding.

The Detroit Community Reinvestment Strategy's assignment was to develop comprehensive recommendations for reinvestment across the entire city, simultaneously; to involve as many people as possible in the process; and to complete the project within one year. CRS's mission was to identify the assets, strengths, land use, and other reinvestment opportunities for individual neighborhoods in Detroit and to recommend reinvestment priorities for the next five to ten years.

The objectives of CRS were to:

1. Identify and prioritize opportunities for reinvestment that offer the most potential for improving the neighborhood, community, and city as a place to live and do business;
2. Identify existing barriers to reinvestment and to recommend the type of reinvestment activity and location where it would be most effective to the community, and;
3. Develop a common community planning database that can be used to attract investments, support project planning, and enhance community decision making.

The results of this effort have been compiled into a series of ten reports released in late 1997. These reports contain a wealth of information. Developers interested in investing in the city can use these reports to determine what type of new developments are desired and where, including the best areas for new housing and rehabilitation potential. Entrepreneurs looking to open a small business can use these reports to see what type of goods and services are missing in different areas. Local community groups can use the reports to assist with grant writing to secure funding for projects. More information is available on the CRS web page at http://crs.cus.wayne.edu/.

Long-Term Financial Goals

- The four cornerstones contribute to the formation of the city's financial goals.
- Maintain balanced operations.

  - Expenditures will not exceed anticipated revenues.
  - Any significant costs for major projects or initiatives will be dealt with in a manner that will not affect the General Fund.
  - The Continuous Improvement Process will be used to reduce current expenditures, improve services and maintain balanced operations.

- A benchmarking effort is beginning that will be used to evaluate various city processes.
- Build financial reserves.

  - Gradual buildup of funds in the Budget Stabilization Fund.
  - Maintain adequate reserves in the Insurance Reserve Fund.
  - Eliminate unfunded liabilities of the Pension Fund.

- Provide tax relief while maintaining essential services.
- Seek permanent funding sources especially in the areas of cultural arts and public transportation.

  - Explore the possibility of a regional dedicated tax and/or merger with regional entities to ensure the existence of quality services at equitable costs.

- Improve revenue collections.

  - An enhanced effort to generate additional revenues and receive new grant or foundation funding will be pursued by departments to increase services to citizens.
  - The city is currently making an aggressive effort to collect delinquent revenue owed to the city. New procedures are being developed to actively pursue the collection of all revenues and maintain an acceptable collection rate.

- Improve financial reporting.

  - The city is nearing the implementation stage of replacing the current financial reporting system (FICS) and the human resource management system.

- Encourage Enterprise Fund self-sufficiency.

  - Develop strategies so that all Enterprise Fund departments will generate sufficient revenues to cover the cost of their operations.

- Utilize resource recovery to its full capacity.

  - Increase the efficiency of the resource recovery facility through the marketing of excess capacity to outside entities.

- Modernize public lighting.

  - Improve reliability and safety at the lowest possible cost.
  - Continue the upgrading of residential and main-street lighting.
  - Attain compliance with all applicable federal, state and local environmental and safety requirements.

- Develop an internal five-year model.

  - While not a substitute for a comprehensive long-term strategic plan, these internal models enable the Budget Department to assess changing conditions and plan for operational adjustments. The new financial system being developed will contain a multiyear forecasting function.

Goals and Budget Guidelines for Fiscal Year 1999–2000 Budget

The 1999–2000 recommended budget is based on realistic revenue and expenditure assumptions. When the budget process began, many additional costs and reduced revenues had to be addressed simply to maintain a status quo budget. Examples include:

- Additional funding for the DRMS project
- Union negotiations for the 1998–1999 and 1999–2000 fiscal years
- Increased general city pension costs and citywide fringe costs
- Need for additional heavy movable equipment throughout the city
- Lower utility user tax collections
- An assumption that no prior-year-surplus carry-forward amount would be available ($.9 million in 98/99 budget)

- Cut in state revenue sharing funds costing millions in growth
- Thirty-sixth District Court funding
- Overall slow growth in major revenues

To provide the mayor with maximum flexibility in preparing the budget, certain standardized constraints were imposed on departments. These included:

- Request no increase to the number of 1998–1999 General Fund–supported positions except where the addition of the position is unquestionably self-funding or where other permanent equivalent reductions in costs can be shown.
- Request no reductions in primary budget that may force layoffs. Vacant positions may be deleted.
- Prepare three prioritized lists on a program or decision-making package basis that:
  - Result in a "net tax total" roughly equivalent to 1998–1999.
  - Reduce 10 percent from your 1998–1999 "net tax total."
  - Add 10 percent to your 1998–1999 "net tax total."
- Prepare a list of operating initiatives and efficiencies incorporated into budget. Also include an estimate of costs or savings associated with each item.

This year the city will continue to prepare a budget revolving around Goal-Based Governance. The Budget Department held a budget training session on November 9, 1998, to explain the changes to the budget and to provide additional technical assistance. Departments were asked to begin placing a greater emphasis on the measurement of activities performed by their agency. They utilized Goal-Based Governance as a tool to establish the benchmarks to be used by the mayor to judge their agency's performance. Departments were also asked to begin a strategic planning process. Departments began firming up their records of key service measures. They are identifying outside forces that may affect their service delivery performance and identifying major programmatic priorities using a three- to five-year planning horizon. Another significant change was converting to a new chart of accounts for the new financial system. This was necessary because the 1999–2000 fiscal year will entirely utilize DRMS.

In many instances, departments were given standardized assumptions to use when preparing their 1999–2000 budget requests. Examples include:

- Utility costs are based on 1997–1998 actuals multiplied by an applicable two-year rate increase.
- Supply costs should reflect the effects of inflation. A general 2 percent inflation rate was assumed unless other specific information was available.

- New or increased revenues were a high priority.
- Agencies were to pursue an aggressive policy with regard to fees and user charges. A serious effort to recover all costs of the inspection or service being provided was required. Special emphasis was given to reviewing fee schedules to ensure that fees and charges for service appropriately reflect the value of the service and the city cost of providing service.
- Salary and wages are based on the negotiated patterns.
- Estimated fringe and pension costs were provided by the Budget Department.
- Travel and training requests should include detailed information.
- Automotive equipment is requested per a prescribed replacement schedule.
- City county building rent rates were provided. Standardized technology cost estimates were provided.

Taking into account the above factors, the city's long-term objectives of meeting the four cornerstones and presenting a balanced budget, the following items and programs are included in the 1999–2000 mayor's recommended budget. This is a listing of major items.

- DETROIT RESOURCE MANAGEMENT SYSTEM (DRMS). The recommended budget includes $23.2 million for implementation of the DRMS project. This project is the replacement of the current financial and human resources system. These funds will be used for equipment, debt service, building rental costs, maintenance and additional contractual personnel.
- SNOW REMOVAL. The recommended budget includes $5 million (Street Fund dollars), an increase of $3.9 million for snow removal. These additional funds will allow for contractual plowing of the center lane of residential streets with a snowfall or accumulation of six inches or more. Perimeter streets around schools, hospitals and senior citizen complexes will be plowed curb to curb. This budget anticipates this service being provided five times a year.

  - An additional $600,000 of General Fund dollars will be used to clear sidewalks in front of city-owned vacant lots and abandoned structures with a snowfall or accumulation of six inches or more. These dollars are in lieu of purchasing executive cars this fiscal year. Executive cars are currently on a two-year replacement cycle. Additional snow removal equipment ($1 million) will be purchased in lieu of general assigned vehicles. General assigned vehicles are currently on a four-year replacement cycle.

- SIDEWALK ASSESSMENT PROGRAM. The recommended budget includes $1 million for a sidewalk assessment program.

- TEMPORARY CASINOS. The recommended budget includes 142 police officers, 11 EMS personnel, 10 fire marshal employees and 27 fire fighters to accommodate the opening of three temporary casinos in 1999–2000 fiscal year. These positions are funded through a municipal service fee provided by the casinos.
- TIPPING FEE. The tipping fee reimbursement to the Greater Detroit Resource Recovery Authority (GDRRA) is recommended at $68.6 million, a decrease of $1.3 million from the current budget.
- ACCELERATED DEMOLITION PROGRAM. The city is continuing the accelerated demolition of dangerous, abandoned and blighted buildings. The recommended budget includes $19 million in block grant float funding to continue this effort.
- TECHNOLOGY. The recommended budget includes $15.72 million for technology improvements. The major expenditures include:
  - Year 2000 Conversion. The recommended budget includes $9.5 million for conversion of the city's computer systems to accommodate year 2000. This is an increase of $400,000 from the current budget. During the last two fiscal years (97/98 and 98/99) the city has budgeted more than $16 million for the Y2K issue.
  - Training. An amount of $520,000 is recommended for citywide and specialized computer training.
  - Departmental. Seventeen departments are budgeted $5.7 million for department-specific technology needs.
- FEDERAL AND STATE GRANTS.
  - Employment and Training. The recommended budget includes an additional $3.2 million for the WorkFirst Program. This will allow contractors to provide more employability skills training, job search and placement activities to eligible welfare clients and other services to two-parent families. The Welfare to Work grant is recommended for an additional $2.4 million. This program is for individuals who are long-term dependant on aid and difficult to employ.
  - Human Services. The recommended budget includes an additional $2.6 million for the Head Start grant. These funds will assist the department with its ongoing expansion of the program, which includes increasing all half-day classes to a full day.
  - Health. An additional $4.1 million is expected in grant awards. This is primarily due to a Medicaid substance abuse grant.

- BOND SALE. The budget includes $40 million in General Obligation Bond Proceeds. These funds will be used in DIA, Fire, Planning and Development, Airport, Health, Public Works, Library, Police, Public Lighting, Recreation and Zoo.
- TRANSPORTATION SUBSIDY. An additional $3 million is provided for General Fund subsidy to support the city's transportation system.
- PAY RAISE. The recommended budget includes $38 million to cover anticipated pay raises for the 1998–1999 and 1999–2000 fiscal year. The 1998–2001 contract is currently being negotiated.
- EMPLOYEE TRAINING. The recommended budget includes $500,000 for Performance Management and Appraisal, Labor Relations Training for Departmental Managers and Supervisors, Labor Management Training and Development, and Middle Management Training and Development. This training has been specifically identified by departments as critical needs. This will teach managers the new concept of performance management and appraisals, increase understanding of labor relations issues and requirements, as well as teach general management skills.

Appendix B: Department of Public Works (DPW) Departmental Budget Information

Mission

The mission of the Public Works Department is to provide excellence in the delivery of essential environmental, infrastructure and automotive services, thereby ensuring a safe and clean environment for our customers in a cost-effective manner.

Description

DPW carries out the city's responsibility to provide excellence in the delivery of essential environmental services and the operation and maintenance of a street system that is safe and reasonably fit for public use.

In order to provide a clean and sanitary environment, DPW provides the necessary services for the collection and disposal of waste generated by residential homes and commercial establishments, snow and ice removal, street cleaning, scrap tire collection, vacant lot cleanup activities, and rodent control. It also provides installation and maintenance of traffic signs and markings, resurfacing, and maintenance of city streets and bridges, demolition and the additional functions performed by DPW to provide a safe environment for the citizens of Detroit.

Additionally, the repairs and maintenance of the city's fleet and inspection of new vehicles to ensure conformity with specification before they are accepted are other functions of DPW.

Major Initiatives

The Administration Division has directed a major planning effort under Mayor Archer's Goal-Based Governance System and is managing department-wide operational improvements. Department Administration is also coordinating significant involvement in the Empowerment Zone, particularly related to vacant land use.

There has been continuous progress with the Traffic Facility Management System (TFMS). The system will use specialized traffic studies to reduce delays in obtaining traffic volume counts. Also, TFMS will provide ongoing data entry for traffic control devices and sign work orders. The first phase of this project has been completed. This phase established information relating to intersections. The second phase is under way and covers midblock information.

Major plans are being developed to improve signal systems in the Central Business District. The system will incorporate state-of-the-art equipment to control signals using a modem located in the traffic engineering building. This will enhance the engineers' ability to monitor traffic conditions and modify signal repetitions for improved traffic operations. With implementation of the system, response time will be reduced, which will translate into cost savings for the city.

Alternative methods and materials for pothole repairs are being explored through discussions with various vendors and institutions. Staff will expedite contract processing for pavement material and milling work for resurfacing jobs.

We are increasing our enforcement of the Refuse Collection Ordinance relating to commercial establishments with additional inspectors. Applying Geographic Information System technology, we have done Route Analysis to facilitate route completion within the workday, hence reducing overtime.

The thrust of street-fund programming continues to be implementing the expanded-street-improvements program initiative. A computerization project continues in the Vehicle Management Division to catalog departmental vehicles, inventories and maintenance records. We are working to develop a program that will facilitate monitoring stock and controlling expenditures.

Planning for the Future

The Administration Division coordinates and directs the future plans of all DPW divisions.

In the Environmental and Commercial Inspection Section we are going to re-educate our citizens with the correct days for both monthly bulk and weekly refuse collection.

We are working with the mayor's office, which is embarking on a code enforcement program that will change the procedures regarding the enforcement of environmental violations.

In the Street Fund Section, since Michigan Department of Transportation is going to assume the responsibility of maintaining city streets (trunklines) effective June 28, 1999, the department can redirect the personnel who were maintaining trunklines to the maintenance of city-owned streets.

In the Solid Waste Section plans are under way to address downtown litter-control cleanup activities 24 hours a day to meet the heavy pedestrian challenges related to the casino/stadium/entertainment mecca.

In the Snow and Ice Removal Section the new snow policy will be evaluated and improved as necessary.

In Street Cleaning the objective is to sweep residential streets three times during the year with a newer and larger vehicle sweeping fleet.

In the Vacant Lot Cleanup Section coordination with community groups will be ongoing.

The Street Maintenance Section continues to explore alternative methods or material for pothole repairs through discussions with various vendors and institutions.

Streets and Traffic and Street Maintenance Divisions of DPW are going to be housed in the same building, enabling them to be more efficient in their operations.

In the Vacant Housing Rescue/Demolition Section all vacant and abandoned structures open to trespass will be knocked down.

In the Vehicle Maintenance Division with the introduction of DRMS, the department anticipates vendors being paid more quickly, which will result in us no longer being put on COD payment status. This would allow for vehicles to be repaired faster while also providing better service to our citizens.

In the City Engineering Services Section we hope to implement an efficient sidewalk replacement program through use of computer technology.

Department of Public Works Budget Information

Table 10.1   Performance Goals, Measures and Targets

Goals: *Measures*	*1997–98* *Actual*	*1998–99* *Projection*	*1999–00* *Target*
Provide optimum refuse collection services and enforcement of environmental ordinances, resulting in a cleaner city:			
Refuse collection routes completed daily during peak	130	150	150
Provide automotive service excellence, thus ensuring optimum vehicular safety and availability:			
Percent of repairs completed within established repair time	100%	100%	100%
Reduce the number of vacant and dangerous structures within the city of Detroit:			
Buildings demolished	2,000	2,500	2,600
Provide high-quality, cost-effective services in the maintenance of city right-of-ways:			
Cycle miles of pothole repairs-roadways	7,000	9,600	10,000
Provide cost-effective and timely design and construction engineering services to our customers:			
Percent of construction engineering services performed within budget	80%	100%	100%

Table 10.2   Department of Public Works Budget

EXPENDITURES

	1997–98 Actual Expense	1998–99 Redbook	1999–00 Mayor's Budget Rec	Variance	Variance Percent
Salary & Wages	$45,672,846	$47,589,360	$50,676,823	$3,087,463	6.49%
Employee Benefits	26,247,680	23,537,797	26,112,313	2,574,516	10.94%
Prof/Contractual	49,443,128	23,759,513	42,379,773	18,620,260	78.37%
Operating Supplies	37,319,686	14,502,138	13,416,246	(1,085,892)	(7.49)%
Operating Services	80,500,158	73,147,377	74,780,010	1,632,633	2.23%
Capital Equipment	5,787,063	9,706,839	9,876,600	169,761	1.75%
Capital Outlays	49,382,730	2,780,033	8,145,500	5,365,467	193.00%
Other Expenses	14,905,620	70,000	70,000	0	0.00%
TOTAL	$309,258,911	$195,093,057	$225,457,265	$30,364,208	15.56%
POSITIONS	1,419	1,428	1,429	1	0.07%

REVENUES

	1997–98 Actual Expense	1998–99 Redbook	1999–00 Mayor's Budget Rec	Variance	Variance Percent
Taxes/Assessments	$55,470,619	$2,869,883	$9,591,093	$6,721,210	234.20%
Licenses/Permits	5,559,543	6,107,500	6,453,600	346,100	5.67%
Fines/Forfeits/ Penalties	25	0	0	0	n/a
Revenue from Use of Assets	4,929,126	1,720,827	1,689,142	(31,685)	(1.84)%
Grants/Shared Taxes	19,879,513	2,087,000	2,237,147	150,147	7.19%
Sales & Charges	62,894,205	44,985,860	48,352,803	3,366,943	7.48%
Sales of Assets	817,256	962,000	856,907	(105,093)	(10.92)%
Contrib/Transfers	14,818,707	0	0	0	n/a
Miscellaneous	2,561,914	1,024,000	20,332,096	19,308,096	1885.56%
TOTAL	$166,930,908	$59,757,070	$89,512,788	$29,755,718	49.79%

How Atlanta Entered into the Largest Privatization Contract in North America

Bill Campbell
Mayor of Atlanta, Georgia

I. Why Privatization was Atlanta's Best Solution

One of the greatest challenges for large cities at the end of the twentieth century is infrastructure. Like a living body, a city must be maintained and nurtured to provide the services and environment to sustain a community's quality of life. Infrastructure systems are the nuts and bolts that hold together the social, cultural and economic fabric of our society. From water and sewer services to power and transportation—if the nuts and bolts give way, so does a community's ability to compete in the global economy.

In spite of the critical role infrastructure plays in the health of cities and the nation, a pervasive and persistent pattern of neglect has brought America to a crisis point. Roads, bridges, wastewater systems, and drinking water systems are crumbling before us. The Rebuild America Coalition estimates that the total price tag of necessary investments is well over $1 trillion.

These realities have put many city governments in a conundrum. To sustain a community's quality of life, massive and immediate investments are needed to bring water systems—as well as other infrastructures—into the twenty-first century. At the same time, local governments, who bear the burden of financing the necessary investments, are facing severe budgetary shortfalls. Failure to act is no longer an option for responsible governments. If we fail to address our community's infrastructure needs today, the costs to future generations will be monumental.

The city of Atlanta was not immune to this national pattern of neglect. For years, the city failed to invest sufficiently in its infrastructure. In 1994, a series of water leaks brought the infrastructure crisis to the fore. Two weeks into my first term, three of the four aging pipes that carry water from our region's only water source, the Chattahoochee River, to Atlanta's largest treatment plant burst within a 16-hour period. This crisis occurred just a few days before 100,000 visitors were expected to arrive for the Super Bowl and amid preparations for the 1996 Centennial Olympic Games. I was forced to impose water restrictions and to ask nearly 500,000 customers to keep their taps closed except for cooking and drinking. Within two days, the leaks were repaired and the crisis was over, but the aftermath was significant.

In July 1994, with the mini–water crisis still fresh on voters' minds, we won approval of a $150 million bond referendum to breathe new life into Atlanta's infrastructure—the first such investment in 30 years. Although the bond referendum went toward repairing streets, bridges, and other infrastructures and did not directly benefit the water system, the mini–water crisis became a symbol of all of our city's infrastructure ills and raised unprecedented public support for the referendum. The crisis also helped shape my administration's agenda. It crystallized for me the urgency of identifying innovative funding solutions to the massive infrastructure problems we faced. Privatization emerged as one possible solution.

Coming to terms with what privatization might mean for Atlanta was a difficult decision. Philosophically, I had never been a proponent of privatization, nor do I subscribe to the axiom that the private sector always performs better than government. For example, Hartsfield-Atlanta International Airport, one of the world's busiest airports and one that is consistently rated among the best by passengers, is owned and operated entirely by the city of Atlanta.

There are compelling reasons for public servants to be reluctant to embrace privatization:

• Traditionally, privatization saves money by firing older, more experienced workers and replacing them with younger workers. As an elected official who has always supported organized labor, I believe all workers should be treated fairly and rewarded according to experience. I was morally uncomfortable with the idea of putting out the street workers who may have 20 years tenure.

- City governments have a compelling interest in ensuring that citizens have access to a clean, affordable and ample supply of water. Beyond its impact on a city's economic competitiveness, water is "the stuff of life," and its supply and delivery carry with it profound health and public policy implications. Inadequate treatment of water can lead to illness and even epidemics, endangering in particular our most vulnerable citizens—children and seniors. The supply of a vital public resource should not be relegated to bottom-line concerns.
- The city of Atlanta has a long-standing commitment to minority participation. My administration had worked hard to keep the city's Equal Business Opportunity Program strong and viable. Unlike city government, private management is not, by ordinance, held to any equal opportunity policy, which could potentially endanger the gains achieved by minority- or female-owned businesses in our city.
- Privatization potentially removes an important layer of accountability. Elected officials' scope of authority and power is balanced by citizen action. Government depends on the participation of citizens. If an official fails to act in the public's best interest, the democratic process guarantees change, through elections for example. The private sector has no such inherent checks and balances.

Though this was my philosophical orientation, I was still faced with the crisis in our water infrastructure. The question remained: how could we pay for the needed capital facilities and improve the performance of the water system without onerous rate increases that would unduly burden citizens? There was no question that a rate increase was imminent. The city faced Environmental Protection Agency (EPA) fines of $100,000 a day for environmental violations by the wastewater system and more than $1 billion in necessary repairs and improvements, including new underground pipe and facility construction and restoration. We have made progress. Phosphorous levels have been reduced by 90 percent and consistently meet state-mandated levels. We have also eliminated $20,000 in daily fines imposed by the EPA by completing construction of two combined sewer overflow facilities. In April of 1999, we completed the largest bond sale ever in the history of our city—$1.1 billion in water and sewer bonds. But after decades of neglect, these are only milestones on a much longer and more expensive journey.

In a city that has a high poverty rate and high percentage of senior citizens, in a city that, after decades of decline, is experiencing a rise in population and economic investment, a quality water system at competitive rates is crucial. Notwithstanding my philosophical inclination, I recognized that a new approach was needed to take our city's water infrastructure into the twenty-first century.

Furthermore, my administration had already established a strong record of successful public–private partnerships. Five years ago, we had one of the worst housing authorities in the country. The U.S. Department of Housing and Urban Development (HUD) had given the Atlanta Housing Authority (AHA) a dismal score of 36 out of 100. In early 1999, we were given a score of 97, but AHA is now designated by HUD as a High-Performing Agency. This reinvention was accomplished through the use of public–private partnerships. The AHA developed the legal and financial model for mixed-income, mixed-finance communities. The Atlanta Development Authority (ADA), the city's economic development agency, has created investment incentives, such as tax allocation districts. Working closely with developers and other private-sector companies, the ADA is attracting major projects and revitalizing neighborhoods. Atlanta's Empowerment Zone uses government dollars to leverage private dollars and investment in the city's most impoverished areas.

This history of successful public–private partnerships, the pending onerous rate increases, and the fear of an infrastructure collapse ultimately caused me to view privatization as the best solution for our water system.

In the meantime, a major regulatory obstacle to long-term contracts for the private management of government services had been removed. Until recently, federal grant repayment obligations and IRS policies impeded the movement to privatize public water systems. In 1992, an executive order (E.O. 12803) changed the allocation of proceeds from the sale or lease of municipal facilities built with federal funds. Now, cities will not be penalized for selling, leasing or structuring contract operations for facilities built with federal support. Moreover, in the past, IRS rules held that municipal water utilities with outstanding tax-exempt debt could not enter contract operations agreements for terms longer than five years and still maintain the debt's tax-exempt status. Because private operators need several years to begin recouping the high costs associated with beginning contract operations, five-year contracts dramatically limited the benefits of private-sector participation. In 1997, however, the IRS changed the policy to allow contracts with terms up to 20 years (Rev. Proc. 97–13).

Now that these obstacles have been removed, cities are able to take advantage of the flexibility of long-term contracts and the full benefits of public–private partnerships in city services. The current circumstances have opened opportunities for the private sector to assist municipalities with reducing operational expenses and improving service delivery quality. With acquisitions or long-term operations and maintenance contracts, both the public and private sector can succeed. The public sector can save on operational costs and attract new funding sources for needed capital improvements. Meanwhile, the private operator has a profit incentive to run the plants more efficiently.

Privatization possibilities need to be carefully analyzed for each situation. What works for one city, both economically and politically, may not be the best solution for another. Privatization could involve a private company purchasing a public water system or a private company taking over the operations of a public water system. Private-sector firms supply the investment needed to improve customer service, the global expertise to employ advanced technologies, and the incentives required for more efficient practices. Particularly in a setting where municipalities confront flat or diminishing budgets, the involvement of private-sector firms is appealing because they lower expenses, improve cash flows, and add new funding sources. Privatization can be partial; it does not necessarily have to encompass the entire system. Water utilities are increasingly contracting out specialized parts of their systems, such as billing, payroll accounting, lab work, or meter reading. It is now common for public water utilities to engage an outside firm to operate a treatment plant or another major part of the system. In cases where the rehabilitating or building of new system elements is required, a variety of well-known arrangements are possible, including Build Own Operate (BOO) and Build Own Operate Transfer (BOOT).

In October 1998, the city of Atlanta made its choice. We completed the largest water operations outsourcing in North America, awarding a 20-year full operations and maintenance contract to United Water Services (UWS) as a result of a competitive procurement process. With annual revenues of $150 million, United Water Services is a joint venture of Suez Lyonnaise des Eaux and New Jersey–based United Water Resources, bringing global expertise to the system. The company offered to operate Atlanta's system at a guaranteed annual cost of $21.4 million, almost half of the city's current operating budget.

While the city will retain ownership of the system, which consists of three treatment plants and a 2,400-mile distribution system, our operations costs will be cut almost by half. UWS will manage the workforce and all operations and will coordinate capital improvements to provide clean drinking water to 1.5 million customers. The contract will save ratepayers $400 million over the life of the 20-year contract—money that can be directly invested in upgrades to the water system.

Beyond these operational and financial benefits, we ensured that the contract protected the interests of the city and addressed our concerns about the possible risks of privatization. The contract specifies clear outcomes and expectations. It provides for 24-hour, 7-day-per-week access and oversight by the city, and a provision for termination of the service agreement without cause after a 90-day notice. Should the contractor fail to meet deadlines, the company—not the city—will pay the fines. The contract also requires prior city approval of all improvements proposed by the contractor. Employees are protected by a "no lay-off" policy for the full duration of the contract. This, in fact, exceeds the three-year, attrition-only requirement in the city's draft operating agreement. UWS also made significant minority participation and community investment commitments.

Privatization is not a panacea, but public–private partnership is an effective means for government to do more with less, to increase efficiency while reducing costs. Rates will still increase, but only on a blended rate of about 8 percent over the next four years. Within the context of a larger reengineering of government services, privatization is a valuable cost-saving and quality-enhancing tool whose time has come. Each city needs to analyze, within its own economic, environmental and political context, the appropriate scope of privatization. In Atlanta's case, contract operation of the entire water system proved to be the solution that best met our local objectives and conditions.

II. How Atlanta Entered into the Largest Privatization Contract in North America

Atlanta's successful entry into the largest privatization contract in North America is a story about expertise, integrity and process. In partnership with a team of expert consultants, we developed a comprehensive, step-by-step blueprint. The process was unique in its speed, thoroughness, openness and integrity. It consisted of two phases: phase I entailed an assessment of current operations and the selection of the best form of operation for our system, and phase II dealt with the actual implementation of privatization and the selection of a private contractor.

We began by hiring a consultant team of Brown and Caldwell, PriceWaterhouseCoopers and Harrington George and Dunn. These engineering and accounting consultants have overseen the technical and financial aspects of the proposal process. We knew early on what our benchmarks and boundaries were.

In addition, Camp, Dresser, and McKee were hired to provide oversight and advice. This company's main function was to ensure the integrity of the process. Working with this company was Washington, D.C.–based Beveridge and Diamond. This team monitored all matters related to the technical, financial, and legal areas.

The city also hired the local firm of Long, Aldridge, and Norman, one of the few major local firms not working with one of the bidding teams, to provide legal advice to the city. This firm created a partnership with Verner Lipfert in Washington, D.C., one of the top firms in the country handling privatization. They have consulted on more than 70 privatizations nationwide. These are all nationally, and in some cases, internationally recognized firms.

A. The First Phase in the Process: Assess Cost-Effectiveness of Current Operations

As a first step, the city commissioned a detailed study to assess the cost-effectiveness of its current water and wastewater operations and identify operational alternatives. This involved analyzing approximately 40 functions and facilities, reviewing documents, interviewing key personnel, benchmarking against similar systems, and identifying long-term goals and strategies. The study identified and examined several operational alternatives, determining their effect on future rates. These options included: (1) light reengineering/outsourcing of noncore operations (such as grounds keeping), (2) heavy reengineering/outsourcing, (3) contract operations of various treatment facilities, and (4) contract operations of all system facilities. We did not consider an outright sale of the assets as an option. It was imperative that we maintain our rate-making authority and ability to protect ratepayers' and the city's interests.

In evaluating alternatives, Atlanta considered a variety of factors:

- Degree of risk
- Experience
- Ease and speed of implementation
- Employee impacts
- Maintaining or improving service quality
- Limitation of local and state laws

Our evaluation methodology also included an examination of financial and operational criteria. We established a benchmark for the savings required. Identifying clear goals helped set achievable benchmarks for the bidding companies. We estimated the range of cost savings that could be derived from each of the options after assembling them into the following savings alternatives:

- **Light Reengineering/Outsourcing**: Making the straightforward changes that can be accomplished within a single system/department. Also included in this alternative was the outsourcing of noncore functions to the private sector.
- **Heavy Reengineering/Outsourcing**: Adding to the light reengineering package those more difficult internal actions that involve the cooperation of two or more departments and/or a basic change in the way that the city conducts its business. Also included in this alternative was the outsourcing of noncore functions to the private sector.
- **Contract Operations**: Selecting through competition a qualified private firm or firms to operate one or more of the five treatment facilities in the system while implementing the heavy reengineering package on the noncontracted facilities and functions that remain under the city's management.
- **System Management**: Selecting through competition a qualified private firm to manage the water system, the wastewater/sewer system, or both, while implementing the heavy reengineering scenario on the remaining system.

The city constructed a financial model to evaluate the impact of these alternatives on the customers. The model simulated the flow of revenues and costs through the systems, including operational costs, indirect costs, capital spending, debt service on bonds, outside revenue sources, and other factors, to demonstrate what future rates would look like under the various alternatives. This analysis determined that a combination of the alternatives would realize the greatest overall potential benefit to the city and its utility customers, at acceptable levels of risk. The chosen combination was contract management of all water system operations and one wastewater plant, with reengineering of the rest of the wastewater and sewer system.

B. The Second Phase in the Process: Choosing a Contractor

The city of Atlanta followed a careful selection process with three phases that took less than a full year to execute: (1) qualification of bidders, (2) initial cost and technical proposals, and (3) best and final offers.

Throughout we had three underlying goals:

- A fair and unbiased competitive process
- Integrity and professionalism in the way the process was carried out
- Obtaining the best value for the city and ratepayers

It was absolutely essential to us that the process was as open as possible. We held 13 public hearings. We researched, produced and made public reams of documents. I also appointed a nine-member Independent Privatization Review Panel. In August of 1997, we held a privatization showcase for city employees, union members and officials. We brought in other cities like Indianapolis, Houston and Charlotte, as well as vendors, to share information on how privatization had worked for them. The event was completely financed by vendors.

The process was also designed to minimize undue influence on the outcome. An evaluation panel of 47 members was established. Based on the city's statutory evaluation criteria and the required scoring system, individual technical teams were assembled to review each aspect of the proposals. The entire process was monitored independently by the consultant team.

In the first stage, we issued a widely advertised request for qualification/ request for proposal (RFQ/RFP), which incorporated a draft Operating Agreement. Five statements of qualification were received. It should be noted that at least one expected bidder declined to bid because of the form of privatization that Atlanta selected. Of the five that did bid, three were from consortia led by French concessionaires and two were from teams led by U.S. firms. Using predetermined criteria, the city evaluated the financial strength and technical ability of each proponent to fulfill the requirements of the contract. The purpose of this stage was to narrow the field by eliminating those contractors who were not substantial enough to meet minimum requirements. All five contractors, however, met the qualification criteria required to continue to the next phase.

At the completion of this qualification phase, all five bidders were invited to submit separate technical and cost proposals. The RFQ/RFP for these proposals provided such information as historical and current Atlanta water utility operating statistics, staffing, budgetary and other related financial data, proposed capital improvement programs and various policies and procedures. In addition, the RFQ/RFP included various required levels of service and performance measures to which the winning contractor would be held during the contract term. In general, the proponents' proposals were to describe the detailed technical project approach, proposed key personnel and staffing plans for the project team, the proposed annual cost for the term of the contract and the mechanism for the escalation of costs over time. Some of the most important aspects of the entire process dealt with the requirement that bidders comply with the city's Equal Business Opportunity (EBO) policy and our stipulation of a "no layoff" policy for the first three years of the contract.

To ensure that the evaluation process was as democratic and unbiased as possible, multiple technical evaluation teams of city staff members were assembled. Each team was responsible for evaluating various specific aspects of the proposals, rather than entire proposals, to further decentralize the evaluation process. As part of the review of the technical and cost proposals, we held personal interviews with each of the bidders. Questions raised by either side that could not be answered during the interview were submitted and answered as a follow-up to the interview process.

In an unusual, open auction, Atlanta provided first-round prices to local newspapers and technical bid summaries to each of the proponents. We then invited the bidders to improve all aspects of their proposals in "best and final offers" three weeks later on August 21, 1988.

In the best-and-final-offer phase, we refined and standardized the final Operating Agreement to include any additional information and requirements that resulted from the entire evaluation process. All of the proponents were required to agree to sign the city's operating agreement as written before submitting revised bids. One bidder was disqualified in the final round for refusing to sign the contract without changes. The technical evaluation teams reviewed all final proposals, ranked the bidders and made recommendations to City Council and to me.

UWS's initial proposal was second lowest on price and ranked third by the technical evaluation committees. Best and final offers were requested for the city's base contract, without the varoius revenue enhancement options offered by bidders in the first round of proposals. UWS had offered the city a revenue guarantee tied to re-metering, and another bidder had offered to buy the water department's inventory, for example.

Sealed, fixed-price bids and the city's revised technical evaluations of the four finalists were opened during a press conference where I announced that UWS had reduced its original price for the first year of a 20-year contract from $27 million to $21.4 million, by almost 21 percent.

In its final determination, the city evaluated bidders using a value index, considering not only cost but also such factors as technical expertise, customer service, minority participation and community investment. UWS had not only the lowest price, but also made a commitment to increase minority business ownership of its local operating company from 15 to 35 percent and to delegate up to 60 percent of the water system management to Atlanta's minority- and women-owned businesses.

In addition, UWS agreed to relocate its local office in Atlanta's Empowerment Zone and to hire 20 percent of its workforce in the Zone. UWS has also committed to providing $100,000 each year for the first five years as seed money for new Zone businesses and $1,000 in down payment assistance for employees who will locate in the Zone. To support research and development, UWS has committed to a $1 million grant to fund an Institute for Water Resource Development at one of our historically black colleges. This investment will establish Atlanta as one of the premier cities in the world for innovative water research and technology.

We realized that a creative public–private partnership could serve as an economic development tool to revitalize our Zone neighborhoods. UWS's investment in the Empowerment Zone represents the most significant contribution ever to some of Atlanta's most historic and most neglected neighborhoods. The company's strong and innovative commitment on public policy was an important factor in its selection.

All these factors made UWS the best choice. As Atlanta's privatization shows, you can combine cost savings with good social public policy objectives in a competitive bidding process.

III. Lessons from Atlanta: Trust the Process

Any city or regional authority considering some form of privatization can benefit from Atlanta's experiences. The key to the success of Atlanta's program has been its comprehensive and rigorous process.

Out of our experience emerged some basic lessons:

1. Begin the process with a comprehensive objective analysis of the alternative ways to reduce operating costs.
2. Make the process open to the public.
3. Make the process fair and competitive.
4. Ensure absolute integrity and professionalism in the process.
5. Obtain not only the lowest cost, but also the best overall value for the city and ratepayers.
6. Make certain the contract protects the city's interests.
7. Trust the process.

Taking the time to develop the process up-front will save time and prevent problems down the road. It will also be the foundation for dealing with the intense media scrutiny that will undoubtedly ensue. Atlanta engaged in an extensive public and employee information campaign, but second-guessing and speculation by the media can easily derail a process if it lacks in focus or integrity. Clear goals and a sound process will provide a firm foundation for major reengineering or restructuring of city service delivery.

IV. A Successful Conclusion

Contract operations are now fully in place as is the city's oversight system. A small team of water department staff has been retained on the city's payroll to monitor contract compliance. Under the direction of a Joint Coordination Committee, baseline conditions are being established, and the scope of the computerized systems is being finalized.

Using Atlanta as an example, it is clear that privatization offers attractive choices to public and private interests. Each privatization opportunity is different and must be evaluated on its own merits, though. Inevitably, however, the water utility of the future will be defined by its ability to deliver better quality and service for lower rates.

Next for Atlanta is the privatization of the wastewater system. We will continue to look for opportunities for public–private partnerships as a catalyst for transforming our city. In an era of limited government—and environmental—resources, economic tools such as privatization may be our best hope for passing on healthy cities to future generations.

The Chicago Alternative Policing Strategy (CAPS)

Richard M. Daley
Mayor of Chicago, Illinois

Introduction

In their landmark study of the effect of physical decay on neighborhood safety, "Broken Windows," James Wilson and George Kelling found that it is not only crime that frightens people, but the appearance of neglect. When neighborhoods succumb to disorder and chaos, the residents have the perception that crime is increasing, even if it is not. Wilson and Kelling state that "at the community level, disorder and crime are usually inextricably linked, in a kind of developmental sequence. Social psychologists and police officers tend to agree that if a window in a building is broken *and is left unrepaired,* all the rest of the windows will soon be broken. . . . One unrepaired, broken window is a signal that no one cares, and so breaking more windows costs nothing."

Chicago's CAPS program attempts to address these concerns. By incorporating the Chicago Alternative Policing Strategy (CAPS) into daily police work, the Daley administration is constantly working to realize the goal of safer streets for everyone. When CAPS was introduced, it was hailed as a new wave in law enforcement. Though the community policing theory can be expounded upon at great length, there is one recurrent theme: improving crime prevention through technology and information sharing. The city of Chicago is doing this by developing and using a computerized crime-mapping program and integrating routine city service delivery into daily police work.

I have been very vigorous in my efforts to make the police department more effective, thereby decreasing the crime rate across the city. Despite actual crime statistics, if a neighborhood is perceived as dangerous, it is difficult to persuade business owners and home buyers to invest money there, and ultimately, crime becomes an impediment to economic development. If a city wants to stimulate development, the onus is on the administration to tackle the high crime rates and negative images.

The city of Chicago has operated proactively to combat crime by combining mapping, an urban planning innovation, with the Community Policing program. The Chicago Police Department (CPD) has implemented a computerized mapping program, called Information Collection for Automated Mapping (ICAM), to aid police in their daily work. The program contains and analyzes crime data, assisting officers in spotting trends and solving crimes. Officers now have the ability to actually see, via maps, where crimes are occurring, what types of crimes occur most frequently, what times or days of the week they occur, and overall crime patterns.

The ICAM system is innovative and effective. There is an emphasis on the relationship between data that cannot be seen in a list and comes across much more vividly in a map format. By employing a point-and-click method, the system has a user-friendly focus. Community information, such as the location of schools, parks and automated teller machines, is also integrated into the maps. All these features make the ICAM system a valuable tool in crime prevention.

The CPD is also integrating routine city service delivery into daily police work. Police are helping other city departments (e.g., the Streets and Sanitation Department and the Buildings Department) by notifying them of problems such as broken traffic signals and abandoned buildings. By working in conjunction with other departments, the police attempt to keep small problems from becoming larger.

Community Policing

Both of these initiatives are part of the CAPS program. The traditional methods of policing had many limitations, so the city was searching for a new technique that would more fully address the needs of the citizenry. Past practices in policing confined many beat officers to their cars, so they were not able to mix with the residents to a large degree. Using patrol cars has some advantages, such as covering a large area and responding more quickly to an emergency, but walking a beat allows the officers to become a part of the scene. Instead of observing the community from the car, they are on the sidewalk, interacting.

Community policing also places more emphasis on citizen involvement. Instead of calling the police to tell them someone is being robbed on the street in front of their house, residents can alert the beat officers that a suspicious character has been lurking about for the past two nights. This kind of intermingling allows police to get to know the players and characters better than they normally would have, and it puts the officers in a better position to notice when something is out of the ordinary.

Introduced as a pilot program in 1993, CAPS was an attempt to involve area residents with the police, use teamwork to fight crime, and build a bridge of trust and cooperation between the police and those whom they were charged to serve and protect. Though police departments across the country have attempted to be more community oriented, the CPD is one of the few to recognize the advantage of instituting CAPS department wide. One of the tenets of CAPS is that every officer, not just one section, should be involved in the partnership with the community, so that everyone acts as a problem solver. To fulfill this mission, CAPS was implemented in all 25 police districts in 1994 and recognized as a permanent policy in 1995.

The effectiveness of CAPS can be seen in the decrease in crime, especially in the five pilot districts: the Seventh, Tenth, Fifteenth, Twenty-second and Twenty-fourth Districts. In 1992, the year before CAPS was piloted, the total number of index crimes in the Fifteenth District, which include homicide, criminal sexual assault, robbery, aggravated assault, burglary, theft, motor vehicle theft and arson, was 10,370. By 1996, this number had dropped to 8,068, a decrease of more than 12 percent. Between 1992 and 1996, criminal sexual assaults and motor vehicle theft declined 17 percent in the Seventh District, and instances of motor vehicle theft declined 40 percent in the Twenty-second District. These numbers demonstrate that CAPS is more than just a slogan. It is an effective crime-fighting tool.

Innovations

The CPD wanted expanded problem-solving tools, including new ways to gather and analyze crime data. The department decided that uniting CAPS with up-to-date computer technology would be a way to anticipate crimes before they happen by looking at trends, such as garage burglaries occurring in the same alley at the same time every day. Out of this need, ICAM, the Information Collection for Automated Mapping, was developed.

The ICAM system was not the first time the CPD had attempted computerized mapping. In 1988, the National Institute of Justice financed a project involving the CPD, the Chicago Alliance for Neighborhood Safety, and researchers from the University of Illinois at Chicago and Northwestern. The group developed a basic crime-tracking and analysis system that was piloted in one of the twenty-five districts. The system was somewhat successful in areas such as recognizing patterns in where specific crimes were taking place and providing information to community groups about increases in certain crimes. However, the maps were only rudimentary, and the project was confined to one district.

The CPD attempted another system in 1991, when they worked in conjunction with the Illinois Criminal Justice Information Authority to create a mapping program that would survey gang activity. This study used the crime data with information about the community, such as where the elevated train stops were, places where teenagers were likely to congregate, liquor stores, abandoned buildings and other trouble spots.

Development of ICAM

The ICAM team, including systems analysts and detectives, used these previous trials to produce a mapping system that would be sophisticated enough to collect the necessary information but elementary enough to be used by those with little or no computer experience. They spent time meeting with officers and detectives from one of the districts to decide how the information should be displayed, so it would be obvious even to the untrained eye. The officers were in favor of using maps, so the next step was not only to design a system, but also to find a way to fund it.

The funding for ICAM arrived from a most unexpected source, the Illinois Motor Vehicle Theft Prevention Council (IMVTPC). The IMVTPC was developed in 1991 by the insurance industry to study possible ways to reduce auto theft losses. IMVTPC awarded the CPD a grant to buy the required equipment with the hope that computerized mapping would reduce auto theft in Chicago.

The system was developed in-house. The CPD staff concentrated on developing a system that would be user-friendly to beat officers. Since most other cities' mapping systems were more complicated, the CPD did not have a model to dupli-

cate. Other departments' mapping systems required a computer analyst to operate; they were not designed as "walk up and use," so they were not effective at
the beat-officer level.

In August 1993, a prototype was unveiled in the Twenty-fourth District, but
the officers voted it too confusing and too slow in the generation of maps. The
creators kept working and in October 1994 the first ICAM was set up in the
Twenty-fourth District; by May 1995, all of the districts had ICAM. Although
initially successful, the first version of ICAM proved lacking in some areas, and
in the fall of 1996 a new version of ICAM was introduced. This updated version
allowed the officers to request more complex analysis.

ICAM was designed for those who are not computer literate. It is a mouse-
based system, meaning that the user only has to point the mouse and click on the
correct icon. The ICAM personal computers do not need keyboards, and when
they are turned on the main screen automatically comes up, so the user does not
have to know how to open a program.

ICAM was developed with two main functions in mind: to create a map of a
particular area and show where a certain type of crime has occurred within that
area, or to produce a "Top 10" list showing the crimes that occur most often on
a particular beat. There were several default categories, such as date and time.
For example, on April 4, ICAM would automatically show all offenses in a chosen beat for the time period of March 4 to March 14, from 00:00 to 24:00 hours.
The user can request a change in the boundaries by clicking on a calendar to
choose the appropriate day and time. The officer might only want burglaries that
were perpetrated in the past seven days on the third watch. The ability to change
the parameters to suit the individual user's needs is the distinctive attribute of
ICAM.

Once the user chooses the information parameters and clicks on "Do It!" both
maps and tables appear on screen. The map can be of the district, sector or beat;
contain the major streets and icons for liquor stores, schools and public transit
stations; and show symbols where offenses have occurred. Crimes are shown as
primary offenses, such as robbery, sexual assault and battery, but they can be
broken down into secondary offenses, like domestic battery or aggravated battery, and each division has a different symbol.

The tables present much of the same information that the maps do, but in a
different format. The tables show the number of occurrences of each type of
crime, the Records Division reference number, date of offense, the beat, time of
day and address. These data are important because looking at a map gives the
officer an indication of where the crimes are occurring in relation to one another,

and matching the data to a table allows the officer to glean valuable details about the characteristics of the perpetrator or incident.

Looking at a series of burglaries listed by address, an officer may not realize how close together they are occurring, or that they are all happening on streets that dead end. Seeing them on a map adds a level of tangibility not to be found in tables. Officers investigating a series of sexual assaults occurring in their beat may notice commonalities when the crimes are mapped on ICAM. The assaults may all be occurring by elevated train stops at certain times. The officer works with that information and discovers that the crimes are occurring after the last nightly train stops at the stations and that women traveling alone are the victims. The offender knows that he will be able to commit the assault undisturbed, because no more trains will stop at the station until the morning. The officers may then stand guard near the train stations while the last trains are running, in order to ensure the safety of the passengers. By incorporating this activity into their beat, the officers have taken away the opportunity for a crime to be committed. The officers were able to use the information they saw mapped on ICAM to determine the trend in those crimes.

Each crime can be looked up individually by its Records Division number if the officer wants more in-depth information. An officer can view tables and maps simultaneously and print them out immediately. The officer can look at community data such as automated teller machine locations, CTA stops, and schools, perform some geographic analysis such as identifying clusters of crimes, or run another query.

If an officer hears about a string of robberies occurring on his beat, he can look up the crimes on ICAM to see where they are occurring. He might see that all of them are occurring near three automated teller machines between 8:00 P.M. and 10:00 P.M. To prevent any more robberies, he may decide to patrol the ATMs more frequently, or advise the banks to install security cameras or guards. With the information from ICAM, the emphasis is on using that knowledge to prevent crimes from happening. Of course it is desirable to apprehend the guilty party, but it is even better if the opportunity to commit a crime is thwarted. Residents will find greater peace of mind in a low crime rate than a high arrest rate.

Training the officers to use the system took time and planning, but access by all officers is key, since the beat officers are the most involved with the community on a daily basis and should know what is happening so they can let the residents know. There was a video produced, and the ICAM team went to all the districts to train officers as well as the district administrative managers. There were user guides written, and the ICAM computers were made available to all officers, not just the superiors. As a result of these efforts, 80 percent of officers use ICAM at least occasionally, and usage has increased the longer the system is in place.

ICAM was instrumental in solving many crimes. In the Twenty-second District, officers learned of a rash of burglaries occurring at schools and used ICAM to map the exact locations of these burglaries and determine patterns about the times they were occurring. Officers established surveillance at the appropriate times and locations and soon arrested a burglar as he was fleeing a school. In the Seventh District, an ICAM map showed that the locations of recovered stolen vehicles were around specific abandoned buildings. Armed with this information, police officials worked with the city's Department of Planning to expedite the demolition of the buildings.

In the past, an officer would have had to look at paper reports case by case to search for commonalities in the crimes and then plot the location of the crimes on a map. ICAM is a time-saver because it shows crime location and gives summaries. Officers can pull up all the information they need in minutes, compared to the hours or days it would have taken previously.

ICAM—Phase 2

Even though ICAM 1 was successful, there were still several features that it lacked, so in September 1995, the CPD began to redesign ICAM. The main difference between ICAM 1 and ICAM 2 is that ICAM 1 computers were all stand-alones; each computer only contained the information that was entered into it. ICAM 2 computers are on a network, and statistics from any district or beat can be accessed through any of the computers. This is valuable because districts working together is one of the tenets of CAPS. An officer may notice a string of burglaries that use the same method occurring throughout his district. This officer can then look at other districts, using ICAM, to see if the same types of burglary are occurring anywhere else. If they are, the officer can cooperate with officers from the other district to apprehend the thieves. Using this method, burglary or auto-theft rings that operate citywide may be more easily recognized.

ICAM is in the districts, as well as the tactical, gang and other special units, so information can be shared between them. Often, units have to coordinate information because many types of crime are related, such as a gang robbing people on the elevated trains. A particular gang may be heavily involved in drug trafficking, so the narcotics unit may want information on the activities of that gang.

By using ICAM, the units have access to the same information that everyone else does, without having to deliver files and fax records. The goals for improving the ICAM system were to create a user-friendly system with more functionality and data access than the original ICAM, to maintain the ease of use that is the key to ICAM, and to strengthen the investigative and problem-solving capabilities of all units in the department.

ICAM was developed with a lot of input from the users, and the enhancements were mainly the result of user requests. ICAM enables officers to plug in an address and search for all crimes committed at that address, as well as enter names and study the offender's record. Pictures of offenders are also available on-screen. In addition, ICAM updates detectives' case status daily, shows arrest activity, allows queries by vehicle or offender description and performs several other tasks.

ICAM has the capacity to store up to two years of information. Having crime records from past years is helpful in spotting trends. A certain park may be quiet most of the year, but it may be the scene of many disturbances during May, June, and December when students begin summer and winter vacations. If officers can access crime history, they may be able to pinpoint certain times when they should increase patrols of the park in order to prevent or discourage disturbances.

ICAM has realized the goals of CAPS: to create a partnership between the police, community members and city service providers to solve crime and disorder problems. By giving the officers a way to analyze up-to-the-minute crime information and generate maps and "Top 10" lists in minutes, ICAM allows the officers to share this information with the community. Officers bring the maps and charts to the monthly beat meetings so the citizens can see where the problems were in their beats and assist the police in stopping illegal activities. Citizen reaction has been positive so far, and citizens go to their beat meetings asking for the crime maps so they can see what is happening in their communities. According to one officer, "ICAM is used for the people, for their knowledge; to give them crime statistics, locations, whether it follows a pattern, to make people aware of what to look out for so they can report back to their beat officer."

The CPD is already working on a more advanced version of ICAM, called Command ICAM, which will be used mainly by the Commander staff. It will support a new management philosophy in police work, called ComStat, which holds the district commander responsible for the crime rate in his or her district. The Command version will be able to analyze more data and be used as a management tool. Command ICAM is less detail-oriented and more summary-based, more of a big picture. Command ICAM will track trends citywide, such as the number of robberies outside currency exchanges, rather than focus on the daily information that is so important to the beat officers. It will support police planning at the citywide level.

For the past six years, crime in Chicago has declined. In 1993, the year CAPS was piloted, there were approximately 287,000 index crimes, which include murder, sexual assault, robbery, battery and arson. By 1996, the last year for which complete statistics are available, there were 263,000 index crimes, a 9 percent decrease. The citizens are also very pleased with the Police Department, giving it an 85 percent approval rating, according to the 1997 Chicago Community Policing Evaluation Consortium. The ICAM system has proven a great asset to CAPS. Since its inception, ICAM has sped up the process for officers to look at and map data. One officer said, "I think it's great. It provides information in two to three minutes that sixteen years ago I would spend two to three hours getting from case reports. Then I'd draw a map."

Examples of ICAM Use

In the fall of 1997 there were several incidents of indecent exposure that occurred in the Twenty-fourth District. On October 6, three girls were victimized while on their way home from school, and one of the parents called the police. One of the girls told police that the same man had followed her home several times in the previous week, and her description of the man matched those given by other victims. Tactical and gang units permeated the area, and surveillance was set up. Two officers from the Twenty-fourth District used ICAM to search for possible offenders and similar crimes armed only with the offender description supplied by the victim. ICAM allowed the search to be conducted for neighboring districts and produced names of possible known sex offenders. Names led to pictures, and a possible match was made. It was determined that a known sex offender matching the victims' description lived just a few doors from the elementary school the victims attended.

On October 7, while on a surveillance mission, two tactical officers observed a vehicle, which matched the suspect offender's vehicle, commit a traffic violation. A stop was put on the vehicle and a subsequent driver's license check revealed the driver to be the suspect. The subject was taken into Area 3 for a lineup. Although the subject was not positively identified by the victims, there have been no more occurrences since that time.

ICAM was instrumental in stopping these crimes. Crimes with similarities were reviewed, and their parameters (in this case "indecent exposure near schools by a white male driving a blue Chevy") were plugged into ICAM. Armed with this information, police were able to be on the lookout and catch the suspect. When certain things about a crime are known, that information can be plugged into ICAM and matched with similar crimes. Officers can work with that data to narrow down the search for the offender or take steps to prevent more crimes from occurring.

The Watch Commanders believe that the ICAM enhances their crime-fighting skills. Lieutenant John Glynn, Watch Commander of the Fourth District, wrote a letter to the ICAM development team, expressing his thanks: "The project has given us the crime and arrest information we need in a readable and usable format. The mouse driven graphical interface is extremely easy to learn. . . . We had to spend no more than two hours of training with any officer before they displayed a mastery of the program. . . . [ICAM is] an extremely useful tool for both crime analysis and CAPS functions."

Effectiveness of ICAM

According to Sergeant Jonathon Lewin, one of the ICAM developers, ICAM has been quite successful. More than 7,000 officers, or roughly two-thirds of the force, have already been trained on the system, with the rest to follow. The officers are enthusiastic about ICAM and enjoy the training. The system processes more than 4,000 requests per day from all districts in the city.

Originally, ICAM was only installed in the districts and then extended to gang and tactical units. However, with its growing popularity and effectiveness, the Youth and Public Transportation units also wanted access. The Public Transportation unit was sending a car to every district in the city on a daily basis to get the most recent crime maps. Having access to the ICAM system makes that information available at the click of a mouse and allows the Public Transportation unit to identify trouble spots on the city's transportation lines.

It is difficult to judge the effectiveness of ICAM, given the many economic and social trends related to crime. The law-enforcement agencies in cities across America, and groups such as the National Institute for Justice, are trying to determine how to quantify the effectiveness of ICAM and crime mapping in general. In this instance, effectiveness can be seen as the ability to assist police in crime fighting and prevention to such a degree that the incidences of crime decrease. Ways to measure effectiveness include whether the system is being used, if the users cite its helpfulness, and demand for access. ICAM 2 also makes people feel safer. When a problem is exaggerated, such as the number of sexual assaults in a district, residents are fearful. When the crimes are mapped or graphed and the information is distributed, people realize that instead of the ten assaults they had heard about, really only two occurred.

Though other municipalities such as Dallas, Baltimore County and Los Angeles have crime-mapping systems, they are centralized and nonautomated. For the most part, they are available only to the data analysts in the department and not the officers. Chicago has the only "walk-up-and-use" system that is accessible to the beat officers and commanders at every district in the city.

Municipalities from all over the country have been inundating the CPD with requests for information on the ICAM system. Though the Chicago model has been successful and is widely hailed, there are still some factors that must be considered by other law-enforcement agencies that wish to pursue this type of crime-mapping system. This includes (1) cost, (2) an agency's capacity to maintain and update the system, and (3) administrative support.

Costs

The computer hardware and software needed to build the system can be a significant investment. For the first version of ICAM the CPD received a $1 million grant from the Illinois Motor Vehicle Theft Prevention Council. When the updated version of ICAM was introduced, it was funded through a COPS grant of $1.5 million, $1 million of which was used toward ICAM hardware. The actual development of the system was done in-house by several data systems analysts. These same people performed the necessary overhaul when the new ICAM was developed.

Not all police departments have the information technology resources that the CPD has in-house. If a department had to pay a vendor to develop a system tailor-made for that department, the consulting costs could easily reach $1 million and may even surpass that. If a department is considering developing a crime-mapping system, it would behoove the managers to research the grant opportunities available rather than attempt to pay for a new system from operating or capital funds.

Buying a ready-made mapping system may be less costly than developing one, but it may not be the best choice in the long run. Departments may find that off-the-shelf mapping systems are not suitable for their purposes, and often, the system needs to be significantly modified to be useful to a department. Also, mapping software can be complicated and not easily learned. System complexity and training time must be considered, as they can add costs and impact eventual success and usability. The more thoroughly the officers are trained, the more effectively they can use ICAM.

Database Maintenance

The data must be updated on a daily basis. Some mapping systems may be able to use data that already exists in a department's computer files, but other systems may not be able to plug into existing data fields. If this is the case, the data entry can be costly and time-consuming, especially if the department wants to enter crime data from before its records were computerized.

The CPD enters crime data on a daily basis at 6:00 A.M., using all the offense reports compiled in the last 24 hours. This was being done even before ICAM, so the CPD did not incur a significant additional cost for this. It is currently done at the district level, but it may be centralized in the future to ensure consistency of reports.

There is an up-front monetary cost as well as time commitment in terms of geocoding the street map of a city. Ideally, the base map that will be the foundation of all this data should be proofed. This entails checking every street to make sure that names are spelled correctly and that the correct modifier (e.g., Avenue, Boulevard, Place, Street) is attached to each address. Though this is time-consuming, it only needs to be done once, as long as it is updated to reflect any name changes of streets and any cul-de-sacs or dead ends that may be created as a result of new construction. Street files are available from the U.S. Bureau of the Census or vendors, but even this information should be checked for accuracy.

Administration Support

If a system such as ICAM is to be built, it must have support from the top down. The mayor or municipal leader needs to believe in the product in order to ensure that it is given top priority. With the support of the superintendent of police, the district commanders and other high-ranking officers will take the time to learn the program and make sure that the officers who go out onto the street are using the maps as well as bringing them to beat meetings so the citizens can use them.

If a system like ICAM is to succeed, it should be institutionalized so that it becomes a daily part of police life, just like roll call.

City Service Delivery

Another act that is becoming part of the police officer's daily routine is the city service request form. This form is also a part of the CAPS program and once again attempts to make policing more holistic, with the belief that officers are there to preserve order as well as apprehend criminals. Following along the lines of the "one broken window" theory, the city of Chicago is using routine city services to combat crime. Though other cities across the nation have developed community policing strategies, only Chicago attempts to fully integrate city services into community policing. Using this tactic, situations that are potentially dangerous, such as streetlight outages, are identified and given the attention that the officer feels they merit. Though this prevention philosophy is not new, it was largely forgotten as the police function became more formalized, and the police used more of their time to actually arrest people and solve crimes.

Crime is often the end result of a cycle. If a neighborhood begins to physically deteriorate, criminals may see it as easy prey. When more crimes are committed, people stop investing their money and time in the community, thinking it is a waste because of the high crime rate. Because of disinvestment, the physical condition worsens, which attracts more criminals, which increases the crime rate, and so on. When police concentrate more on solving crimes rather than preventing them, they may have become more effective at crime solving, but the link between order maintenance and crime prevention is forgotten.

With the city service request process, officers can point out problems that they feel contribute to an atmosphere conducive to crime. The city service request allows the officers the opportunity to work with other departments in order to eliminate small problems before they fester. Citizens can also let the police know what is broken or missing, and when they see that the police have processed their request, their faith in the police is strengthened. People may have been disappointed in the past by what they perceived as police ineffectiveness. When residents see that a neighborhood problem such as abandoned cars or graffiti has been taken care of due to police action, they think of the police as their partners in keeping the community problem-free.

Response

There is a process apart from the city service request form for situations where serious danger is posed to the public and requires immediate responses, such as street cave-ins and broken traffic signals. In these situations, officers notify dispatchers, who send the appropriate city department to handle the matter. The officer would still inform their supervisor of the matter, but they would not have to fill out a city service request form.

For situations that are serious but not dangerous, yet require a city agency to respond immediately, officers present a city service request form to their supervisors immediately. The supervisor decides whether an immediate response is merited and, if so, contacts the supervisor's desk at the Mayor's Office of Inquiry and Information (MOII). MOII records the reference number of the request and forwards it to the Neighborhood Relations section of the Police Department. MOII enters the request into its database and electronically transmits a work order to the proper city department. If Neighborhood Relations receives a regular request for service but decides that it needs immediate response, it can upgrade the request to "immediate response." Streetlight outages, missing stop signs and one-way signs are examples of situations that would be managed in this way.

The city service request form is the exclusive tool of the Police Department. The premise of the city service request is police being able to determine what is a dangerous situation so that their requests receive top priority. If citizens cooperate with the police, their concerns will receive attention. Officers can solicit suggestions from residents, but only police employees are to use the form to focus rapid-response resources on public safety concerns.

The service request status reports are kept in the beat plan binders at each district. Beat officers and supervisors review reports so that they can classify areas that have the same problem occurring repeatedly, such as stolen refuse containers, and formulate a strategy to combat it or find out why it keeps happening. The CPD does not fully have the capability to map all the city service requests now, because it does not have access to the appropriate database, but it will be doing this in the near future. The officers can also let the residents know the status of their city service requests. To tie up any loose ends, the district commanders meet quarterly with city departments to discuss any unresolved issues and possible new procedures.

The city service request program has been quite popular with residents. Citizens are building relationships with their beat officers, realizing that they cannot only stop crime, but accelerate the delivery of city services. Approximately 88 percent of all CAPS city service requests have been completed, more than 103,000, since 1993. This high completion rate proves to the citizens that they can trust their beat officers to work with them and help them with problems. If residents realize that they can work with police on an issue such as graffiti, they may have enough confidence to work with the police on more serious issues, such as identifying drug sellers.

According to the Chicago Community Policing Evaluation Consortium, it is the quality-of-life issues that worry people the most. These issues, including things like abandoned buildings, prostitution and graffiti, were addressed at 67 percent of the beat meetings. The most commonly requested services are the towing of abandoned cars, demolition of abandoned buildings and replacement of traffic signs.

Conclusion and Lessons Learned

If a municipality is interested in embracing community policing, city service delivery can easily be combined with such an effort. An initiative such as this must have the support of all members of a city's administration because there are so many departments involved. The community policing city service requests must be given priority or there is no point to doing them, and the officers' efforts at helping citizens clear up problems will not seem legitimate. Also, the officers must be able to check the status of a request at any time. They are acting as ambassadors to the community, and they must not be put in the position of giving incorrect or false information. If there is commitment from all departments to ensure that police requests receive resources and status reports are easily accessible, the program should be successful anywhere.

When things are let go, such as broken streetlights and missing sewer covers and street signs, an aura of neglect and lawlessness pervades the air. It is the mission of CAPS, through the city services request, to break the cycle of physical decay leading to crime. If a neighborhood appears well tended, criminals will be scared off, knowing that the residents care about their area and will notice any criminal activity, no matter how small. If Chicago wants to maintain its identity not only as a world-class city, but also as a very safe, livable city, criminal activity must be stopped before it starts.

In the past, people were more likely to stay in their community, most likely because they did not have the financial means and also could not move too far from their workplace. Now that more people have more choice in where they live, due to increased income and improved transportation, a low or decreasing crime rate can be used as a marketing tool to entice suburbanites to move into the city. While the impetus for any concentrated crime-fighting effort must come from the administration, citizens must also do their part and realize that if community policing is to succeed, whether it uses mapping or city service delivery, it must have the cooperation and support of everyone.

CHAPTER THIRTEEN

Reforming New York City

A New Chapter in Reinventing Government

Rudolph W. Giuliani
Mayor of New York City

In the twenty-first century, the United States increasingly will depend on strong and dynamic cities to thrive in a global economy because America's cities have always been crucibles of the nation's cultural and intellectual life and are the generators of much of its wealth.

Our strategies for the next century are developing today in cities across the country as municipal governments remake themselves and pioneer management strategies that will become models for the rest of the nation. In an era of declining public resources, local elected officials are creating leaner, more efficient systems for delivering vital services.

When I came into office in 1994, the city of New York was struggling with twin burdens: a bloated bureaucracy and a massive budget gap. A legacy of unchecked government growth and spending threatened to stymie New York City's ability to take full advantage of its natural preeminence in the world economy. In only a short time, we have regained our position as the capital of the world. We did this by reordering the balance between government and the private economy and initiating a series of programs to improve the quality of life for all New Yorkers. The breadth and number of accomplishments achieved from this strategy have been dramatic.

At the outset of my administration, we began to implement the largest and widest-ranging privatization program of any city in the country. We have completed dozens of projects, spanning virtually all city services, from parks maintenance to homeless-shelter management. These projects are fundamentally changing the way we deliver basic city services to 7.5 million New Yorkers.

Our comprehensive effort to reinvent New York City government also includes the nation's most significant welfare reform program. As part of this initiative, we implemented the nation's largest and most successful workfare program. In exchange for welfare benefits, our 35,000 workfare participants help maintain streets, parks, and city buildings and gain work experience in more than 20 city agencies. To date, this program has generated more than $500 million in additional services for the city.

Finally, we downsized city government through a landmark severance and redeployment agreement with our municipal unions—eliminating more than 17,000 government jobs and reducing the city's payroll by 8 percent without layoffs. Recognizing this accomplishment, *Business Week* cited New York as the nation's leader in government downsizing.

But we went beyond just making government more efficient and cost-effective. We also created strategies to improve the city's quality of life and stimulate economic growth to attract investment and broaden our tax base. Again, the results of these strategies have been striking.

New York City is now the safest large city in America. Since I took office, serious felony crime has declined by 46 percent. This dramatic drop in crime has been achieved through a number of unique policing strategies. These include using daily crime statistics as a management tool to respond directly to specific problems and emerging crime trends on a block-by-block basis. Building on the "broken windows" theory of James Wilson and George Kelling, we used these crime statistics—which include quality-of-life offenses—to address problems virtually the moment they occur and thereby raised the standard of public behavior throughout the city.

The dramatic reduction in crime goes beyond mere statistics: our citizens and visitors to New York now enjoy a sense of security and confidence for the first time in a generation that New York's streets belong to them, not to the criminals.

By reducing or eliminating onerous taxes, we are stimulating economic growth. Corporate investment in New York is rising, tourism is booming, and since I took office, we have added more than 320,000 private-sector jobs to our local economy. As evidence of this success, *Fortune Magazine* named New York City the number one city in America for international business.

New York City's success is being realized because we have simultaneously implemented a mix of programs designed to give us the flexibility to achieve three simple and related goals:

1. Innovate to improve the way we deliver services.
2. Improve the quality of life in our city to retain and attract residents and businesses, and create more jobs to broaden our tax base.
3. Downsize government and cut debt so we can reduce taxes and invest in our future.

We began working toward these goals by asking each city agency to think "outside the box" and identify services that they were no longer equipped to perform well: where we could benefit from a public asset sale, where the private sector had better expertise for delivering a service, where we needed to reengineer services, or where in-house employees could become more productive through a competitive forum.

We now have a broad array of privatization programs that impact nearly every aspect of the city government. We have privatized custodial services for public schools, job placement services, security guards, vehicle fleet maintenance, data entry services, tax billing services, medical labs, road resurfacing, office supply delivery, and reproduction and mail room services and numerous other city services.

As part of our privatization program, we divested ourselves of businesses that more appropriately belong in the private sector. In addition to the sale of our two radio stations and a television station, we have sold a city-owned luxury hotel and several municipal parking garages. Now, these properties generate tax revenue and private-sector jobs.

We also looked to the experience and expertise of the private sector to help launch our reengineering program to improve the city's in-house service delivery. To streamline time-consuming and absurd bureaucratic processes, we coordinated numerous reengineering projects, including partnering city agencies with some of the nation's most prestigious corporations.

For example, the Xerox Corporation joined with the Department of Health to tackle the city's chronic problems in issuing birth and death certificates. The city was operating under an enormous certificate request backlog. With the help of Xerox, we developed a plan that reduced response time from fourteen weeks to one week, and through the use of new technology we will bring this response time down ultimately to twenty-four hours. Other corporations such as Bell Atlantic, United Parcel Service, and ITT Sheraton have also been instrumental in successfully working with us in reengineering other agency services. This program has allowed us to vastly improve the delivery of core services without incurring additional costs.

In a short time, we have learned some valuable lessons from the combination of our privatization, reengineering, workfare and quality-of-life initiatives. We have found that using a mix of programs produces the flexibility needed to increase productivity, reduce costs, manage risk and set new performance standards for both the private and public sectors.

For example, one of the areas we targeted for privatization was custodial services for our 1,100 public schools. Custodial services in our schools were notoriously poor, and the Board of Education was running its operation with more than 50,000 backlogged repair orders.

We took a two-pronged approach to this problem. First, we rejected the Board of Education's preliminary contract with school custodians, which would have forced the city to increase spending on a system riddled with inefficiency and waste. We went back to the negotiating table and forged an agreement that did away with outlandish perks and privileges, tied productivity to pay for the first time ever and placed school custodians under the control of school principals.

Working with a blue-ribbon private-sector committee from the real estate industry, we then developed a privatization program in 52 public schools. We solicited proposals from the private sector to maintain clusters of school buildings, where, acting as property managers, contractors would maintain and repair the school facilities. In addition, no one company could bid on all the schools, to avoid the complacency that comes from private-contract monopolies.

The winning vendors produced an initial $700,000 in annual savings as well as a guaranteed 70 percent increase in productivity. Thus with this approach, we raised performance standards and substantially reduced costs. At the same time, we are creating a model that promises to provide the type of improvement and cost-effective service we desperately need in our schools. Again, the statistics are impressive, but having cleaner, safer, and better schools for our kids is the real payoff to these reforms.

In other cases, we have found that our in-house forces can be competitive with the private sector if given the opportunity to compete. For example, when we proposed privatizing a portion of the Department of Transportation's traffic-sign program, we wound up instead with a landmark agreement to keep all sign work in-house. Unionized city workers came back to us with a proposal to complete the additional sign work offered by the private contractor for no additional cost by increasing their own productivity by more than 50 percent and saving taxpayers $1 million annually.

At the same time, we began implementing our comprehensive workfare program. Of the 35,000 participants in this program, more than 5,000 are being assigned to the Parks Department alone. This program augmented park crews and enabled Parks Department employees to increase productivity by working with workfare participants.

In turn, this coordination between unionized employees and the city's workfare program, combined with streamlined management of capital work, is laying the groundwork for Parks Department employees to compete successfully with the private sector in the future. And the program is already proving effective: thus far, this initiative has produced a 48 percent increase in the city's overall park cleanliness ratings. It has also resulted in many of the workfare participants moving from a culture of dependency to gainful employment. Once again, the key to better services was a flexible approach.

Improving service delivery and downsizing, however, constitute only one side of the equation—the other is to improve the quality of life so we can stimulate economic growth. For too long the quality of life in New York City had been permitted to deteriorate, driving people and businesses out of the city. To reverse this unhealthy trend, we focused on improving public safety, reducing taxes and developing policies and programs aimed at encouraging economic development.

We initiated numerous new police strategies targeting specific types of crime including drugs, youth crime, illegal guns, quality-of-life crimes, family violence, car theft and police corruption. And we merged our transit, housing and regular police forces to reduce administrative duplication, free more officers for law-enforcement duties, and coordinate our citywide anticrime efforts. Most recently, the New York City Police Department assumed control of school safety to ensure that our schools continue to provide a safe environment for learning.

While implementing these police strategies, we innovated new management methods to ensure results. For instance, instead of passively tabulating crime statistics on a quarterly basis, the New York City Police Department began to compile the data so it could be used more effectively to deter crime. Now, crime data from each of the city's 76 precincts is monitored daily and used to redeploy officers throughout the city to target crime trends as they occur, neighborhood by neighborhood. This strategy has allowed us to actually manage crime down, and it marks a revolutionary approach to reinventing the way government delivers police services. Finally, we have delegated most day-to-day decision making from police headquarters to the individual precinct commanders so that accountability for routine policing is where it should be—in the community.

This comprehensive effort has produced an unprecedented drop in crime: serious felony crime is down by 46 percent. In fact, our declining crime rate and our commitment to deterring quality-of-life offenses make New York City the safest big city in America. Improving the quality of life in our city also led us to look at our services through the eyes of our taxpayers. This led to an effort to make New York City more business-friendly by eliminating or reducing taxes and regulations that have been particularly onerous to businesses.

Now, companies are once again investing in New York City's future. Viacom, Bertelsmann, Disney, Conde Nast and others have made substantial new commitments to Times Square, heralding the rebirth of our city's midtown business district. Large retailers are also investing here, like Virgin Records and Warner Brothers.

Reducing our hotel occupancy tax—once the highest in the nation—has fueled a tourism boom. Hotel occupancy is at record levels and tourist spending is expected to increase to $14.5 billion in 1999, the most profitable tourism year in the city's history. And we've seen real job growth in the private sector, generating more than 320,000 jobs since we took office.

Making change in a city like New York is by no means an easy task. New York City has a budget larger than that of many countries ($34 billion); serves roughly 8 million people; educates 1.1 million schoolchildren; maintains 5,600 miles of roads, 866 bridges and tunnels, 26,000 acres of parkland; and supports the world's largest financial, banking, publishing and fashion industries.

In this context, our pragmatic, flexible approach has produced substantial, quantifiable success. We have dramatically reduced the size and cost of government, stimulated job growth, found ways to run government more efficiently and cost-effectively and improved the quality of life for all New Yorkers.

The lesson we have learned is that there is no simple answer to the challenges we face, and herein lies New York City's unique approach. Privatization and workfare programs, downsizing, and reengineering all comprise a means toward our larger goal: to deliver quality services at a reasonable cost and to eliminate functions better performed by the private sector.

To prepare the nation's cities for stability and growth in the twenty-first century, we must continue to explore new ways of making government run efficiently and effectively. To achieve this we must use every tool at our disposal and develop fiscal and social policies that produce long-lasting, positive results. In time, we will refine and develop superior strategies based on the important lessons we are learning right now. In the end, it will be the people of New York City who see and feel the benefits of a smaller, smarter, and better government dedicated to real results and continuous improvement.

The City of San Diego's Multiple Species Conservation Program

Restructuring Government through a Community Partnership

Susan Golding
Mayor of San Diego, California

The challenge of good government is not to dictate, but to build coalitions to jointly solve the tough questions that have no easy answer. An example of this type of partnership was created in San Diego when I used the office of the mayor to bring to the negotiating table divergent parties who had historically disagreed on the long-standing issue of open-space preservation.

The Multiple Species Conservation Program (MSCP), the first of its kind in the nation, was the end result of this process. The MSCP is a road map for the preservation of thousands of acres in San Diego, acres that would not be saved today if it were not for this historic agreement and partnership.

San Diego's construction boom of the early 1980s came to a crashing halt in the late 1980s as part of an economic downturn felt by a broad sector of our community. However, due to the continuous and very visible development of the early 1980s, the construction industry was tainted with a "black hat" by a public that saw bulldozers at work and didn't understand that all the undeveloped land along our freeways was not public and therefore not preserved as open space. A "prevent Los Angelization now" mentality turned into a heated campaign that gained momentum and culminated in a loss at the polls for several future urbanizing area (FUA) proposed developments. These proposals for areas along the northern reaches of our city boundaries were identified in the growth management strategy established by then–Governor Wilson's administration and were intended to be held from development until the "urbanizing" areas were completed. A public vote in the early 1980s added the requirement of a public vote for these lands to be released for development. All it took was a distrustful electorate and a very small amount of environmental funding to kill a multimillion dollar campaign in support of these projects. Voters in San Diego were labeled as antigrowth and antidestruction of open space.

So here's where the problem began. Taking their cue from the public, the city's planning staff began to approach every project from the perspective of "protect the city from development." Development proposals of all sizes were routinely declined and turned down by the Planning Commission. These projects inevitably found their way to the City Council on appeal, which, as a result, became inappropriately inundated with even the simplest home-expansion issues. The development approval process with all its many layers had become daunting.

It became even worse if the project needed an environmental impact report (EIR) or if a sensitive species was on the site requiring a state and federal permit. San Diego, at that time, had both the blessing and the curse of being identified as one of ten "hot spots" in the nation identified by E. O. Wilson because of our biological species diversity. We still have more than 1,500 species in our 300-square-mile area. Regrettably, all the activity created developers who were beat up and frustrated with local government and it only minimally benefited the environment with patch-size pieces of land and habitat unconnected to other open space. Piecemeal planning, as it was called, was not beneficial to anyone.

This was the status and climate of our city's open-space protection processes when I became mayor in 1993. Another serious issue, completely unrelated, was quickly gaining momentum and would ultimately become the catalyst for my creation of the Multiple Species Conservation Program—an upgraded sewer system. When I took office, San Diego had for many years been in need of an upgraded sewer system. Several alternatives were in the design phase to provide this upgrade, but there were problems. The federal government, specifically the Environmental Protection Agency, had sued the city, claiming noncompliance with its requirement for a secondary treatment level of effluent. These projects, designed to respond to the federal government's secondary requirements, were enormous and would have required billions of dollars of public monies to build. The magnitude of the project also raised the question of mitigation requirements for "growth-inducing impacts." Due to the considerable size of mitigation the federal requirements would have required, it meant that an extremely large amount of resource mitigation would have to be provided. I floated the concept of mitigating all the requirements together to create one open-space preserve footprint, and the City of San Diego's Multiple Species Conservation Program (MSCP) was created.

Fortunately, the city of San Diego was ultimately successful in winning the lawsuit, and the federal requirements to carry out the MSCP evaporated. However, the spirit of cooperation I had created was not dispersed, and soon, this interesting coalition was put to the test again when another issue arose, adding a new level to the discussions and eventually to the creation of our adopted plan and new ciy policies. This issue was caused by the California gnatcatcher. This smallest of creatures resides in the coastal sage scrub found in southern California, specifically, on the very mesa tops that had been our prime locations for new development in San Diego. Since our existing regulations had been directing development away from the hillsides and valley bottoms to preserve the character of our region, a "train wreck" was about to happen. The needs of San Diego's growing population were headed for a full-blown crash with our desire and need to preserve our natural resources.

The gnatcatcher was listed as a threatened species, and this action brought the state and federal wildlife agencies to the MSCP table, through the direct involvement of Federal Interior Secretary Bruce Babbitt and California State Resources Secretary Doug Wheeler. Both secretaries were immediately interested in the MSCP because it was already under way and had the potential to be a setting for the proactive set-aside of enough habitat to not only protect the gnatcatcher, but also 84 other sensitive species.

The MSCP was built over the course of six years around a stakeholders table, the "working group," that was key to the partnership establishing trust. A process for consensus grew out of this trust, and no votes were ever taken at the working group. The private development and business sector would not have continued to be a part of the consensus had it not known that what it was headed to as an outcome would be guaranteed. Likewise, the environmentalists were looking for the same guarantees. What was before us was a huge project with ramifications that would be felt for generations if decisions were not made fairly and for the good of the entire region. Even with the entire working group at the table, it became very apparent that I needed to take something from each side and create an alternative to the options currently on the table upon which everyone could agree. The three alternatives under discussion were: (1) a biologically preferred alternative of approximately 197,000 acres, (2) a coastal sage scrub alternative of 33,000 acres, and (3) a public lands alternative (proposed by the developers) of 85,000 acres. I built the "mayor's alternative" around publicly owned lands with critical acres added, where necessary, to provide 75 percent coverage of the critical core areas and linkages and 75 percent coverage of the 93 targeted species. My plan was also within a monetary framework that could be accomplished without "stealing" or taking property. Private mitigation and public acquisition and dedication were the only tools to be used; condemnation was forbidden.

It was a huge task getting all these groups to work together, but I believed that by bringing all the right players to the table we could hammer out a process for future development that would be less burdensome and would result in the largest amount of contiguously preserved land in San Diego's history—a gift to our future generations.

In the end, the building industry supported my mayor's alternative after there were assurances that there would be no additional land required to protect the endangered species and that "a deal was a deal" as it pertained to permitting. These guarantees were all part of the ensuing negotiations among the partners and were ultimately codified and signed off on in March 1997.

Through the MSCP, we essentially restructured our government to minimize steps and hassles in the development process and to ensure a biologically sustainable, open-space preserve system by partnering with development interests. San Diego can now be assured a sustained quality of life by the preservation of our natural resources while still providing housing and amenities for our residents. It took a community partnership as well as a three-way public partnership (local, state and federal) along with the private sector and environmental community.

The results of this partnership are as follows: (1) our permit grants us "take authority," enabling us to make good on our promise of expedited permitting with no second "hits"; (2) the state and federal agencies are out of local permitting procedures, which expedites the process and provides a one-stop shop for the clients of the city; and (3) a consolidated set of regulations has been established.

Our public–private partnership also required a sharing of the assemblage of the preserve. Certain amounts of acres were assumed to be obtained through private project mitigation and certain other acreages were presumed to be acquired through public purchases. Through a sharing of assemblage responsibilities, a mutual desire to see MSCP's completion was created.

The challenge left to all the jurisdictions now is how to maintain the "paradigm shift" that took place during the negotiation days of the MSCP. This is imperative to the long-term success of the program, so as to not allow "business as usual" to retreat back into our attitudes.

This partnership has also provided the framework by which several development projects, previously denied by the voters, have won approval and begun to move forward. You need look no further than the future urbanizing area, mentioned earlier, for examples of this partnership's success.

- Sub Area 5, passed by the voters, included a transfer of density, enabling the preservation of a large section of important habitat while still maintaining the community-planned goals. The Del Mar Mesa area Bougainvillea, a residential resort, garnered public support after agreeing to an "environmentally sensitive land tax" on hotel room nights that will go toward the acquisition of adjacent open space and toward ensuring that the development area will continue to be noteworthy for habitat purposes.
- The largest, and probably the most significant, of the examples is the recent success on the November 1998 ballot of the area known as Sub Area 3 and the adjacent project in Carmel Valley known as Neighborhood 8a. The same MSCP partnership paved the way to a long negotiated agreement being on the ballot and winning voter approval, with the signatories of support coming from both the environmental community and the business community—something unheard of in the early 1990s! The project agreement provided more than 1,600 acres of protected open space while allowing the development of well-planned acres of housing and community amenities, such as schools, parks, commercial areas, trails, and civic places.

Through a joint partnership, San Diego has laid the all-important groundwork for a sustained quality of life—furthering the desirability of our city into the future. The city of San Diego has many unique and valuable natural resources both from a biological perspective and a people perspective. Finding a way to protect these natural resources, while also accommodating the economic vitality of our region, was paramount in the success of turning our region from one of no growth to one of smart growth.

I am proud of the groups who came to the table and were willing to put aside their own preconceived notions of each other, roll up their sleeves, and create a plan to help ensure that our region's children will enjoy this area's wildlife and open space for generations.

City Services in the Competitive Marketplace

Stephen Goldsmith
Mayor of Indianapolis, Indiana

Observing the Private Marketplace

Every day, the private sector introduces new products, improves old ones, expands services, and, in general, reduces costs. The desktop computer on which this chapter is being written, for example, was nonexistent 25 years ago and essentially unaffordable until very recently.

Government, on the other hand, becomes less responsive and more expensive over time. Spending by the federal government increased from $92 billion in 1960 to $1.5 trillion today. Yet almost no one would say that government services are better today than they were 40 years ago.

Why are private-sector companies more efficient, more customer-oriented, and more innovative than government? The answer is that these companies must compete in the marketplace, and they will go out of business if customers do not like the goods and services they offer. No matter how successful a company is today, if it loses touch with its customers' needs or charges too much, someone will steal its customers away tomorrow.

Government, which has a lock on the delivery of a wide range of services and the management of many assets, is not only a monopoly, but a particularly effective form of monopoly:

- Government cannot go out of business. Every citizen of the United States, like it or not, is a customer for government services—and a new customer is born every eight seconds. Poorer Americans in particular are customers for government services because they cannot afford to go elsewhere.
- Government controls revenue. If more money is needed to provide a service, government can and will raise taxes to pay for it. Whereas the private sector must persuade people to make purchases, government simply takes dollars. If a citizen decides not to buy what government is selling by refusing to pay taxes, that citizen will wind up in jail. General Motors would never close a plant if it could seize the assets of people who do not buy their cars.
- Government is allowed to spend more than it takes in. While many states and cities are required by law to enact balanced budgets, many government entities are not—including the federal government. And even governments that by law must balance their budgets nevertheless avoid doing so by borrowing, deferring capital spending, and employing bookkeeping devices. Private companies and families can only deficit spend in the short term before going out of business; government can go into debt indefinitely.
- Government delivers "essential services." Whenever reform-minded managers or elected officials exert pressure to reduce costs, status-quo managers can mount an effective defense by pointing to the essential nature of their task. A call for budget cuts in a municipal Department of Public Safety, for example, might be met with a cry that the streets will be less safe. Attempting to slow the growth of education spending might be met with a challenge such as, "Aren't our kids worth a few extra dollars a month?" This is a strategy that resonates powerfully with constituents, who have neither the time nor the inclination to scour budgets to see if savings are possible without cuts in service quality.

What limits government's incentive to be efficient is not public ownership per se, but the monopoly that government enjoys over the services it provides. The key issue is not public versus private—it is monopolistic versus competitive delivery. This is why in Indianapolis we prefer the term "marketization" to the more commonly used "privatization." As a rule, one can predict the responsiveness and efficiency of a company by the amount of competition its products face. The more rigorous the competition, the better the product. Utilities and large monopolies, for example, tend to be less efficient and customer-oriented. To the extent that we move services into the marketplace, or create markets for their delivery, we can increase efficiency, improve service quality, and reduce costs.

Moving Services into the Marketplace

One of the challenges in moving services into the marketplace is that governments at all levels diversified over time in order to support the services we think of as fundamental. For decades, governments vertically integrated themselves into performing services that would be best performed by the private sector. And it will probably take decades for governments to peel back the layers and return to providing only the services that are their proper province. Still, some services are more obvious candidates for competition than others, and identifying these "low-hanging fruit" can provide governments with lucrative and relatively straightforward competitive initiatives.

This can be a confusing and controversial task, because managers always insist that their jobs are fundamental to government operation. There are a few basic questions that managers can ask themselves to determine a given service's "ripeness" for competition, however. Based on what we in Indianapolis observed during our on-the-job training, figure 15.1 is a useful tool for thinking about services to be competitively bid.

Core vs. Ancillary

The horizontal axis of the graph below (figure 15.1) describes whether an activity is a "core service" that government must provide for citizens—a necessary, non-divisible public good—or whether it is an "ancillary service" performed, presumably, to support the provision of core services.

The core service behind any given activity can often be determined simply by repeatedly posing the question, "Why is this service necessary?" Each iteration

Figure 15.1   Thinking About Services to be Competitively Bid: Core vs. Ancillary.

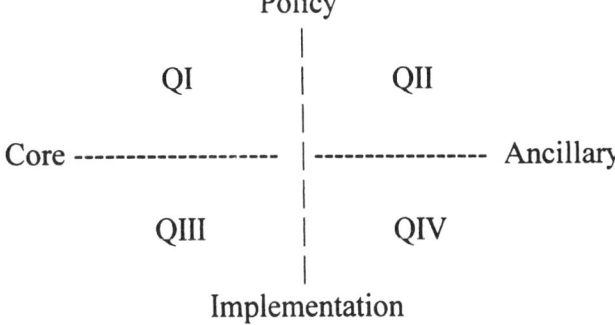

will move the answer closer to a core service. For example, Indianapolis operates a Central Equipment Maintenance Division that, among its other duties, changes the oil in police cars. Why does it do so? Because the city's Police Department needs a well-maintained fleet. Why? So that police officers can patrol, make emergency runs quickly, and pursue suspects if necessary. Why? So that the Police Department can protect the public. Why? At this point, the answer is: protecting the public is a core service.

Therefore, the position of a given activity along the horizontal axis of this graph is determined by how closely it relates to the performance of a core government service.

Policy vs. Implementation

This is similar to the distinction David Osborne described in *Reinventing Government* as the difference between "steering" and "rowing." Does the activity by its nature require the making of policy, or is it an activity that involves the implementation of policy that has already been established?

The distinction between policy and implementation is often difficult. Reasonable people could differ about whether a police officer recognizing a certain behavior as domestic violence and making an arrest is making a policy decision or implementing policy. However, some activities are easily identifiable as more policymaking than others: deciding to equip city buses with lifts for the handicapped is a policy decision; installing the lifts is implementation. The position of an activity along the vertical axis is determined by how much policymaking it requires. Plugging various services into figure 15.1 results in the figure 15.2.

Quadrant IV: Ancillary, Implementation

Any service that falls into Quadrant IV is a candidate for immediately moving to the marketplace, with the presumption that the private sector can probably provide it better and cheaper. In Indianapolis, one of our first successful marketizations was the city's microfilm division, which employed 22 workers and had an annual budget of $700,000. We discovered that it cost the city of Indianapolis 10.5 cents per page to microfilm a document. The lowest private-sector bid offered a price of 3.3 cents per page, and produced higher-quality copies. The decision to privatize was easy, and over the first four years of the contract the city saved more than $1.3 million as a result.

It is important to note again that even though it is probable that the private sector can provide any Quadrant IV service better and at lower cost than govern-

Figure 15.2   Thinking About Services to be Competitively Bid: Policy vs. Implementation.

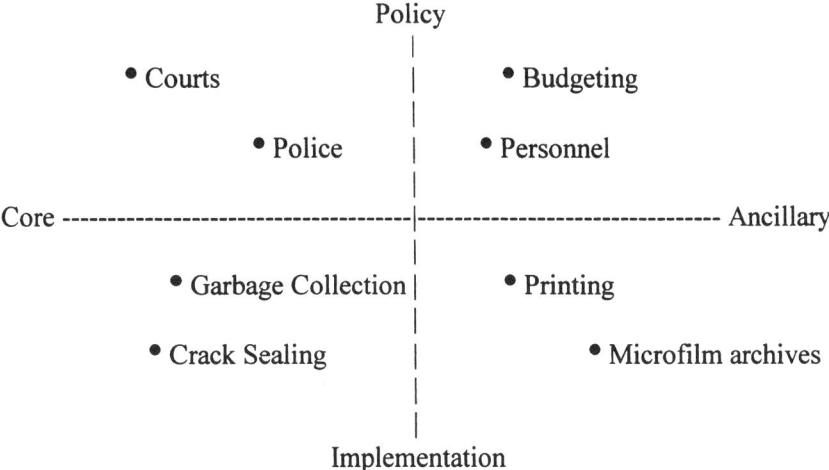

ment, it is the process of competition, and not merely provision by the private sector, that produces cost savings.

Indianapolis provides an example that illustrates this point as well. Each month, the Department of Public Works sent out bills to its customers for sewer service; this service cost the city $3 million each year. Since this activity almost exactly parallels the billing procedure of our local water utility, we approached the utility about taking over the city's sewer-user billing. The water utility made a proposal that would have saved us 5 percent annually on our sewer billing. Not satisfied, we approached other utilities in the area and asked them to bid with the water utility to provide our sewer billing. When forced to compete for the service, the water utility creatively found a way to lower its bid by 70 percent. Last year alone, the city saved more than $3.5 million on the cost of billing its sewer users.

There are enough government services in Quadrant IV that any level of government could generate substantial savings simply by moving all these services into the marketplace.

Quadrant III: Core, Implementation

Activities in Quadrant III are also good candidates for moving to the marketplace. But because these activities are closer to core services of government, government may actually be able to provide them cheaper than the private sector. Therefore, Quadrant III services provide the best opportunities for public employees to win contracts. It is also probable that if Quadrant III activities are competitively bid, private-sector companies will develop competencies in these activities and either capture contracts or stimulate improved service by public-sector providers.

Garbage collection is a Quadrant III activity because it is one of the core services of most municipal governments, but the actual picking up of trash does not involve policy decisions. In Indianapolis, the Department of Public Works (DPW) used to collect garbage through a patchwork system that divided the city into 25 districts, which were serviced by DPW's in-house crews and four private haulers. DPW had franchise agreements with the various trash collectors that gave each a monopoly in its service area. Not surprisingly, haulers' prices increased every year.

When the time came to renew hauler contracts in 1993, we opted instead to reconfigure the service districts and compete them out. After reducing the number of districts from 25 to 11, we guaranteed DPW at least one district to ensure that the city retained the capacity to collect trash in case problems arose. We also limited private collectors to a maximum of three districts to prevent monopolistic situations and predatory pricing.

Empowered and cost-conscious DPW employees found ways to provide more service for less money and won the maximum three districts in the process. Competing out garbage collection resulted in more than $15 million in savings over the following three years, and more than $9.5 million in additional savings was projected for 1997 alone.

Quadrant II: Ancillary, Policy

Our experience is that most of the activities in Quadrant II are carried out by the Department of Administration. Decisions about personnel policies and budgeting are several steps removed from the provision of core government services but involve reasonably important policy choices.

Quadrant I: Core, Policy

Quadrant I includes services and activities that could be considered both "core" and "policy"—such as zoning, police and fire protection, and the courts. These activities will probably be the last that an entrepreneurial government examines in its efforts to move services into the marketplace.

Activity-Based Costing

Regardless of the service being considered for competition, governments must possess a thorough understanding of the costs associated with its existing operations in order to move services into the marketplace. But whereas private companies must keep a close eye on costs at all times, government tends to monitor only expenditures. Although this may seem a subtle distinction, it is a critical one. A car manufacturer, for example, would not stay in business long if managers knew only how much they spent making cars, without knowing how much it cost to manufacture a single car. Yet for government at all levels, this tends to be standard procedure.

Every year Indianapolis produces one of the best-looking, four-color financial reports of any city in the country. But when I took office in January 1992, no one in city government could tell me how much it cost to fill a pothole, pave a street, plant a tree or pick up trash. If we were simply interested in privatization, this might not have been such a significant problem. However, our interest is in marketization, and any reasonable evaluation of competitive bids requires that we know how much a given activity costs us to perform in-house.

In the spring of 1992, we hired KPMG Peat Marwick to lead a process called activity-based costing (ABC). For every identifiable activity of government, ABC would determine the cost of everything that went into producing that activity. The process used private-sector definitions of depreciation and loaded in all the costs of idle equipment, building space, and other fixed costs.

Our Department of Transportation's snow-plowing operation was one of the first services we subjected to the activity-based costing process. The results provided a good example of how the simple act of measuring costs can by itself improve the quality of service. We divided the snow-plowing groups into regions and then analyzed the costs of each activity associated with plowing snow. First, the consultants examined all of the equipment used, then all of the materials, then all of the labor for every mile of snow plowed. Managers discovered that the cost of plowing snow varied wildly from region to region. The labor cost of plowing a mile of snow was $39.90 per mile in the central region, but only $13.20 in the southeast region. The cost of materials varied from $48.97 in the southwest region to $9.25 in the northeast region. Total cost for plowing one mile of snow ranged from $117.59 in the southwest region to $39.96 in the southeast.

Now, it may be that differences in topography, road layout, or miscellaneous other factors contributed to some of the difference in cost between regions, but it was clear to us that they could not account for such a huge discrepancy. By examining the numbers and applying the best management practice in each region to all the regions, we were able to improve the mix of equipment, resources, and training in each location.

As this example shows, there are benefits to the costing process wholly independent of competition. Because every dime of government spending is allocated to some outcome, managers scramble to reduce waste and overhead.

Although we did not compete out Indianapolis's snow-plowing operations, we did compete out more than 70 other city services, none of which would have been possible without activity-based costing. Using private-sector rules for our accounting allowed city workers and managers to prepare legitimate internal bids and provided us with a meaningful standard against which to compare private proposals.

Maximizing Value

Simply saving money is not enough. Government must respond to customer preferences and maximize value from every tax dollar it spends. Toward this end, measuring and rewarding performance become indispensable, requiring officials to pay close attention to what government actually produces and not simply the amount of money it spends on a given service. This task is complicated by the previously mentioned vertical integration of government, which makes it difficult for managers to distinguish between outcomes and outputs.

For example, everyone expects the Police Department to make the city safer—an outcome. Yet somehow this led the Indianapolis Police Department to operate a full-service print shop that prints the department's own tickets and arrest warrants—an output. Everyone expects the Public Works Department to dispose of sewage in a way that enhances water quality—an outcome. Yet somehow this led Indianapolis to spend tens of thousands of dollars assembling a television studio just to make training tapes—an output.

Distinguishing outcomes from outputs can be extremely difficult. Early in my administration, at a meeting of the city's department directors I expressed my frustration at our progress in being able to measure our performance. I told the director of the Department of Transportation that I wanted to know exactly how many potholes his crews filled in a week. "I thought you wanted to measure performance," he replied. "You shouldn't care how many potholes my department fills. You should care how smooth the roads are. How do you know we're not doing such a poor job filling potholes that we have to go back out and redo them later?" He was right—smooth roads are the outcome; filling potholes is the output.

Because government simply confiscates dollars rather than competing for them, government managers do not get good information about their customers' needs and wants. Therefore, government must invent processes to determine preferences, including neighborhood forums, focus groups, and public-opinion surveys. In contrast, in the private marketplace it is a relatively straightforward task to determine what outcomes people desire: follow their dollars. Do they spend their earnings on vacations? A mortgage? Their children? Marketplace activity demonstrates what outcomes people value and how much they are willing to pay to produce them.

In Indianapolis, our goal is to produce added value for our citizens. It is therefore our responsibility to shift resources toward activities that produce desired outcomes for citizens. Whenever we produce more of a desired outcome without increasing cost, or produce the same outcome at a lower cost, we add value for our customers. If we cannot produce a dollar's worth of outcome for every dollar's worth of government spending, then we must not spend the dollar. For our managers, this equation is the bottom line.

An example from my days as a prosecuting attorney illustrates the point of the value equation. Having determined that making an arrest for domestic violence made the recurrence of violent activity less likely, we set up an enhanced prosecution effort and devoted substantial resources to it. Eventually, a researcher asked what should have been an obvious question: Does the additional sanction of prosecution over and above the initial arrest further reduce the recurrence of violence?

As we soon discovered, the answer in most cases was *no*. We were devoting substantial resources to do something very effectively that did not produce the outcome most desired by citizens—a reduction in domestic violence. Clearly that does not mean we should not fully prosecute and seek convictions for those who commit domestic violence. But if our desired outcome is to decrease domestic violence, and if we have limited financial resources, then we should know how to focus our resources to achieve the desired outcome most frequently.

Only by identifying a clear and specific set of outcomes can managers truly begin to maximize value. Of course, measuring and pricing these outcomes are useful only insofar as managers are willing to act on that knowledge to improve service delivery. Government bureaucracies are notoriously rigid, and it takes powerful incentives to motivate government employees to break with traditional practices and implement creative solutions.

Competition Is Key

It is competition that causes managers to take the activity-based costing process seriously and use the new information at their disposal to make prudent choices about service delivery.

When we announced that we were going to open up a part of our Department of Transportation's (DOT's) crack-sealing operation for competitive bid, the drivers' union made the legitimate point that if we wanted it to compete for the bid, we had to free it from all the unnecessary overhead that was loaded into its budget. It turned out that in this particular division, there were 32 managers supervising 94 workers. This was not a good ratio by anybody's standards, so we complied with the union's request and eliminated 14 of the 32 managers. Armed with greater decision-making authority, front-line workers found creative ways to improve efficiency dramatically. For example, union workers determined that they did not really require eight men working with two trucks to seal cracks. By removing a certain piece of equipment from the second truck and adding it to the first, DOT could seal cracks with one truck and five workers. The union bid for the job and won. When asked about the competitive process afterwards, one of the DOT workers said, "It was like going from darkness into daylight."

The DOT example taught us that if we are serious about allowing public employees to compete for contracts, it is our duty to free them from as much unnecessary bureaucracy and cost as possible. To encourage city workers to seek out unnecessary costs, I established a Golden Garbage Award to be given on a regular basis to city employees who find egregious examples of government waste.

The December 1992 winner of the Golden Garbage Award was a manager at the city's Advanced Wastewater Treatment (AWT) plant. Several years ago, the Department of Public Works set up a full-service television studio to make training tapes for new AWT employees. At the press conference announcing that we would get rid of this equipment, the manager was asked why he had identified the studio as government waste. The manager answered: "We aren't in the business of video production. We're in the business of training employees. Eventually, we will be asked to compete against private-sector providers of training services, and all of this equipment—and the cost of this wasted square footage—will be loaded into my overhead. If I'm going to compete, I need to get rid of all this." He answered exactly the way an efficient government manager should.

Conclusion

In addition to getting more value for tax dollars, properly structured marketization can also provide business opportunities for citizens, especially minority and women business owners and enterprising residents of poorer urban neighborhoods. For example, contracts with private companies can require vendors to use their best efforts to do business with minority- and women-owned enterprises. In Indianapolis, many vendors exceed the targeted participation levels specified in their contracts and surpass the city's previous commitment to these businesses— not as set-asides, but through market-driven, value-added decision making.

Likewise, competing out city services can offer real business opportunities for residents of poor neighborhoods. In the current system, we tax people in poor neighborhoods, accumulate their limited wealth, and then use that wealth to hire a worker from outside their neighborhood—a Parks Department worker from a middle-class neighborhood, for example—to come in and provide a service that the neighborhood may not want in the first place. By competing out the delivery of services, municipal governments can provide opportunities for neighborhood-level business development, as neighborhood groups can bid to perform their own services and use the revenue stream to leverage other possible business opportunities.

Perhaps most important, to the extent that marketization reduces the size and cost of government, it leaves more money for families to spend themselves. Moving services into the marketplace can be the fairest, most populist way to approach city services.

CHAPTER SIXTEEN

Managed Competition in Charlotte

Patrick McCrory
Mayor of Charlotte, North Carolina

Municipalities are corporations. While there are significant differences between public and private-sector corporations that preclude absolute comparisons, they face, even if not for the same reasons, similar challenges in the areas of balancing expenditures and revenues, providing excellence in customer service and "doing more with less."

For more than a decade, the city of Charlotte, North Carolina, has been fortunate to enjoy a strong local economy and a healthy amount of growth. The population has nearly doubled (now 513,000) in the last 20 years. At the same time, there were, and still are, increasing demands on municipal services, particularly in the areas of public safety and transportation, and a firm "no-tax-increase" City Council policy. The city faced significant challenges to reduce expenditures, devote substantial financial resources to hire more police officers and invest in major road construction and neighborhood improvement projects.

In response to these challenges, the city embarked on a major restructuring initiative that included changes in everything from employee pay, benefits and safety programs to process reengineering, selling city-owned property and introducing managed competition. As a result the city has reduced the number of non-public safety employees by nearly 600 and added more than 550 police officers since 1992. In November 1996, Charlotte voters overwhelmingly approved a bond package of $98.6 million to fund roadway, sidewalk and neighborhood improvement projects, and in January 1997, the Charlotte City Council unanimously approved an ambitious five-year transportation plan that includes goals for mass transit, bikeway and roadway projects. All of this and more has been accomplished without a property tax rate increase in more than ten years.

The total impact of all the changes made in recent years calculates to more than $20 million in savings and cost avoidance. While it is the combination of initiatives the city has undertaken that contributes to this bottom line, few changes have had more of an impact than injecting managed competition (public–private competition) into public services.

This chapter focuses, then, on how the city of Charlotte is using managed competition as part of an overall strategy to create a more efficient, effective and smaller government. Specifically, this article will review the components of Charlotte's managed-competition program, including the guidelines and methods used to reduce costs, make municipal services competitive with the private sector, monitor contracts with both private and public-sector contractors and, ultimately, offer citizens the best services at the lowest possible costs.

Background

The term *privatization* means many things to many people, and this is where some confusion may arise in comparing the activities of cities nationally. At one end of the political spectrum, privatization is touted as the "cure" for bloated government bureaucracy. The private sector can provide service better than the public sector, this perspective argues, so the public sector should get out of the business of providing some services with its own employees and, in essence, become contract monitors for the private-sector firms hired to do this work. This perspective, at least in Charlotte, has been met with considerable resistance, particularly from public-sector employees who maintain intense pride in their work and fear politicians will simply "take" their jobs and "give" them to the private sector. At the other end of the political spectrum are those who believe privatization has no place in public service. Private companies, they reason, have profit, not the public's interests, at heart and would therefore gouge the unsuspecting taxpayer, leading to inflated costs for services and, perhaps, lesser quality.

Charlotte has taken a middle-ground approach to privatization, preferring to use managed competition as the method for determining service providers. Managed competition includes the entire spectrum of service delivery options:

- "Pure" privatization—the city gets out of the business of and commits no funding to providing a service (e.g., leaf collection).
- Public and private competition and contracting—the city competes with the

private sector for the right to provide a service (garbage collection, vehicle maintenance).

* Outsourcing—the city decides to provide a service using contracts with private-sector firms and invites potential bidders to respond to a request for proposal (RFP). This may be a service the city currently provides with city crews or a new service authorized by City Council.

The basic premise underlying the managed-competition approach is that the "who does what better and cheaper, the private or public sector" argument is recast as competition versus monopoly. No monopoly, public or private, delivers the totality of advantages (financial, service-related, quality, etc.) that comes when competition is the means used for determining service providers. Charlotte has also included asset management as a component of its overall privatization strategy.

Services contracting is not new to Charlotte. Like most other cities and counties across the United Sates, Charlotte has for some time contracted with the private sector to provide many services. As early as 1978, the city began outsourcing such services as street resurfacing and business garbage collection, then multifamily garbage collection (1980), custodial services (1984), golf course management (1985) and ground maintenance (1986). Many of these services have just recently appeared on the privatization "radar screens" of other municipalities. In fiscal year 1995, Charlotte awarded a total of $204 million in service and construction contracts to the private sector, up from $151 million awarded in the previous year.

What is new in the city of Charlotte is how the entire process of services contracting and competition is defined and approached. Managed competition is the way we do business: it is systematic and institutionalized. Benefits are derived when traditional public services—that is, those delivered by enterprises owned and wholly operated by municipal workers—are subjected to head-to-head competition with the private sector. Aside from the significant financial advantages, other benefits are realized, such as increased efficiencies and renewed pride in public service when municipal employees demonstrate performance levels meeting or exceeding those of the private sector.

Competitive bidding of public services is not, however, without potential pitfalls. Private-sector firms that default on contracts, for example, can cause major problems and result in added costs, particularly if the city has not retained any capacity to provide a service it has contracted out. The inevitable protests from unsuccessful bidders to field and a tendency to politicize a bid process can obscure the basic goal: to provide the best service at the lowest cost, whether that service is performed by city employees or a private firm.

These issues notwithstanding, several examples will serve to set the stage for the essential premise of Charlotte's restructuring government initative: competition works.

Residential Garbage Collection

In 1995, the city of Charlotte took bids for providing garbage-collection services to one-quarter of the city's residential households. While the city's Solid Waste Services Department was excluded from submitting a formal bid on this initial contract, it did submit, for comparison purposes, its costs for providing residential garbage-collection services. The successful low bid was submitted by a private firm whose costs were approximately $70,000 a year below those of the city department.

Two years (and lightyears of change) later, the city of Charlotte put up for competitive bid a second quarter of the city's residential garbage-collection service. When the bids were opened February 24, 1997, the city of Charlotte's Solid Waste Services Department was the apparent low bidder, beating the lowest private-sector bid by more than $2.5 million over the five-year contract period.

The city's Solid Waste Services Department had reengineered garbage-collection services for the quarter of the city it was bidding on, including making route changes and upgrading equipment to increase capacity and decrease trips to the landfill. While these and other changes contributed to the city's ability to lower its costs, it is important to note that even if the city had made no changes to garbage-collection services, it would still have submitted the low bid.

Water and Wastewater Treatment Plants

On June 10, 1996, the Charlotte City Council unanimously approved an agreement with CM-ConOp for the operation and maintenance of a city-owned water treatment plant and a wastewater treatment plan. Under the five-year agreement, the city pays CM-ConOp $7.5 million, and water and sewer customers will save $4.2 million. CM-ConOp's proposal beat those of eight international firms experienced in water and wastewater contract operations. CM-ConOp stands for Charlotte-Mecklenburg Contract Operations, a team composed of and representing the employees of the city of Charlotte and Charlotte-Mecklenburg Utilities, a city department.

CM-ConOp looked at every aspect of plant operations in preparing its bid, including evaluating best-practices learned from privately run plants in other areas of the country and Canada. The bid team focused on four major areas to improve operations and reduce costs: energy and utilities, treatment processes, control and automation, and personnel. The final bid contained a reduction of the total staffing for the two plants from 29 to 16, with the 16 operators cross-trained to increase overall plant performance. The bid also reflected changes in chemical treatments and automation and contained an incentive system that was, until then, unprecedented in Charlotte city government.

On the basis of private operating practices, the bid team believed that strong incentives were necessary to maintain plant operators' interest in the success of the plants. As proposed, the incentive plan returns one-half of any operational savings beyond the bid amount to the plant staff (savings being the bid amount minus the actual costs). The remaining one-half is retained by the plant, accumulated as an operating buffer or used for minor purchases and improvements. Goals for operating costs are set quarterly, but half the amount due is held back for payment annually. Cost overruns are deducted from accumulated savings. For monthly savings to accrue to employees, two performance goals must be met: the plant has to be in full regulatory compliance and there can be no lost-time accidents. Employees at both plants have received incentive awards.

Landscape Maintenance Services

Early in 1997, the city competitively bid several contracts in the area of landscape maintenance. Several firms and the city submitted bids in each case. A contract for grounds maintenance at city-owned buildings was awarded to the low bidder, a private firm. Another contract for grounds maintenance at two other city-owned facilities was also awarded to a private firm that submitted the low Bid. Seven city employees who had been providing these services lost their jobs as a result of the lost bids. The city was able to successfully place all but one of these employees in other vacant city jobs. One employee left voluntarily to start his own landscape business, and one was laid off.

A third competition involved right-of-way shoulder mowing. Initially, a private firm won the contract. Within a month, the private contractor defaulted on the contract and the three-year contract went to the next low bidder, the city.

Installation of Police Radios

City staff benchmarked its costs for installing radios and electrical equipment in police cars against what firms were charging for these services in other cities and counties. On that basis, staff concluded that the city would be the low-cost provider of that service and expected to win the bid. When the bids were opened, the low bidder was a firm that offered Charlotte prices one-fifth of those it was charging others.

These four examples highlight several issues related to public–private competition. First, when given the opportunity, municipal employees can successfully compete with the private sector. Second, there are areas in which, for a variety of reasons, the private sector is able to deliver a service more cost-effectively.

Generally speaking, the city has major cost advantages over private firms. It pays no taxes (income, property, sales, or gas) and does not need to make a profit. On the other hand, when the city bids, we must reveal our total costs and our bids must reflect those costs. The city does not have the latitude to underprice a bid (or "lowball" or "buy the bid" or propose a "loss leader"), as private firms might choose to do for a variety of sound business reasons. In several instances after a bid was awarded, losing firms or city staff asserted that the winner "bought the bid." The city's response is that as long as the performance criteria of the contract are met, the winners are the taxpayers who are receiving the "best service at the lowest cost."

Managed Competition

The city of Charlotte's evolving competitive culture is based on a single premise: provide the "best service at the lowest cost for our customers." To this end, since February 1994, the city has put 34 services out for competitive bid. Twenty-four contracts were awarded to the city and ten were outsourced to private firms. Over the next five years, the city plans to put out 132 services with a total dollar value of $39.6 million for competitive bid or outsourcing.

The initiatives have involved all "key businesses" (Charlotte's term for departments) whose services are also available in the marketplace. These areas include residential garbage collection, landscape and grounds maintenance, fueling of the city fleet, printing and copying, administering the new false-alarm ordinance, special transportation services, street widening and resurfacing, replacing traffic-signal bulbs, tree trimming and removal, building maintenance, water meter reading, maintenance of the city's vehicle fleet and others. Even the police and fire departments, often considered off-limits when discussions of privatization arise, have identified services they will bid competitively.

Savings have been achieved in most areas, whether the city or private firms won the competition to provide the service. Examples include $70,000 annual savings in garbage collection, $95,000 annual savings in print shop and copier services, $4.2 million savings in the operation and maintenance of water treatment and wastewater treatment plants, $413 annually by contracting with a private hauler for multifamily solid-waste collection, $180,000 annually through the City's successful bid for specialized transportation services, and $62,000 over a three-year contract to read 28 percent of the residential water meters.

More important, competition has changed the day-to-day focus and functions of the city's workforce. Employees now constantly look for ways to reduce costs and improve services. In fact, lessons learned through managed competition are being applied in other operating areas of the city, adding up to another $2.4 million in savings.

Asset Management

Asset management means identifying and analyzing all physical assets (land and buildings) and evaluating alternative arrangements for ownership and management. Charlotte's goal is to maximize use and/or return on existing and future assets.

Since 1995, 125 parcels of land have been sold or ownership transferred to adjacent property owners for a total of $15 million in addition to returning these properties to the tax rolls. Additional city-owned properties are on the market, including the city's old Convention Center (which, as of this writing, has interested buyers).

Over the last few years, the city has also considered selling a wastewater treatment plant (it did not) and evaluated whether the city should remain in the cemetery business (it should). Today, a debate about the future of the Charlotte Coliseum is under way, as its anchor tenant, the Charlotte Hornets, has argued that the facility cannot provide it with the revenues necessary to be competitive in the National Basketball Association.

Evolution of the Privatization Policy

With the exception of two categories of contracts, local governments in North Carolina are free to bid against the private sector without complying with any statutory procedures. When local governments contract for construction or repair work and for the purchase of equipment, the North Carolina General Statutes require bids if the expenditure exceeds $5,000. For most other services, however, governments can exercise broad discretion in developing procedures for obtaining competition and determining the best method of delivering services.

In 1992, Charlotte's then-Mayor Richard Vinroot appointed a Citizens' Privatization Task Force to "evaluate services and facilities provided and managed by the city of Charlotte and determine whether they could be delivered more effectively and efficiently by the private sector." After a year of study, the task force reported to the City Council, recommending that the council foster competition between the public and private sectors in providing municipal services. The task force wrote, "Competition is the primary force that keeps private businesses efficient and focused on customer needs. The city should have to compete and perform in the same manner as demanded for private business to continue performing services."

In November 1993, the City Council approved a policy statement and goals for Services Contracting (see appendix A), which can be summed up as follows: the city will seek the best service at the lowest cost either through city forces or the private sector. A competitive procurement process will determine who the service provider will be. The City Council also established a Citizens' Privatization/ Competition Advisory Committee to monitor progress toward these goals.

Implementing the Policy

Adopting a policy is one thing. How the policy and its concomitant elements play out in real life often presents unforeseen challenges and opportunities. Elected officials, city staff and citizens alike sometimes struggled with the real implications of changing service providers, of making major service delivery decisions on a low-cost basis, and (for some) of the wisdom of subjecting key services to competition at all. These and other issues come to life when specific services and approaches are debated.

Following the approval of the privatization policy, the city organization began wrestling with how to prepare a workforce of 4,800 to compete, especially when competition could mean the loss of jobs. Some organizational systems needed to change or be eliminated to support competition.

Several strategies have been used over the last three years to address these and related issues and concerns: organizational changes, communication, and changes in systems and policies.

Organizational Changes

Citywide Reorganization

In September 1993, before the City Council established the privatization policy, the city's 26 departments were reorganized into nine "key businesses" and four "support businesses." The goals of the reorganization were to focus on "essential service" areas, to run each department more like a private business and to make the departments (now called key businesses) more accountable. Key businesses were required to develop business plans, and many decisions formerly made by central administrative staff (human resources, budget, finance, purchasing) were delegated to the key business executives (formerly department heads).

The change was significant and, in hindsight, critical to competing successfully with the private sector. Specifically, key businesses have had three years of experience with business planning and operating more "autonomously" (e.g., making decisions about buying technology, redesigning jobs and reclassifying employees).

Citizens' Advisory Committee

The Privatization/Competition Advisory Committee (PCAC) created by the City Council in 1993 has played an important role in providing detailed guidelines on services contracting and asset management. The guidelines prescribed a broad role for the committee, and, as a result, its members have been involved in the competition process from beginning to end. They participate in preparing requests for proposals, review the city's costing methodologies, evaluate proposals and bids, and make recommendations to the City Council. Perhaps because its role was so broad, at times, the committee was controversial and itself the center of the issue instead of the service.

In the early stages, the committee and city staff had a somewhat adversarial relationship: committee members tended not to trust city staff and city staff members were wary of what they perceived to be the committee's "real" agenda: turn public services over to the private sector. Over the years, however, the committee and city staff have worked to establish what has become a generally positive and productive working relationship. The committee provides invaluable feedback on the structure and content of requests for proposals and objective review of bids submitted.

Steering Committee

The city established two steering committees to oversee the privatization and competition effort: one for services contracting and competition, another on asset management. Each committee includes key business executives and an assistant city manager.

Bid Preparation and Evaluation Teams

For each city service competitively bid, the city employs a bid team, consisting of city staff who put together the city's bid, and an evaluation team, which consists of other city staff and members of the Citizens' Advisory Committee. The clear directive is to keep these two teams separate so as to ensure the integrity of the process and the ultimate recommendations.

Support Staff

During fiscal year 1995, positions were reallocated to provide support and assistance to key businesses in competition, to track the progress of competition and privatization citywide, and to work with the Citizens' Advisory Committee. Staff help key businesses prepare requests for proposals, determine the cost of services, prepare bids and proposals, and learn how to become more competitive.

Communicating a Future with Competition

From a Charlotte employee's perspective, the whole world was changing. One day, work with the city was fairly secure. The next day, one's future was contingent on competing successfully with the private sector. The city employed several strategies to communicate that competition was here to stay in the organization, that city workers could compete successfully, and that the city could improve the organization, its services and its value in the community.

A Picture of Our Future

In August 1994, the city manager initiated a process to answer the question, "What might the city's services and workforce look like four years from now?" In an attempt to answer the question, a group of employees and managers developed a "picture." The picture was based on an examination of local, state and national trends and the expectations of political leaders, citizens and city employees. It included the following points:

1. Government will be addressing community problems through partnership arrangements and by brokering services, placing less emphasis on new government programs as solutions to problems.
2. Government will be competitive in cost and quality with the private sector for services provided by city employees.
3. All city services that are available in the private sector will be put up for competitive bid.
4. There will be fewer employees providing direct services to citizens, except for public safety.
5. Competition will change the way in which the city approaches human resource issues: recruiting, pay and benefits, training, scheduling, promoting, and the like.

The "picture of our future" became the focal point for explaining the coming changes in how the city would conduct its business.

Privatization/Competition Update

The city also began to publish a monthly newsletter distributed to employees, City Council members, members of the Citizens' Advisory Committee and interested citizens. It chronicled the city's competition and privatization efforts and listed upcoming contracting opportunities.

Competition Plans

Each key business—even police and fire—has developed five-year competition plans that include the following:

1. A listing of the services provided by the key business that are also available in the private sector.
2. A schedule for subjecting services to competitive bidding.
3. Strategies for making the key business more competitive.
4. A listing of services (and reasons) the key business will not compete but will retain in-house.
5. Services that the key business elects to outsource without competing for the service itself. Appendix B contains a summary from the competition plan for the Charlotte-Mecklenburg Utilities.

System and Policy Changes

The city understood early that if it were to compete successfully to provide services to citizens, changes would be necessary. Indeed, changes to the existing way of doing business have occurred at the work unit level, the key business level and citywide. These include activity-based costing and management and workforce preparedness.

Activity-based Costing and Management

In order to control costs, activity-based costing and management is being implemented on an organization-wide scale. Activity-based costing requires each of the key businesses to identify all services or "activities" and to identify all resources (staff, tools, office space, supervisors) necessary to deliver the service. The goal is to put all cost information (including all "overhead") at the activity or service level. For the purposes of competition, activity-based costing provides the most accurate accounting for costs associated with a service. Over time this will change how the city prepares and administers the budget and tracks financial information.

Workforce Preparedness

While there was never an explicit guarantee of employment until retirement with the city, like municipal (and even some private-sector) employees nationally, there certainly existed an implied guarantee of employment. That has changed. The effort to prepare employees and communicate a different message has several components.

1. The new Human Resources philosophy states: "The city of Charlotte is committed to providing quality services at market-competitive costs through service delivery by city employees or, when costs would be lower, through privatization. The city is also committed to the skills development of its employees, both to enhance their services to citizens, or when necessary due to organizational changes or privatization to prepare them for opportunities within or outside of the city organization."

2. Several years ago, the city moved from the traditional "step" system of providing set raises every year to a merit-based, pay-for-performance system that ties an employee's pay to his or her performance and bases pay on market data for that particular position. These changes have enabled Charlotte to become more competitive both in recruiting and retaining employees and in terms of overall costs.

3. Implementing incentive programs similar to the private-sector practice of profit sharing.

4. Offering new training programs. City employees may enroll in a course called Competition 101. In the training, employees are assigned to groups, each of which forms a business to compete against the city. They are asked to identify what they would do differently (in running their new business) than what the city does today. Then they explore how the city might implement those things itself. Competing successfully means adopting a new approach and fresh perspective.

   Employees are also asked to think about what he or she can do differently. Two-way responsibility is stressed. The organization's responsibility is to ensure that the environment (resources, work rules, etc.) exists for successful competition, and the employee's responsibility is to do what is necessary to be competitive. Both the employee and organization win with this arrangement.

Lessons Learned

Seldom does change come without resistance, roadblocks, challenges and opportunities. As the city of Charlotte pursues privatization and competition initiatives, it encounters new situations and issues to work through. Lessons learned along the way have helped the city make whatever changes might be necessary to have successful outcomes.

Know the Competition

The city knows its competitors much better than it used to. In the past its efforts to establish benchmarks focused on comparing Charlotte to other cities and counties. Charlotte wanted to compare its service levels, staffing, and costs with Raleigh; Winston-Salem; Greensboro; Richmond, Virginia; and so on. In the heat of competition, however, these comparisons are irrelevant. The city compares itself to its private competitors—in sanitation, with BFI or Waste Management; in wastewater treatment, with JMM or Wheelabrator; for fleet management, with Ryder or Penske. Competition also leads to sharing. Charlotte has found many private firms willing to provide information they use to improve the city's posture prior to formal competitive bidding.

Know Your Costs

Charlotte city government understands and recognizes the cost of services better than it used to. There is a difference between budgets and bids. Budgets are prepared on the assumption that they must be all-inclusive and absorb any changed conditions or events that may occur in a fiscal year. Finishing a year under budget is acceptable and encouraged. A bid, however, needs to be precise to respond directly to the requirements of the request for proposal and not inflated to account for events or conditions outside the request for proposal.

Key businesses are also required to reflect the total cost of a service, which includes their overhead and citywide overhead (finance, human resources, training, city manager, city attorney, and the like). Attention to costs has created many positive changes in the city organization. Some examples include a key business closing an operations yard in order to reduce costs in the delivery of residential garbage collection; several key businesses turning in vehicles (which were barely used) to reduce their fleet ownership costs; and several key businesses reducing the amount of office space used since it was now being charged on a per-square-foot basis.

Analyzing costs has affected internal services. Key businesses question the amount and nature of the costs allocated to them from internal support services (purchasing, finance, human resources, information technology, fleet management, and the like). As a result, charge-back systems are being changed to be more closely linked to consumption (of the service), and market-based support services are also getting smaller.

Pay Attention to Morale

Privatization and competition require an organization to change. As noted earlier, Charlotte has entered into a new "contract" with employees, which has affected morale. Some employees long for the organization of yesterday. Some are energized by the opportunities that change brings. Although morale is taken seriously because of its obvious and direct impacts on everything from productivity to service, Charlotte refuses to retreat to the old, somewhat patriarchal ways of yesterday.

The goal is to focus on what can be controlled and on creating the kind of environment that affords opportunities for the workforce. Is the environment open enough for calculated risk-taking and a free exchange of ideas? Do employees have the staff, tools, and technology to be efficient? Do they have time and resources for training? In short, is the organization supporting employees as they compete? Charlotte's aim is to answer all of these questions affirmatively.

Involve Employees and Citizens in Making Service Decisions

Charlotte's elected officials are keenly aware of how important it is to receive feedback about services from the people who know them best: the people who receive them and the people who provide them. The employees know better than anyone the things the city should be doing differently to be more competitive. Those employees who are providing the services day-in and day-out (and those whose jobs are at stake) are the ones who need to be involved in the competition process.

At the same time, the citizens of the community have a major stake in the nature and extent of services provided by local government. As such, Charlotte takes a customer-service orientation whenever possible, asking its citizens what services they want and how they perceive the quality and consistency of those services. The city routinely surveys its customers in order to assess and make decisions about service delivery issues.

Recognize That Competition Works

This article began with the conclusion that competition works. It is Charlotte's greatest lesson learned. The city is accomplishing things today that it could not have without competition. Over the last five to six years, it has rightsized, downsized, reengineered, restructured and, ultimately, improved. Our efforts resulted in reduced staff and reduced costs. Competition has taken the organization to a new level. Charlotte has shown that local governments—when given the time and resources—can compete successfully with the private sector. The winners are our taxpayers and customers who rightfully expect the city to deliver to them the "best service at lowest cost."

Appendix A: City of Charlotte Privatization/Competition Advisory Committee Guidelines for Services Contracting (Adopted by Charlotte City Council, July 25, 1994)

City Council Policy for Services Contracting

The City Council will evaluate whether an individual city service should be considered a "public" or "private" service. If the council determines that a service is a public service (involving a citywide standard of service, determined and administered by the city and paid for by a tax or governmental levy), the following policy shall apply:

> The City Council wishes to provide appropriate public services at the highest quality and the lowest cost, whether provided by city forces or by private contracts. In evaluating the most efficient and effective way to provide public services, the city shall use a competitive process in which private service providers are encouraged to compete with city departments for the opportunity to provide such services, and in which the option of delivering services through public employees and departments must be justified through the competitive bidding process. The city shall encourage the provision of public services through contracts with private service providers, wherever this offers the lowest cost, most effective method of service delivery consistent with service level standards and other adopted city policies.

City Council Goals for Services Contracting

1. The City Council will systematically assess current city services to determine the appropriate level of service to be provided, whether by city forces or by private contract.
2. The City Council will assess the relationship of a service being considered for competition with other council priorities and policies. Council will use this assessment to determine whether the services will be subject to competitive bid and in what amount, to determine any special provisions that may need to

be included in specifications and to address other council priorities and policies.

3. Current contracts for city services will be reviewed to ensure that existing private and city service providers are being held accountable and are providing effective and efficient services as specified by individual contracts. This review may result in placing a service out for competitive bidding.

4. The City Council will make an assessment of how to best provide a "level playing field" for the city and all potential private-service providers. This assessment will include defining the public values of city services and how these values will be addressed in the bid process and specifications.

5. Efforts should be made to minimize the impact on current city employees affected by competition. Each competition recommendation should include an assessment of the effect on employees and recommendations for handling any negative impact.

Guidelines

Guideline I—Level Playing Field

The Privatization/Competition Advisory Committee (Committee) is responsible for determining that the services contracting guidelines provide for a "level playing field." The definition of a level playing field, for the purposes of these guidelines, is one that neither favors nor disadvantages any bidder (including any city department) to any extent over another party. City management and the Committee shall assure that specific procedures are in place for each specific bid. Certain general guidelines to establish a level playing field are summarized in Guidelines II through VI that follow.

Guideline II—Organizing for Contracting

1. All key business units (KBU) should have a Five-Year Competition Plan that will be updated annually. Services to be contracted out or subjected to public–private competition should come from these plans.

2. Prior to starting a competition process, the city contracts administrator should be notified and provided with a proposed schedule of activities.

3. An evaluation team should initially be formed to assist in developing specifications, conducting prequalification screening, and evaluating all bids received. This review should include substantiating the reasonableness, com-

pleteness and accuracy of cost figures and cost comparisons set forth in the bid contract; evaluating the quality assurance and customer complaint procedures proposed; and reassuring conformity to other elements of the request for proposal (RFP). The members of the evaluation team will be established based on the annual contract value.

- Contracts less than $100,000. The responsible key business executive (KBE) may establish an evaluation team and review process within a key business unit.
- Contracts of $100,000 to $500,000. The evaluation team shall consist of representatives from Purchasing, Contracts Administration, Budget and Evaluation, and City Attorney. For contracts in support areas, a representative of a major user may also serve.
- Contracts more than $500,000. The evaluation team shall consist of at least two members of the Committee, a representative from the city Manager's Office and the staff KBE liaison to the Committee.
- If the evaluation team determines that additional technical expertise is required, it may obtain that expertise from any source including requesting that the KBE of the bidding department serve on the evaluation team. In that case, the bidding KBE must be excluded from the bidding process and demonstrate a "wall of separation" from the bid team.
- Contracts for similar work should not be divided to avoid the threshold stated above.

Guideline III—Content of Requests for Proposals

1. The scope of the services to be provided, in the form of "work statements," the length of the contract period, and all other pertinent information should be clearly and explicitly set forth in the request for proposal.
2. Each RFP should specify the desired outcome/result of the service in accordance with City Council policy and any other governmental mandates. Emphasis should be on describing the desired results in lieu of the means/methods used to obtain the result. RFPs should encourage responders to demonstrate creativity and innovation in describing their method for delivering the service instead of describing how they would perform the city's existing program.
3. Each RFP should include a formalized quality assurance and customer complaint resolution plan, which shall seek to assure quantitative and qualitative

measures of service delivery to be followed by the successful bidder during the contract period.

4. Each RFP should request that all bidders provide their approach to using current city employees who may be displaced by privatization.

5. Each RFP should include the performance standards and other contract monitoring requirements as described in Guideline IX—Contract Monitoring.

Guideline IV—Development of Request for Proposals

1. The service providing the key business executive is responsible for developing the RFP.

2. For contracts less than $500,000/year, the responsible KBE may use Business Support Services Key Business or his/her own department staff to develop the RFP. However, the KBE must demonstrate the "wall of separation" between the RFP development team and the in-house city bid team.

3. The responsible KBE will use the services of Engineering Key Business, Business Support Services Key Business and/or an outside consultant to prepare RFPs for contracts exceeding $500,000/year. The responsible KBE should create a "wall of separation" between the city bid team and the RFP development team by minimizing his/her department's involvement in the RFP development. That involvement should be limited to providing the historical data necessary to compete for the service and any technical support necessary to describe the desired outcome.

4. A draft of each RFP for contracts in excess of $100,000 should be reviewed by all qualified bidders prior to publication.

5. There should be a clearly designated staff resource, who is separate from the city's bid team, responsible for responding to general inquiries about the contracting process from private service providers and other interested citizens. After the issuance of an RFP for a specific service this individual is responsible for making available to private service bidders the information/data relevant to or needed by them in the preparation of bids.

6. Procedures should be developed for ensuring that any information or data that is requested by one bidder is made available to all bidders. Under such procedures, all information that is requested or that is made available to a city department for its use in preparing an "in-house bid" shall also be made available to private bidders. This will not mean that private bidders may request or have access to the working papers prepared or developed by a city department

in order to calculate or decide upon or prepare its proposal for performing the service in-house.

Guideline V—Proposal Review

1. Where appropriate in relation to the size and scope of the service that is being considered for contracting out, a prequalification screening analysis of private-sector bidders should be conducted to evaluate the potential bidder's business plan and resources committed to the plan, prior performance history (if any), financial and organizational ability to perform the scope of services, and the ability to obtain any necessary bonding. The use of prequalification screening and the criteria for such screening shall be decided on a case-by-case basis with input from the Committee on the appropriateness of such screening and the criteria for screening.
2. All bids submitted in response to an RFP shall be sealed and submitted at the same time. The bid evaluation process shall be conducted in accordance with the city's "Standards of Conduct" set forth in City Code Section 2–73 and in accordance with these guidelines.
3. Costing for city "in-house" bids shall be reviewed by Internal Audit prior to bid submittal.
4. The results of all bids more than $100,000 will be shared with the Committee.
5. All bid proposals more than $500,000 will be shared with the Committee. The Committee may make its own comments and recommendations, if any, on such bid proposals independent of the staff evaluation and recommendation. Such comments and evaluation by the committee will be transmitted to the city manager and to City Council along with any staff recommendation and report on the bids. In addition, in the event the Committee and city staff are unable to agree on other issues during the course of the process, the Committee may, at its option, seek further guidance and directions from City Council.
6. In addition, the Committee anticipates that it will make quarterly reports (verified by an internal auditor) to City Council on the overall progress of the contracting-out effort, including the selection of services for consideration by the city manager and City Council, the schedule for consideration of contracting out, and the progress on the cost elimination plans.

Guideline VI—Costing Methodology

Cost Methodology for Preparation of "In-House" Bids

1. Bids submitted by a city department shall include the following cost calculations and components of total cost:

- All direct or variable costs associated with performance of the service that would not be incurred if the service were not provided "in-house."
- An allocation for capital costs (including depreciation and actual or imputed financing costs) for capital equipment and assets used or required in order to provide the service.
- An allocation for semivariable and fixed costs whose amount is related to and may be affected by the number, scope and level of services that the city provides "in-house."

2. A reconciliation of the "submitted bid" to the current budget. This reconciliation should be verified by Internal Audit.
3. There shall be excluded from these calculations those fixed costs that, regardless of the extent to which services may be contracted out to private bidders, could not be eliminated. An example of these excludable costs would be allocatable expenses for the Office of the Mayor and City Council, or expenses for services that are purely regulatory functions.
4. Costing for city "in-house" bids shall be reviewed by Internal Audit prior to bid submittal.

Comparison of "In-House" and Private Bids

1. In comparing bids prepared by private contractors with "in-house" proposals to provide a service, certain adjustments will be necessary in order to "level the playing field." Because these guidelines require that "in-house" proposals include an allocation for certain semivariable and fixed costs, simple comparison of the bottom line totals for "in-house" proposals with the price quoted in private bids may not be an accurate reflection of the city's possible savings or costs from contracting out a service. In order for the city to make a proper comparison of "in-house" proposals with private bids, the following possible factors and adjustments may need to be considered:

- The extent to which the "in-house" proposal includes an allocation for semivariable or fixed costs that may not be eliminated or phased out over the short term if the particular service is contracted out. The key to this comparison will be the cost elimination plan provided in Guideline VIII.
- Transitional costs and/or savings (i.e., potential gains or losses from the disposal of any capital assets, employee impact costs).
- The costs of contract monitoring and oversight. Where these costs are different for "in-house" proposals and private bidders or as between different pri-

vate bidders, the city should provide full justification and rationale for any such differences.

2. Applying these factors in particular instances may have the same effect as an adjustment in the "bid price," either up or down. The goal of such comparison is to ensure that the various proposals and bids are evaluated on a "level playing field," regardless of the cost basis used in their preparation and to ensure that the ultimate total costs to the city of providing a service is as low as possible, consistent with the quality and service level standards specified in the approved RFP.

Guideline VII—Employee Impact Statement

1. Consistent with the goals for services contracting established by the City Council, efforts should be made to minimize the impact on current city employees affected by decisions to contract out services.
2. After receipt of the bids, the city manager shall prepare and submit as a part of the evaluation package a personnel impact statement, setting forth for each prospective bid the cost of any personnel severance programs associated with the acceptance of such bid, the potential for absorption of displaced employees by other city agencies, and any other plans for dealing with displaced employees, including the cost of any such plans.
3. "In-house" bids shall include a statement setting forth the number, grade and pay ranges of current employees assigned to the service that is being put for bid and the number, grades and pay ranges of employees who will be needed for performance of the contract awarded "in-house."
4. Private-sector bids should include a statement of the anticipated needs, if any, of the bidder for additional personnel if selected as the service provider and may include, at the election of the bidder, a proposal for providing qualified "in-house" employees access to future jobs that may be available in connection with the services to be provided.

Guideline VIII—Cost Elimination Plan

1. In the event the city enters into a contract with a private contractor to provide a service previously provided by the city, the city manager shall develop and implement a cost elimination plan to eliminate the avoidable costs related to that service during the first annual budget period of the contract.

2. The cost elimination plan shall be based on the concept of variable, semi-variable and fixed costs. This concept recognizes that certain semivariable costs that cannot be eliminated due to the privatization of a single service will become available in stages when more services are privatized. Whenever practical the cost elimination plan should provide an analysis of the next level of semivariable costs that can be reduced or eliminated and the applicable phase-out period, if specific additional services or combinations thereof are contracted out to the private sector.

Guideline IX—Contract Monitoring

1. Monitoring is the process of overseeing performance after a contract has been signed to ensure that cost and service specifications are met. Monitoring procedures should address the general requirements for post-award assessments of all contracts and should also address the unique requirements for city-awarded contracts.

2. The KBE for the contracted services is ultimately responsible for monitoring the contracts for cost compliance and service delivery. The Business Support Services contract administrator serves as the central source for the collection and reporting of monitoring data. In addition, effective independent auditing of monitoring activities and verification of compliance with policies and procedures should be part of the internal control system to ensure that the processes put into place are working as intended.

3. There are additional monitoring considerations when the city is the successful bidder. To encourage competition, the city should be accountable both to the taxpayers and to the nonsuccessful bidders for evidence of compliance with proposed costs and service delivery. This evidence should include an audit (independent of the bidding team) to ensure that cost overruns are not passed on inadvertently to other city departments.

4. The best way to monitor contracts is to set explicit and quantifiable performance standards in the contract and then clearly state what the city will require of the contractor to ensure that those standards have been met. All contracts should include a mechanism for evaluating the contractor's performance as defined in the RFP. For some contracts, recording satisfactory completion within the time and cost constraints will satisfy the monitoring requirement. Larger multiyear contracts with complex specifications and performance criteria will demand more extensive monitoring procedures.

5. Monitoring requirements should include some form of contractor-prepared

statements of progress that provide information on work completed and information relative to performance standards. These statements of progress should identify problems encountered and any contractual adjustments believed necessary. The size and complexity of the contract will determine the frequency of reporting, but the reports should be verified (audited) for accuracy.

6. The feasibility of on-site inspections will depend on the contract and on the type of monitoring conducted. Inspection results should be reported comparing the observation and accomplishment of work to prescribed specifications. The contractor should be informed of the nature of these inspections, and a standard rating or scorecard should be used to record findings.

7. The method for obtaining feedback from citizens, user departments, or service recipients should be identified in the contract monitoring requirements.

8. The PCAC member(s) assigned to a proposal evaluation team (contracts of more than $500,000) should receive monitoring reports of the awarded contract.

9. The full PCAC should be provided an Annual Summary Report on contracts awarded in accordance with these guidelines that will have an annual value of more than $100,000.

10. The information in the Annual Summary Report on city-awarded contracts should include the following:

- Summary of comparisons of current contract performance requirements with work completed to date.
- A forecast of future contract performance requirements and expected work completion.
- Expenditures to date and any variances between budget and actual.
- A narrative description of any problems encountered.
- Any contract adjustments considered necessary.
- Summary findings of any independent audits performed.

Appendix B: Charlotte-Mecklenburg Utilities Services Competition and Contracting Plan, FY 1998–2002

Service	Comp/Cont	# Positions	1998	1999	2000	2001	2002
Hydrant Maintenance	Compete	8	$478,000				
Meter Maintenance	Compete	1	$126,000		$126,000		
Tying Sewer Lines	Compete	3	$180,000				
Laboratory Services	Compete	13	$775,000				
Instrumentation Maint	Compete	2	$111,600				
Routine Water Main Repairs	Compete	5		$128,000			
Soils & Materials Testing	Compete	5		$192,750			
Lateral Installation/Replacement	Compete	10		$600,000			
Mgmt-wastewater facility	Compete	24		$5,144,000			
Meter Reading	Compete	5		$198,000			
Water Locates	Compete	3			$160,000		
Wastewater Treatment Facility	Compete	10.5				$1,565,000	
Wastewater Treatment Facility	Compete	16				$1,941,000	
Residuals Land Application	Compete	0				$680,000	
Residuals Compost Mgmt Facility	Compete	4				$1,300,000	
Water Treatment Plant	Compete	7.5					$912,000
Water Treatment Plant	Compete	10					$980,000
TOTAL		127	$1,670,600	$6,262,750	$286,000	$5,486,000	$1,892,000

CHAPTER SEVENTEEN

Privatizing Government Services in New Orleans

Marc H. Morial
Mayor of New Orleans, Louisiana

Robert K. Whelan
University of New Orleans

In our view, privatization should be approached on a case-by-case basis. In any privatization decision, a local government will find that there are many trade-offs in service provisions. Often, it is difficult to evaluate whether a service should be provided by government, the private sector, the nonprofit and voluntary sector, or some combination of the three sectors.

It is our opinion that there is no universal approach to the privatization question. Cities' responses should be determined by the administrative and political realities surrounding individual cases. Cities should not simply accept the widespread American myth that "private is better." Neither should they believe that all services delivered by cities in the past should be provided by the public sector in the future. In brief, when a city is examining a service for privatization, our response is that *it all depends.*

Some functions lend themselves better to being privatized. For example, services with few production function uncertainties are prime candidates for contracting. In services of this type, there can be clear standards, which result in tightly written contracts and performance monitoring. If service quality can be defined clearly, that service is more susceptible to contracting. Such services as solid-waste collection, water supply services, street paving and maintenance, ambulance services, and transportation can have clear performance standards and easily measured output. Thus, they are candidates for contracting out. In contrast, services with less tangible performance standards and outputs are less likely to be contracted.

The literature tends to agree that the services that are best prospects for contracting out are those which have the following characteristics:

1. They are new. Therefore this involves no layoff of current city workers.
2. They have easy-to-specify outputs. As in the collection of solid waste, easy-to-specify outputs make monitoring and contract preparation easier.
3. They require specialized skills or equipment. An example is the provision of city legal services. In smaller communities, especially, many types of skills and equipment have to be obtained on a part-time or irregular basis. For example, Alexandria, Ontario, has only four full-time employees, with a town clerk as the main professional employee. If a small city of this type has to produce a comprehensive plan, it will, inevitably, need private planning consultants and assistance from higher-level governments.[1]
4. They have large numbers of low-skilled workers. An example is the provision of janitorial services. These areas seem to show the greatest differences in pay and benefits between public and private sectors.[2] We hasten to add that this last point is not necessarily good from our point of view; we are just reflecting the findings of the literature.

In general, we believe that privatization is not a panacea for local government. Since experience varies in each case, we believe that more analysis is necessary at both the micro- and macro-levels. Some years ago, an Urban Institute study listed advantages and disadvantages of private delivery of public services. This list was not exhaustive; it was merely suggestive. We have chosen some of these alleged advantages and disadvantages as the basis for organizing our paper. The topics that we will discuss include governmental effectiveness, specialized skills, size of government, costs, flexibility, evaluation and information, management and efficiency, and specificity in drawing up contracts. In each section, we provide examples based upon our experience in New Orleans. Since the New Orleans case is paramount for us, we preface our discussion of advantages and disadvantages with a presentation on the context of service delivery in New Orleans.

New Orleans: The Context of City Service Delivery

All cities are limited by fiscal constraints in their ability to deliver services. New Orleans is especially hampered in this area for several reasons. First, the city is more than usually handicapped in its ability to tax. The property tax is the major source of income for most local governments. However, the state of Louisiana has a homestead exemption of $75,000 guaranteed by the state constitution. This is a high figure. It means that homeowners in New Orleans do not pay any significant property taxes until they are assessed above the $75,000 figure.

About 68 percent of owner-occupied homes in New Orleans are covered by the homestead exemption and pay only a special 10.47 mill tax for enhanced police and fire protection services. Various efforts to change the homestead exemption have failed. This is compounded in New Orleans by a system of assessors elected on a district basis. Elected assessors want to win the support of voters in future elections. Thus, they tend to undervalue home assessments. For example, a homeowner might have a house that would sell at a market price of more than $100,000. However, the assessor sets a value of $60,000 on the house. It is easy to see how a house that might sell for more than $100,000 might pay no property tax in New Orleans.

Second, the city has been more than usually impacted by federal-aid cutbacks. For a number of reasons, New Orleans was a late starter in the 1950s and 1960s generation of federal-aid programs. During the administrations of former Mayors Moon Landrieu and Ernest "Dutch" Morial, the city pursued federal grants vigorously and successfully. Just as these grants came to fruition, federal aid was decreased.

Third, the city has a high incidence of urban poverty. Generally, citizens with low incomes do not generate as much in tax revenues as citizens with higher incomes and require additional governmental services. Given our fiscal constraints, it's easy to see why the city needed to look for methods of efficient service delivery.

Governmental Effectiveness

More efficient and effective service delivery by the private sector is the prime reason given for privatization. Perhaps the best example in Orleans is the Touro-Shakespeare Nursing Home, which is owned by the city. This facility was operated for many years by the city's Department of Human Services. During the

administration of Mayor Sidney Barthelemy (1986–1994), this function was privatized by lease. At present, Mayor Marc H. Morial's administration is finalizing
a new lease for redevelopment of the facility.

There are a number of people, particularly in the city's Human Services Department, who think that the city should continue to operate this facility. The fact
is that in a scarce resource situation, the city simply can't do everything. Moreover, the skilled labor necessary to run a nursing home runs counter to a civil
service system on pay scales and other issues. The lease in negotiation provides
for redevelopment, combining housing for elderly with the nursing home function. The city's goal is to serve only as a landlord and, in so doing, to capture a
revenue stream for 20 to 25 years. In this instance, the private sector can generate
a profit and provide effective services.

The absence of a profit motive on the part of government can be viewed as an
obstacle to innovative and effective management. Since the early nineteenth century, the city of New Orleans has operated a system of public cemeteries, but the
city has never done a particularly good job of operating and maintaining them.
Recently, a citizen's task force appointed by Mayor Marc H. Morial conducted a
comprehensive review of the city-owned cemeteries and recommended privatization.

A key reason for the task force recommendation to privatize was its belief that
an entrepreneurial approach to cemetery management would result in increased
revenues from cemetery operations. In turn, increased revenues would result in
better maintenance of the city's historic cemeteries. At this writing, the city is
preparing a request for proposal for privatization of cemetery operation and management.

While privatization may improve service (as above), sometimes contracting for
services results in worse services for the public. Private contractors may save
money by hiring staff at low wages, but the private staff may be less qualified
than public-sector providers. In New Orleans, our transit authority had an experience of this type with para-transit. There were many complaints about time
and bus breakdowns. The transit operators who won the contract were nonpro-
fessionals. In brief, the profit came out of the low salaries and benefits paid to
the workers. The quality of service suffered. At present, the transit authority
has taken para-transit back in-house. Perhaps the original failure was the length
of the contract, which may have been too short to attract professional transit
operators.

Specialized Skills

Privatization and contracting out often provide specialized skills that are not ordinarily found in city government. The nursing home situation described above is one example. Another instance occurs in the Community Development Block Grant (CDBG), the largest federal urban program with money from the U.S. Department of Housing and Urban Development going to build housing and for community development.

In New Orleans, much of the work under CDBG is done by private and not-for-profit contractors. Several grassroots groups, for example, provide social services. Grassroots organizations have developed specialized skills that might not be found in the routine bureaucratic situation. Moreover, as will be discussed, government has goals other than efficiency and effectiveness. Citizen participation and a sense of empowerment are also important values in public administration.

Specialized skills, however, are not always easy to find. Many proponents of privatization assume that there will always be vigorous competition in the marketplace (or between public and private agencies) for service contracts. In the real world, this is often not the case. Many functions that might be privatized have markets that are monopolistic or oligopolistic.

In such situations, the city government loses leverage because without a competitive market, the city doesn't have a lot of options. This is especially true in a large, capital-intensive area like sanitation. In larger cities, there are basically two firms providing sanitation services: BFI and Waste Management. In New Orleans' case, sanitation was largely contracted out in the 1980s. If the city chose to return to delivering the service itself, it would have to purchase new trucks and other new equipment and hire new employees. This would be very expensive.

While specialized services are likely candidates for privatization, we must also remember that cities can be somewhat hamstrung by public bidding requirements and that diligent monitoring of a contractor's performance is essential for successful completion of a contract. In some instances, a contractor may not complete the terms of a contract.

In St. Tammany Parish, Louisiana (a New Orleans suburb), a small building contractor was the lowest bidder to build a new public library in the city of Slidell. The library was badly constructed, and it had a leaking roof ten years after the building opened. In the meantime, the contractor went out of business, leaving the parish library system with a messy situation physically and fiscally.

While there is a legal process to address responsibilities and rights, service delivery may suffer in the short run. The point is that any contractor may not fulfill obligations.

Costs

Another alleged advantage of privatization is that it limits the growth of government. By privatizing, permanent employees are not added to the city payroll. Through privatization, a city may be able to limit direct pension and health-care costs. Instead of adding new bureaus, departments, and functions within city government, overall size and costs may be limited by privatization.

Privatization may help to avoid large initial or upgrade costs in capital expenditures or in human resources. An example from New Orleans city government would be the recent decision to contract out the print shop. In that case, the city was operating with outmoded equipment. The kind of modern equipment needed would have cost the city over a quarter of a million dollars. While the purchase of new equipment was an alternative, the city decided that it would be wiser to privatize in this situation. Moreover, printing is an area in which there is a great deal of competition within the private sector. Thus, the city expects to have competition when the contract is up for renewal.

Obviously, if privatized services may cost less, they may also cost more. For example, a city might privatize legal services, and it might find that private-practice costs increase more than the old city attorney's office with its staff. Or, a city might contract its auto repairs and find that costs increase. Admittedly, the more costly private service might be superior to city-provided services. Decisions of this type present a series of trade-offs for city decision makers.

Our next point seems rather obvious, but privatization often results in the reduction of the public-sector workforce. Unions such as AFSCME and the AFT, which represent many public-sector workers, tend to oppose privatization efforts and may provide campaign workers and funds to do so. Union interests and concerns are taken seriously by city officials where employee groups are a major political force. Although public-sector employee unions are not as powerful in New Orleans as they are in many other cities, their views would need to be taken into consideration before making major personnel reductions or before changing workloads in departments with active employee organizations.

Civil service boards may also have concerns about privatization's effect on the public workforce. In New Orleans, our Civil Service Commission has adopted a rule, which has the force of law, that addresses privatization contracts. The rule requires specificity in a contract as to the effects of privatization on current civil service employees, and it requires safeguards to prevent discrimination or arbitrary disciplinary actions against government employees. The New Orleans Civil Service Commission must approve privatization contracts and gives strong consideration to a proposed contract's effect on current city employees.

Flexibility

Privatization is said to allow mayors more flexibility in adjusting the size of urban programs. In particular, the thinking is that it is easier to terminate a contract than it is to lay off city employees. Similarly, it might be advantageous to have some work done on a contractual basis rather than add additional permanent employees to the city payroll.

However, privatization and contractual obligations may reduce the flexibility that is needed to respond to emergency situations and to other changes in the environment of service delivery. For example, New Orleans experienced a major flood in the spring of 1995. With a private contractor handling most of the service delivery in sanitation, there were problems in increasing the number of available trucks and workers during the flood emergency.

This illustrates the point that contractual agreements should provide for effective and efficient methods for coping with foreseeable emergencies. The most recent solid-waste-collection agreement negotiated by the city of New Orleans contains specific provisions to address emergency situations such as our flood of 1995.

Evaluation and Information

Some privatization might provide a yardstick for comparison with productivity in the private sector. Research by Miranda and Learner uses the term "benchmarking" to signify the idea that joint contracting allows sponsors to play service producers against one another.[3] Their results, taken from a 1982 survey of alternative service delivery by the International City Managers Association (ICMA), support the argument that benchmarking is associated with reductions in expenditures.[4] To some extent, sanitation in New Orleans is an example of benchmarking. The great majority of trash pickup has been privatized. However, the city retains a small sanitation workforce (about 90 people) that provides daily refuse pickups in the French Quarter and central business district and other special services (e.g., emergency pickups, concentrated efforts in neighborhoods). This opportunity for benchmarking must be monitored very carefully, however. There are great differences in the French Quarter, with all the debris of tourists, restaurants, and bars, and the normal residential pickup, which comprises most of the rest of sanitation work by a private firm.

On the other hand, local governments usually do not have the time, staff or money to devote to a comprehensive analysis and evaluation of alternative means of providing services and to monitoring contractors' performance. There is little hard data on the costs and benefits of contracted services. The information is often sketchy and anecdotal, with serious methodological problems. Although solid-waste collection is one area where the data clearly suggest that contracting reduces costs, even in this area information is inadequate for a definitive conclusion.

Local governments always have to proceed in the face of uncertainty and partial ignorance. It is ironic that government evaluation efforts have been cut back because of fiscal constraints just as we begin to look at new, different, and sometimes promising approaches to service delivery.

Management and Efficiency

It is often argued that privatization enables better management. Certainly, in a sense, this can be true. If a city saves money, and if services are delivered more economically and effectively, then, in those respects, it has better management. The expectations are that contractors will compete vigorously with one another, that government officials will presumably have access to the information necessary to evaluate the bids and choose the best provider. If contractors fail to provide the service at the agreed cost, the local government can move on to another provider. Through competition, local government services become more effective, more efficient, and better managed.

Carefully drafted and monitored contracts can provide better management information for local governments. Certainly, the competitive process should produce more information than is often available. Private-sector service providers are also likely to have better computer resources than most local governments have. Indeed, contracting out and benchmarking could encourage unified management information systems in many local governments.

In addition to efficiency, there are many values that are important in public administration. In many instances, these differing values are in conflict. Herbert Kaufman, for example, notes the shifting emphasis among these major values (representativeness, politically neutral competence, and executive leadership) in the administrative history of the United States.[5] The market model of privatization assumes the primacy of efficiency as a desired value. Certainly, efficiency has always been an important value in American public administration.

Let us illustrate with an example from the New Orleans experience. Several recent administrations have felt that it was important to have city workers reside within the city, and domicile for city employees in the city limits is required by law. This was thought to be important for several reasons. If middle-class city employees reside within the city, they will pay taxes and spend money inside the city. Furthermore, the thinking is that residence will make city employees more responsive and more involved with city problems. Concern for the residence requirement can be lost if government functions are privatized and the private contractor has no similar residence requirement.

Efficiency goals may also conflict with the public's need for accountability. In New Orleans, as in many cities, social services provided under the Community Development Block Grant (CDBG) program are delivered by competitively selected nonprofit and community organizations with experience in the delivery of social services in specific geographic areas or to a particular client base. The use of community organizations serves other governmental purposes such as enhancing community empowerment and providing training and employment opportunities at the grassroots level.

The problems come in the accountability to the public. Effective monitoring can be difficult and may require a significant commitment of personnel. What is the system of ensuring accountability to the public in cases such as this? There are many positives in having community-based service providers, but often accountability and efficiency can conflict.

Another factor to consider is that when there are contracts and competitive bidding, there are more chances for corruption to occur. When a city provides a service, there is no competition in the process. Every contract presents an opportunity to reward friends. Competitive bidding creates a situation where businesses may seek to influence the process through campaign contributions or more direct inducements.

Specificity in Writing Contracts

The more specific the standard for the contract, the easier it is to privatize. Drawing up contracts is a difficult task. Important items may be omitted from contracts. Cities do not always have the expertise to cover all possible contractual eventualities in the original experience. After one contractual period, cities are better aware of possible limitations, problems, and difficulties when they enter a second round of negotiations.

For cities considering contracting out a particular government service for the first time, we would suggest that contracts used for similar functions in other cities be carefully reviewed and that officials in those cities be contacted for insight into their experiences with such contracts. Cities should also consider seeking the advice of consultants, particularly in specialized areas such as emergency medical services.

Conclusion

We would like to offer some thoughts to other local governments, based upon our experience in New Orleans, about where and when to privatize:

1. Privatize when the contractor provides highly specialized services that cannot be easily accommodated by the city's personnel system, as in the nursing-home situation.
2. Make contracts for long enough duration, and provide enough incentives to attract bids from high-quality professionals in the field. Our local transit authority didn't do this in para-transit and ended up taking the function back.
3. Privatization in the social services area may produce additional benefits in community empowerment and in developing skills and careers at the grass-roots level. At the same time, there must be accountability when public dollars are involved.
4. Privatization decisions are often extremely difficult for a city, as it trades off, for example, the potential long-range cost of new equipment and the loss of long-term, public-sector employees against an immediate savings.
5. Quality of service delivered is an important value and must be weighed against cost considerations.
6. Contract language should anticipate potential emergency situations.

7. Benchmarking and other modern evaluation techniques should be used in monitoring privatization.

We believe that public officials and citizens should recognize that privatization is not a panacea for all the ills of government or society. In some cases it makes sense, but in others it may not. The public and responsible officials should carefully scrutinize proposals to privatize services.

Notes

1. The Alexandria example comes from David Rayside, *Small Town in Modern Times* (Montreal and Kingston: McGill-Queen's University Press, 1991).
2. This discussion is developed from David R. Morgan, *Managing Urban America,* 3rd edition (Pacific Grove, Calif.: Brooks/Cole, 1989), p. 189.
3. Rowan Miranda and Allan Learner, "Bureaucracy, Organizational Redundancy, and the Privatization of Public Service," *Public Administration Review* 55, no. 2 (March–April 1995), p. 198.
4. Miranda and Learner, p. 199.
5. Herbert Kaufman, "Administrative Decentralization and Political Power," *Public Administration Review* 29, no. 1 (January–February 1969), pp. 3–15.

References

DeHoog, Rich Hoogland. "Competition, Negotiation or Cooperation: Three Models for Service Contracting." *Administration and Society,* November 1990, pp. 3, 22, 317–340.

Eggers, William, ed. *Competitive Government for a Competitive Los Angeles*. Los Angeles: Reason Foundation, 1994.

Eggers, William. *Rightsizing Government: Lessons from America's Public-Sector Innovators*. Los Angeles: Reason Foundation, 1994.

Hatry, Harry P., et al. *Excellence in Managing: Practical Experiences from Community Development Agencies*. Washington, D.C.: Urban Institute, 1991.

Lineberry, Robert L., ed. *The Politics and Economics of Urban Services*. Beverly Hills, Calif.: Sage, 1978.

McClendon, Bruce W. *Customer Service in Local Government*. Chicago: Planners Press, 1992.

Miranda, Rowan, and Allan Learner. "Bureaucracies, Organizational Redundancy and Privatization of Public Service." *Public Administration Review* 55, no. 2, March–April 1995, pp. 193–200.

Morgan, David R. "The Pitfalls of Privatization: Contracting without Competition." *American Review of Public Administration* 22, no. 4, December 1992, pp. 251–270.

Morgan, David R. *Managing Urban America*, 3rd ed. Pacific Grove, Calif.: Brooks/Cole, 1989.

Osborne, David, and Ted Gaebler. *Reinventing Government*. Reading, Mass.: Addison-Wesley, 1992.

Poister, Theodore H., and Gary T. Henry. "Citizen Ratings of Public and Private Service Quality: A Comparative Perspective." *Public Administration Review* 54, no. 2, March–April 1994, pp. 155–160.

Reason Foundation. *Privatization '94*. Los Angeles: Reason Foundation.

Rehfuss, John. "A Leaner, Tougher Public Administration?: Public Agency Competition with Private Contractors." *Public Administration Quarterly* 15, no. 2, Summer 1991, pp. 239–251.

Seals, Gerald. *Taming City Hall: Rightsizing for Results*. San Francisco: Institute for Contemporary Studies, 1995.

Shenk, Joshua Wolf. "The Perils of Privatization." *Washington Monthly,* May 1995, pp. 16–23.

Stein, Lana. "Privatization, Work-Force Cutbacks and African-American Municipal Employment." *American Review of Public Administration* 24, no. 2, June 1994, pp. 181–192.

Stone, Clarence N., et al. *Urban Policy and Politics in a Bureaucratic Age*, 2nd ed. Englewood Cliffs, N.J.: Prentice-Hall, 1986.

Whelan, Robert, and Robert Dupont. "Some Political Costs of Coprovision: The Case of the New Orleans Zoo." *Public Productivity Review* 40, Winter 1986, pp. 69–75.

Competitive Contracting

The Philadelphia Story

Edward G. Rendell
Mayor of Philadelphia, Pennsylvania

"Government should run more like a business." In this era of widespread fiscal difficulties for governments, taxpayers—with much justification—are increasingly demanding private-sector productivity from their public-sector leaders. Not surprisingly, the management concepts and buzzwords of the corporate world—total quality management, reengineering, and rightsizing among them—have gained increasing currency among government managers and elected officials.

These contemporary management theories emphasize the development of a highly skilled, flexible workforce with decision-making ability and authority pushed down throughout the organization. Traditional hierarchical organizational models are giving way to decentralized, fluid *teams* that can quickly adapt to rapid change. Faced with new, global competitors, companies from Motorola to Harley-Davidson—often staring down the threat of bankruptcy—have dramatically reorganized the way they do business and have reemerged as high-performing success stories.

But government is not and will never be exactly "like a business." In a competitive marketplace where feedback is manifest (consumers can simply buy from Burger King instead of McDonalds, or vice versa), organizations must continually refine their operations, increase efficiency and productivity, and minimize their costs—or risk the loss of their customers. Because the public sector generally exists to address needs that the marketplace cannot meet effectively, however, governments do not feel the same pressures. With no fear of going out of business, governments, like all monopolistic organizations, tend to grow bloated and soft—with civil service protection and union work rules too often shaping an incentiveless environment for government workers.

Here in Philadelphia, however, we have been reminded all too clearly that even public-sector monopolies can face bankruptcy—and lose businesses, people, and opportunity—if they fail to deliver services competitively. When I took office in January 1992, our government faced a cumulative operating deficit of more than $200 million, projected to grow to $1.4 billion at the end of five years if uncorrected. In just my first week on the job, it took a court ruling permitting us to stretch out mandated pension payments to keep us from missing payroll. Perhaps even worse, after 19 major tax increases in the preceding decade, many Philadelphia homeowners and businesses were packed up and ready to leave town for good—on top of the many good jobs and more than half a million people who had already left us. Had we attempted to tax our way out of these troubles, or to have dramatically cut city services, we would have destroyed whatever credibility and hope that we had left. Notwithstanding our monopoly on city services or even our singular power to tax, Philadelphia was, and remains, in a very real competition with other places to do business and to live. Our customers—both businesses and residents alike—may not be able to vote with their pocketbooks, but, over time, they can and do vote with their feet.

Since 1992, Philadelphia has begun to turn the corner. Our budget is now balanced, showing a $128.8 million General Fund surplus at the end of fiscal year 1997—achieved without a tax increase or major service cuts. In fact, over the three years, we initiated a gradual reduction in our business and wage tax burdens while enhancing basic services. Our new world-class Convention Center and a host of exciting cultural and entertainment projects under way have sparked unprecedented increases in new hotel development and our growing tourism and hospitality sector, which have in turn produced thousands of new jobs. As but one measure of our progress in the "competition" that we face, in November 1996, *Fortune* magazine ranked Philadelphia among the top three communities nationwide—and number one on the East Coast—in its "Best Cities for Work and Family" survey.

There has been no single secret to this turnaround, but there has been a lot of hard work and sacrifice by a lot of dedicated people—among our unionized workforce, our managers, and our civic and elected leadership. To survive, and to begin to thrive, we all needed to work together to make fundamental changes in the way that we, as a government, did business.

Of the many areas in which we made fundamental changes, competitive contracting has been one of the most important. Over five years, the city has subjected 45 functions to a competitive process, with a cumulative estimated savings from July 1, 1992, to June 30, 1997, of $140 million—over $10 million more than our cumulative surplus at the end of that same period. Total annual savings are estimated at $42 million, with equal—and in most cases better—service levels provided to the public. Of these 45 projects, 41 are contracted with the private sector while 4 have been retained in-house by the city workforce. Perhaps most important, the simple fact that we have engaged in this process has helped to foster a new, more competitive dynamic within city government. It has provided real incentive to our workforce to be more productive, to save more money—in short, to do a better job. The private sector's new, team-oriented management theories are absolutely on target—however, to build a strong team, there has to be someone to play against.

Philadelphia's Program to Foster Competition

In Philadelphia, the first step in beginning our program was the appointment of a senior-level Competitive Contracting Committee to spark, implement, and monitor all potential competition initiatives. Initially, the Competitive Contracting Committee surveyed all city departments and identified several dozen possibilities. These initiatives cut across numerous departments and all types of services—both white and blue collar alike—with the potential for multimillion dollar savings. As the program has matured, departments now bring initiatives to the committee, and—more than five years and forty-five implemented projects after the committee was first established—nearly two dozen new competitive contracting initiatives are in the pipeline.

When this committee first evaluates whether to open a service up to competition, the initial step is to identify both the service's end user—the customer—and the desired end result. The process begins not by trying to replicate simply and solely what is done today, but rather by assessing exactly what the customers need from the service and what should be delivered. This understanding, in turn, guides the development of a meaningful scope of services, with quantifiable standards for performance.

Next, our managers undertake a rigorous economic analysis of the projected cost for delivering the service desired. In so doing, our analysis compares the estimated cost using in-house resources to meet the scope against the projected cost using a contracted service provider. Then, before a service delivered by public employees is even put out for a bid, we share our economic analysis with the city union(s) representing these employees, and the unions are given a chance to critique and counter the city's analysis. If proposals are eventually solicited, the city's employees are invited to compete, and the economic analysis and comparison are continually refined as actual bids come in and contract negotiations move toward closure.

Through this process, competitive contracting evaluates both the private and public sector on a fair and realistic "apples-to-apples" basis, seeking to determine the very best alternative for delivering the very same standard of services. In this regard, we hold no ideological bias toward privatization for privatization's sake. If the government's monopoly on providing a given service is merely transferred to the private sector without ongoing competition, then prices will tend to escalate and services to decline. Further, if a government's own employees are not afforded a real opportunity to compete, then a contracting program will only alienate and discourage the government's remaining workers—rather than generating the creativity and performance that can be achieved.

Therefore, we are committed not only to having our own city workers competing on every bid, but also to having our employees working with us on an ongoing basis to improve our overall governmental productivity. Similarly, we expect our managers to work side-by-side with our unions to develop competitive proposals and to increase our efficiency before a private contractor ever knocks on our door. Nationally, the experience of Phoenix offers a tremendous example for all of us in the public sector. In a competitive environment comparable to Philadelphia's, after several years of learning from private competitors, Phoenix city sanitation workers became increasingly efficient and began to win back areas of the city that they had lost to private companies. Now, after several years of competition in Philadelphia, our own local unions and city employees are showing similar creativity and results.

At our Water Department's Biosolids Recycling Center, for example, before putting the plant's operation out to bid in 1993, we gave our workers and managers a chance to turn this sludge processing and composting facility around. While a study of this facility at that time showed that efficiency savings of up to $6 million were possible through privatization, our own employees developed a plan in response with the potential to do even better. Given the opportunity to implement this plan, our Water Department adopted an aggressive strategy, including the following: investment in more efficient equipment, such as higher-performing centrifuges; the implementation of streamlined work processes negotiated with the city's largest municipal employee union, AFSCME District Council 33; partial outsourcing of functions not performed cost-effectively by the utility, such as long-distance hauling to landfills; and the adoption of a total quality management program, including strengthened cost accounting and performance measurement systems. As a result of this transformation, the Biosolids Recycling Center has reduced its budget from $31.6 million in fiscal year 1993 to $16.9 million in fiscal year 1997—more than doubling the annual savings projected from privatization.

Building on examples such as this, Philadelphia entered into a new project with its municipal unions in 1996—the Redesigning Government Initiative (RGI)—intended to foster in-house initiatives to increase the competitiveness of the public-sector workforce. Working with Harvard University's John F. Kennedy School of Government, we are already piloting one successful such initiative, helping to improve our services in Philadelphia's Department of Recreation.

In May of 1997, our managers began working with Recreation Center staff and union representatives from AFSCME, District Council 47. As a first step, this labor-management team has focused on improvements to Philadelphia's summer meals program for low-income children. Through the efforts of both labor and management to promote and improve this service, in 1997, 30 more facilities participated in the meals program than during 1996, a total of more than 106,000 additional free lunches were served to Philadelphia kids, and breakfasts were added to the program for the first time. In addition, frontline city workers were given a chance to suggest program changes, and their ideas for improving the distribution of meals and cleanup at participating centers were successfully adopted. Finally, because existing Recreation Center staff members already in place were able to integrate this program into their overall duties, and because food and administrative costs are reimbursed by the sponsoring Commonwealth of Pennsylvania, this strengthened program has not burdened the city's own budget.

Clearly, the benefits of competition are pro-citizen and pro-taxpayer. But also of vital importance to us—and contrary to the claims of some opponents—Philadelphia's example demonstrates that competitive contracting need not be antiworker. While we have eliminated or avoided nearly 1,600 city positions through competitive contracting to date, fewer than 15 employees have actually been laid off—and all of these workers have subsequently been offered a chance to return to city service. This has been possible because we have accomplished much of our competitive contracting program through attrition, because we have worked aggressively to redeploy all displaced workers in other unfilled city jobs (even rewriting our transfer policies to make redeployment easier), and because we have made it a universal requirement for contractors taking over city services to provide any displaced employees the first shot at any new jobs these companies may create.

Moreover, as Philadelphia's municipal government has become more competitive and begun to stabilize its fiscal position, we have been able to reinvest a portion of the savings that we have achieved in strategic increases to other needed services. As a result, while our municipal General Fund workforce declined by more than 3,600 positions over the four fiscal years prior to the initiation of my competitive contracting program in fiscal year 1993, we are no longer forced to downsize today. In fact, at the end of fiscal year 1997, we added back more than 500 net municipal workers since fiscal year 1993 to help us deliver needed service improvements for our neighborhoods, and we have pledged not to contract out any services that would result in layoffs or demotions for our workers.

Finally, in terms of labor considerations, one of the greatest surprises that we encountered in our program was that much of the initial resistance to competition came at first not from our workers or the unions, but from some of our own city managers. For too long, bureaucracies have allocated stature, prestige and career advancement on the basis of how many people and how big a budget a manager oversees. As a consequence of this perverse structure, some managers, perhaps subconsciously, have resisted competition that results in a smaller and more efficient government. To counter this long-standing culture, we have had to push and prod and propagandize. But we are also working, for the long-term, to change our incentive structure. In small ways, this simply means recognizing and applauding managers who take the risk to manage creatively. More fundamentally, however, this means moving toward better performance measurement, performance-based budgeting, and a performance-based compensation system. Today, Philadelphia department heads and deputies no longer all receive the same raises. Under a new compensation system implemented in 1997, we now provide raises based on results, not merely inputs, and our managerial culture has changed no less profoundly than our culture on the shop floor.

Contracting Out as Outsourcing

In addition to the fundamental impact of competition, contracting can also be about leveraging specialized expertise and experience that may be difficult, if not impossible, for government itself to develop and maintain. Government is not and cannot be expert in every field, and—much like private-sector organizations outsourcing noncore business processes—government can benefit in two major ways from outsourcing ancillary services. First, government can gain from access to the skills and economies of scale that may be possessed by outside specialists. Second, and perhaps even more important, outsourcing can free up a government's managers to focus more of their energies on core city responsibilities.

For example, both cost and service improvements have been realized as Philadelphia has gotten out of the business of managing its own city warehouse. In 1992, when we still sought to deliver this service directly, it would often take weeks just to get an order of pencils—even for me as the mayor. Now we do business directly with office-products suppliers who deliver straight to city departments, typically within 24 hours. This arrangement is not only much quicker, but it also saves us nearly $1.2 million per year, as the city no longer carries excessive inventories of outdated products nor maintains and operates its own facility. Similarly, new contracts have also eliminated the need for the city's print shop, for savings of an additional $500,000 annually as multiple contracted vendors now meet the printing needs of the city.

Another example of the benefits to be gained by outsourcing is our programs to assist our own city workers injured on duty. For many years, Philadelphia was notorious for the mismanagement of its disability and workers' compensation claims. Historically, the city failed to deliver professional safety and injury prevention programs, effective rehabilitative treatment, or responsive medical case management to its own employees hurt on the job. At the same time, poor system management enabled a handful of abusers to exploit system loopholes and drive the city's costs through the roof. During these years, there is little question that the city officials and workers administering such programs held the best of intentions. Nonetheless, the management of a complex health-care network was simply too much to handle.

In contrast, Philadelphia today contracts with a private firm that seeks to be the best in disability claims management—not only for the City, but also for other companies and organizations. This vendor invests in the infrastructure of technology and highly trained personnel to actively manage claims. The firm coordinates a broad managed-care network of professional medical facilities and physicians, and it uses licensed nurses to manage the cases of our injured employees. As a result of such professional care, under the city's new system, total incurred workers' compensation liabilities have decreased by more than $100 million, the number of paid workdays lost because of injuries declined from nearly 80,000 in 1991 to approximately 30,000 by 1996, and the city has been able to invest in improved workplace safety programs. In recognition of this turnaround, Philadelphia received *Risk & Insurance* magazine's 1997 award for Best Workers' Compensation Program nationwide, public or private sector.

Lessons of Contract Management

Whether contracting out is done more as a matter of sparking competition or more as a matter of leveraging core competencies, it is critical to recognize that the process never ends with the award of a private contract. Contracting out a service does *not* mean that city management can forget about the service. The focus simply changes from managing people to managing a vendor. Regular reporting and monitoring remain essential, and, for this very reason, our Competitive Contracting Committee requires that departments provide a comprehensive status report to the committee after the first 90 days of contracting out a service (in addition to whatever regular and ongoing department-level reporting may take place). It is not enough to make the "right" decision; it is also essential to work to make the decision right.

For example, our success with contracting for employee disability management services would not have been realized had we also not strengthened our in-house expertise to a level sufficient to manage this contract. Just prior to putting our city disability management out to bid, we centralized our in-house expertise in a newly created Risk Management Division, consolidating key staff formerly fragmented in our Law, Health, and Finance Departments. To further strengthen our internal contract management capacity, we conducted a national search to fill our top positions in this new division with veteran industry professionals. Because of these steps, the work of our contractor better meets our organizational needs, and we have been able to prevent unwarranted cost escalation for these services over time.

In this example, as in all government contracting, one of the keys to preventing cost escalation has also been to *maintain* competition. Unfortunately, there are contractors who will lowball to get a contract, then look to inch their prices back up over time. A private monopoly is no better than a public one, so it is absolutely critical to rebid services periodically. Of course, if the service in question requires a contractor to invest heavily in capital equipment or to hire a lot of specialized people, it may be in the public interest to enter a longer term agreement. If the deal is long enough for the balance of these up-front costs to be amortized, the taxpayers will get a better price. Nonetheless—well in advance of a contract's expiration—public-sector managers have an obligation to review what services are needed, to again research the marketplace, to again evaluate the possibility for doing the service in-house, and to again open up the service to a meaningful competitive process. For these reasons, Philadelphia's Competitive Contracting Committee also requires that contracting departments prepare and submit a formal service evaluation at least 180 days before each contract is set to expire.

Conclusion

Philadelphia is home to tremendous architectural treasures—from historic Independence Hall to the contemporary Pennsylvania Convention Center. I am fortunate to work in one of these treasures, Philadelphia City Hall, one of the finest examples of Second Empire architecture in the country. Yet when I first came into office, years of neglect had left City Hall covered in grime and full of foul odors. During my campaign, one of my most well-received promises was that we would quickly get City Hall smelling, if not like roses, at least like Lysol. And soon after my election, more than a thousand Philadelphians came forward one spring weekend to volunteer with me to scrub, paint, and clean up City Hall.

Now, more than five years after this first spring cleaning, City Hall looks, if anything, even better. Over this period, City Hall maintenance has been opened up to competition twice and is now under contract with an 80-year-old family-run business. According to a clearly defined scope of services, unionized workers clean City Hall's 750 rooms, wash its 1,400 windows, and scrub down its courtyard, apron, and the subway concourse beneath it. As a result, City Hall is markedly cleaner and brighter, while Philadelphia taxpayers are saving approximately $477,000 per year. Further, every municipal custodial worker initially displaced by this contract has been redeployed to another good city job. To achieve such model results, substantial time and effort must be applied, but such effort can make a real difference. Whether cleaning up City Hall or trying to clean up a government, competition may not solve every problem, but it is a very powerful tool.

Index

About the Contributors

George Allen was governor of Virginia from 1993 until January 1999. Before his tenure as governor, he practiced law in Charlottesville, served in the Virginia House of Delegates, and was a member of the U.S. House of Representatives. He was named the American Legislative Exchange Council's first Jeffersonian Scholar in 1998 and is currently practicing law in Richmond. He announced his candidacy for the U.S. Senate in April 1999.

Paul J. Andrisani is director of the Center for Labor and Human Resource Studies and codirector of the Privatization Research Center at Temple University, where he is also professor of management in the School of Business and Management. He has served as a consultant to numerous government agencies and major corporations, including Boeing, Martin Marietta, the *New York Times,* Coca-Cola, and the U.S. Department of the Army.

Dennis W. Archer began his tenure as mayor of Detroit in 1994 and was re-elected in November 1997, with more than 83 percent of the vote. Previously, he spent fifteen years as a trial lawyer and eight years as a Michigan Supreme Court Justice. Archer serves on the Board of Trustees of the U.S. Conference of Mayors and as president of the National Conference of Democratic Mayors.

Page Boinest works on independent research and public relations projects for corporate, political, and nonprofit clients. She served as press secretary and spokesperson for Don Beyer, Virginia's two-term lieutenant governor, and was director of public affairs for the National Governors' Association. She worked as speechwriter and then press secretary for Maryland Governor William Donald Schaefer from November 1990 to August 1994.

Terry Branstad was elected governor of Iowa in 1982 to become the youngest governor in Iowa's history. He served for four consecutive terms, leaving office in January 1999. He served as chair of the Republican Governors Association and the Governors' Ethanol Coalition. He now runs his own company, Branstad and Associates, L.C., and teaches at the University of Iowa's School of Business.

Jeb Bush was elected governor of Florida in November 1998. Before that, he helped launch and served as president and chief operating officer of the Codina Group, now the largest full-service commercial real estate firm in south Florida. He served as Florida's secretary of commerce from 1987 to 1988 and is the coauthor of *Profiles in Character,* a book profiling fourteen of Florida's civic heroes.

Bill Campbell became Atlanta's fifty-seventh mayor, as well as its third African American mayor, in a landslide victory in 1993. He was reelected to a second term in 1997. Previously, he received his law degree from Duke University, worked as a prosecutor for the U.S. Justice Department, had a successful career as a trial lawyer, and served on the Atlanta City Council.

Arne Carlson was governor of Minnesota from 1991 to 1999 and achieved an impressive array of reforms, including greater accountability in state finances and $3 billion in tax relief for Minnesota citizens and businesses. Although he was the state's longest-serving Republican governor, Arne Carlson's record reflects ideals that span the political spectrum. He is currently chairman and chief executive officer of American Express Funds.

Keon S. Chi is a Senior Fellow for the Council of State Governments and professor of political science at Georgetown College. He is the author of articles on state government and coauthor of "Private Practice: A Review of Privatization Activities in State Government." He received the James E. Webb Award for the most outstanding paper on privatization at the 1994 National Conference of the American Society for Public Administration.

Richard M. Daley was elected mayor of Chicago in April 1989 to complete the term of the late Harold Washington and was reelected in 1991, 1995, and 1999 by overwhelming margins. In 1997 he ws named Municipal Leader of the Year by *American City and Country* magazine, a Public Official of the Year by *Governing* magazine, and Politician of the Year by *Library Journal.*

John Engler was elected Michigan's forty-sixth governor in 1990. First elected to public office in 1970 at the age of twenty-two, Engler began a series of nine straight election victories, including those for state representative, state senator, and Michigan Senate majority leader. In 1994 he was awarded the Thomas Jefferson Freedom Award by the American Legislative Exchange Council Board of Directors.

Geni Giannotti became director of the Buildings and Safety Engineering Department of the city of Detroit in April 1998. For four years prior, she served as executive assistant to Mayor Archer, overseeing and coordinating government reengineering and other improvement programs. Before joining Mayor Archer's transition team in 1993, she was a financial and operational consultant to underperforming organizations with Jay Alix and Associates.

Rudolph W. Giuliani was elected mayor of New York City in 1993 and was reelected in 1997. A native of Brooklyn, before serving as mayor he attended law school at New York University, was associate attorney general of the Department of Justice, the third highest position in that department, and served as U.S. attorney for the Southern District of New York.

Susan Golding was elected mayor of San Diego in November 1992 and was overwhelmingly reelected in 1996 with 78 percent of the vote. Golding spearheaded the largest redevelopment project in San Diego's history and the development of San Diego's Habitat Conservation Program, which the *New York Times* called "the most ambitious effort ever undertaken in this country to reconcile the competing needs of environmental protection and economic development."

Stephen Goldsmith was elected mayor of Indianapolis in November 1991. He was the recipient of *Governing Magazine*'s Public Official of the Year Award and the prestigious Innovations in American Government Award from the Ford Foundation. He is also the author of *The Twenty-First Century City: Resurrecting Urban America* and is currently serving as an advisor to Governor George W. Bush of Texas.

Simon Hakim is professor of economics and codirector of the Privatization Research Center at Temple University, where he has worked since 1974. He is the author of several books on privatization and crime, including the 1997 *Securing Home and Business: A Guide to the Electronic Security Industry* (as coauthor).

He has also conducted major research projects for several government agencies and corporations on privatization and security issues.

Eva Leeds received her doctorate in economics from Princeton University. She taught economics and finance at several schools, including Temple University. She also taught as a Fulbright lecturer at the Prague School of Economics and later became advisor to the Minister of Economy of the Czech Republic. She has written many articles about housing finance and privatization and is currently a visiting assistant professor at Moravian College.

Patrick McCrory began his second term of office as Charlotte's mayor when he was reelected in 1997 with 78 percent of the vote. He began his political career in Charlotte in 1989 when he was elected to the Charlotte City Council and was mayor pro tem from 1993 to 1995. A part-time mayor, he has worked at Duke Energy Corporation since 1978 and currently serves as manager of Business Relations.

Zell Miller was elected governor of Georgia in 1990 and reelected in 1994. The *Washington Post* in 1998 called him the most popular governor in America, and *Governing Magazine* named him Governor of the Year in 1998. He has served as chair of many national associations, including the Council of State Governments and the Education Commission of the States, and is the author of four books.

Marc H. Morial was elected mayor of New Orleans in 1994 to become the city's first African American mayor. He was reelected in March 1998. He is the chair of the Advisory Board for the U.S. Conference of Mayors and also chairs several of its committees. Previously he ran his own law firm, served as state senator, and taught political science at Xavier University.

Edward G. Rendell took office in January 1992 as mayor of Philadelphia and served two terms during the 1992–1999 period. Previously, he graduated from Villanova Law School, served as chief of homicide in the Philadelphia District Attorney's office, and was elected district attorney in 1977, becoming the youngest district attorney in the city's history. In September 1999, he was elected general chairman of the Democratic National Committee.

Thomas Ridge was elected governor of Pennsylvania in November 1994 and was reelected in 1998 by the largest victory margin accorded to a Republic governor in state history. He served as assistant district attorney in Erie County before his election to the U.S. House of Representatives in 1982. The first enlisted Vietnam veteran to serve in the House, he served six consecutive terms before his election as governor.

William Donald Schaefer was mayor of Baltimore from 1971 to 1987 and governor of Maryland from 1987 to 1995. He served on the Baltimore City Council from 1955 until 1971. Schaefer currently serves as Maryland Comptroller of the Treaury and holds the Schaefer Chair at the University of Maryland's School of Public Affairs in conjunction with the Johns Hopkins University Institute for Policy Studies.

Robert K. Whelan studies urban revitalization, development, and public management in the United States, Canada, and France. He was honored with the Donato J. Pugliese award for service to SECOPA. Dr. Whelan has published in the *International Journal of Public Administration, Public Administration Quarterly, Public Administration Review,* and the *Journal of Urban and Public Affairs* as well as coauthored *Urban Policy and Politics in a Bureaucratic Age.*